23.00

D1242868

License for Empire

License for Empire
Colonialism by Treaty in Early America

Dorothy V. Jones

The University of Chicago Press
Chicago and London

Dorothy V. Jones is a research fellow at
the Newberry Library in Chicago.

The University of Chicago Press, Chicago 60637
The University of Chicago Press, Ltd., London

Library of Congress Cataloging in Publication Data

Jones, Dorothy V.
    License for empire.

    Bibliography: p.
    Includes index.
        1. Indians of North America–Government relations–
    To 1789. 2. Indians of North America–Treaties.
    3. United States–Territorial expansion. 4. Indians of
    North America–Government relations–1789–1869.
    I. Title.   II. Title: Colonialism by treaty in early
    America.
    E93.J63   323.1'197'073   81-19700
    ISBN 0-226-40707-1   AACR2

In memory of
Myra Perrings
Poet, Scholar, Friend

Contents

Figures and Tables

Figures

Tables

Preface

This is a study of the way that traditional diplomacy helped to create an early American example of colonialism. The world "colonialism" is a deliberate choice. Despite its distortion in the mindless vocabulary of abuse, no other word expresses so well the distinctive blend of uplift and exploitation that was one result (and only one) of Europe's long invasion of the world. How then did colonialism become established in North America?

To answer that question I have looked at the means that were available to Europeans for dealing with other peoples. For the most part these means were diplomatic, and they followed set forms of contact, negotiation, and agreement, usually in the form of a treaty. This was the pattern that was followed in North America, and we are all familiar with the outcome. It is graphically portrayed by two maps that hang on the wall of my study. On one of the maps, the land claims of the many different Indian groups that were native to this continent cover the entire area of what is now the United States. The other map shows present-day Indian reservations: scattered spots of land, mostly small, mostly west of the Mississippi River.

The maps are a useful reminder that a treaty system, like the law in Justice Holmes's formulation, is what the majority wills it to be. In the past, the majority in this country was determined to have the Indians' land, and have it they did. Outright land-grabbing was not nearly so widespread as is commonly believed. There was no need. The treaty system itself was the primary vehicle of transfer. After 1796, when the treaty system was well established, with the federal government of the new United States as the dominant member, the system functioned— for the most part, legally—to reduce the landholdings of the Indians. (After 1871, treaties were no longer made with the Indians, and their landholdings were reduced by other means.)

The legality of the proceedings was, of course, within the Western European legal tradition. But more than that, the means used (until 1871) were negotiated means. They were not imposed by fiat or by unilateral enactment. They had the form, if not the substance, of diplomacy. One of the marks of colonialism is that it bends traditional diplomatic structures to exploitative ends. This can happen because accountability is not built into the diplomatic system. The only check is the assumption of countervailing force. When that is absent, as it invariably is in situations of colonialism, the whole treaty system becomes a weapon in the arsenal of the stronger power.

Again, the results are familiar and depressing. In return for their land, the American Indians received goods, which were quickly consumed; money, which was soon spent; and certain rights and privileges, which few Indians had the knowledge or power to use effectively at the time the rights were granted. The rights still exist, however, and are today the focus of legal battles between some of the states and Indian groups that are both knowledgeable and determined to defend what the treaties have left to them. It is a situation that generates confusion as well as lawsuits.

Of all the social and political groups that make up present-day America, only the Indians have a treaty relationship with the federal government. As individuals, Indians are all (since 1924) citizens of the United States. As members of Indian nations or tribes, they are part of corporate bodies with a unique legal status. That status is defined in part by the many treaties that are still in force between Indian groups and the United States. If those treaties grant certain privileges, such as fishing rights, that seem unfair to other Americans today, it may be well to remember that the same unique legal status imposes tremendous disabilities on the corporate groups of which the Indians are a part. Any municipal mayor, who must look to Washington for permission to sneeze, can sympathize with the Indians' corporate plight. By the time permission is granted, the sneeze has long since passed into history, and the guidelines from Washington no longer apply.

All of this is to say that the treaty system that exists today between the federal government and the various Indian tribes and nations is not the same as the system that is described in this study. The form is the same, and the participants are the same, but the social and political context has changed. As a result, the system functions differently—so differently that many Indians today look on their treaties with the

United States as the best guarantees of their rights. It was not always so. This study explores the how and why of the differences at a time when diplomacy helped to create a classic case of colonialism in America. The chief debt in a study such as this is to that ancient and honorable company of scholars that is usually mentioned only in commencement exercises. Every work with any claim to substance rests so solidly on the labor of the general body of scholars that it becomes a cooperative venture even if the author seems to stand alone. When others are actively involved at various stages along the way, the supporting linkages of scholarship become more evident. It is a pleasure to make plain here how much I owe to others. My thanks go to: the trustees of the Eugene F. Saxton Memorial Fellowship Fund, Harper and Row, for a fellowship that got this study underway; Orval J. Liljequist of the Milwaukee Public Library for much help in the early stages of research; Lewis Atherton, Imtiaz Ahmad, and John Lankford of the University of Missouri-Columbia for stimulating forays into the world of modern scholarship, and Lankford, in particular, for coaching that made further graduate training feasible; members of the awards committee of the history department of the University of Chicago for a fellowship that made further graduate training possible; Akira Iriye, Barry D. Karl, Raymond D. Fogelson, and Arthur Mann of the University of Chicago for the vistas of intellect that they shared and for kindnesses that made more bearable the shock of discovered ignorance; members of the fellowship awards committee of the Newberry Library, Chicago, for their vote of confidence in my work; and Francis Jennings, director emeritus of the Newberry Library Center for the History of the American Indian who has, with editing pencil in hand, twice worked his way through this manuscript in its various revisions. A better-written, more tightly argued book is the result.

The reader may have noticed that there is no woman's name in the foregoing list. That is a fairly accurate reflection of women's past position in the formal linkages that support scholarship, but it is not an accurate reflection of their contributions to this particular scholarly endeavor. I should like to record here my great debt to women who were, for the most part, outside the institutions of scholarship. First, my mother, Margaret M. Vincent, whose eighth-grade-only education did not prevent her passing on to her children a love of learning. Then, Marie C. Jones, Elnora Huyck, and Winkie Turner, who tended my small children, as well as my dreams, at a time when these seemed to be an insoluble contradiction. There are four more for special mention: Ruth Hunt, Ruth Lowery, Lela Barnes, and Myra Perrings. Each of these women—the living and the dead—has a share in this book.

Finally, there is my husband, Bob. Expressing thanks to him for the layer upon layer of intricate involvement in this enterprise is a continuing, but private, pleasure. What needs to be acknowledged publicly is a rare virtue that I would commend to other spouses. At every stage, he helped when asked—helped far beyond any reasonable measure. Beyond that, he had the restraint and the wisdom to leave me alone and let me make and learn from my own mistakes. It was an incomparable training. I trust that few mistakes will see the light of day in this book, but for those that remain I alone am responsible.

1   The Great Theater of the World

By the close of the Seven Years War in 1763, Europeans and American Indians were well acquainted in certain respects, while in others they were as strange to each other as they had been at the time of their mutual discovery. They could and did meet together and negotiate binding agreements, but at the deepest levels of belief they saw the world with different eyes and had different expectations. For many Indians, these differences were no problem. "We must hang upon our ancient rules," said the Seneca leader, Red Jacket, "and the white people upon theirs. We can then as well agree together as if we followed one rule."[1]

On the face of it, this was an attractive approach to the problems that the two peoples posed for each other. There was even a time after the Seven Years War when the approach seemed possible and the problems manageable. But in 1790, when Red Jacket spoke, that was no longer true for the Senecas or for many of the Indian groups east of the Mississippi River. From 1763 to the mid-1790s, the whites did indeed follow their ancient rules, and the Indians followed theirs. The result was expansion of land and opportunity for the whites, and a shrinking of both for the Indians to the point where they found themselves virtually captive to the rules of a society that they still saw as alien. The situation was legally constituted within the European tradition, and there were legal safeguards for the Indians, but to once independent people and nations, it was captivity all the same.

The Oneida leader, Good Peter, saw more clearly than Red Jacket what was happening to the Indians. He and other Oneidas had been prevented from disposing of some of their land as they wanted, because New York would not allow it. Even if New York officials had been willing, there was still the federal government to contend with since federal laws also forbade the private land lease that the Indians wanted to make.

1

This was in 1792, only twenty-nine years after the close of the Seven Years War. On behalf of the Oneidas, Good Peter protested:

> It seems to us that we are not really free men, nor have we had the real disposal of our property. If we understand what is meant by a person's being free and independent, as to his own property, he may either lend, or sell his property, or any portion of it, as he pleases.[2]

This distinctive blend of aristocratic pride and condescending preachment was a mark of Good Peter's distinctive background. He was first an Oneida and, second, a member of the Iroquois League of the Six Nations. Furthermore, he was a survivor of *l'ancien régime* of the Iroquois, that time when the Iroquois League, of which the Oneidas were a part, dominated the entire Northeast and managed the diplomacy of the area to its own advantage. When Good Peter was a young man, the League was the heart and center of a complex system of colony and Indian alliances that was called the Covenant Chain. For more than sixty years, the Covenant Chain had acted as a diplomatic stabilizer in the Northeast, with the Iroquois as magnetic north.[3]

By 1792, the Iroquois were part of a different treaty system, one with the new United States as its center. This system functioned chiefly as a legal mechanism for the transfer of land from Indian to white ownership. As one treaty followed another, and land was ceded piece by piece, the League was increasingly restricted, increasingly hemmed in both by white settlements and by legal limitations on its actions. Where land was concerned, the Indians could not rent, could not lease, could not sell without the permission of their "partners" in the treaty system that defined and structured the Indians' exterior relations. Caught within this net of legal restrictions, Good Peter traveled to Philadelphia to make his protest. The trip was futile, and he knew it, but from posterity's point of view the trip was not wholly wasted. While Good Peter was in Philadelphia, John Trumbull painted his portrait. Not only the words but the face of the man are thus on record, and Good Peter continues to look out with calm disdain upon the world that, even in 1792, was rapidly replacing the world he knew.[4]

What had changed in Good Peter's lifetime? By what steps had the possibilities of 1763 been eliminated? In 1763 there had been hope on all sides that the end of the long years of fighting in North America offered an opportunity for Indians and whites to work out means of peaceful coexistence. Yet by 1796 the treaty system that had developed

between whites and Indians in the eastern United States was so unequal
that it can only be called colonial. How had this happened?

From Accommodation to Domination

Part of the story is well known. The rise and fall of Great Britain as
the leading imperial power in North America, the weakness of the new
American nation, and the subsequent three-way scramble between Great
Britain, the United States, and Spain have been thoroughly studied.
Less well known, but beginning now to be studied in detail, are the
Indian elements of change. The crumbling of the power of the Iroquois
League, which occurred during the same period, set off intense competition among the Indian nations north of the Ohio River. South of the
Ohio, the struggle was scarcely less intense as Creeks, Cherokees, Choctaws, and Chickasaws fought for dominance, for prestige, and, in some
cases, for survival. What has been studied very little is the way that all
these factors acted and reacted upon one another in the period from
1763 to 1796 to create a treaty system that was little more than an
instrument of colonialism.

The term "colonialism" is used in this study in a broad descriptive
sense to mean the domination of one culturally distinct group by another group with a different culture. Beyond that, the term's meaning
is determined by context. The colonial situations created by European
expansion varied so greatly and changed so rapidly that, as Georges
Balandier has observed, detailed definitions of colonialism are of limited
value at this stage of knowledge. Instead, it is necessary "that the situation be studied in an historical manner, that the dates be specified."[5]

More specifically then, in 1763, at the close of the Seven Years War,
France and Spain withdrew from active competition with Great Britain
in eastern North America. The way was opened for the Indians and the
British to exercise on a broad scale the diplomatic skills they had gained
in their long years of contact with each other. They took advantage of
the opportunity. In the five years from 1763 through 1768, they put
together a comprehensive treaty system with all that the word "system"
implies about the various parts forming a connected whole. The treaties
dealt with many different subjects, but they had one binding, common
element: the definition of a boundary to divide Indian lands and jurisdiction from the lands and jurisdiction of the English.

The treaty system of 1763-68 was an accommodation system, worked out by mutual agreement and compromise. It was deliberately created

to provide a means of adjusting the many differences between Indians and Europeans. In the end, the accommodation system failed. It began to come apart when the Iroquois League and Great Britain, working in mutually advantageous partnership, ignored the land rights of the Shawnees and Delawares. The efforts of the Cherokee nation to turn this situation to its own benefit accelerated the process of disintegration and helped to destroy the whole central section of the Indian-white boundary. From 1768 through 1775, the accommodation system was gradually transformed into a system for transferring land ownership.

The system was more important than its duration might suggest, however. Its effects were felt far beyond the short period when Europeans and Indians negotiated on a basis of relative equality to work out trade and boundary arrangements. When U.S. officials turned to the task of administering the backcountry that had been transferred to the United States at the close of the war with Britain, they discovered the persistence of the influence of the prewar system. In two regions in particular, in the South and in what came to be called the Northwest Territory, the Indians were ready to fight to preserve what they had accomplished with Great Britain before the war. The Ohio section of the general boundary of 1768, and the Creek-Georgia section, were the rallying points for the militant Indians' determination to prevent any further loss of land.

Right from the start of its national existence, the United States was thus forced to adjust its policies to the conditions created by the short-lived treaty system of 1763–68. Indian resistance to U.S. assertions of total sovereignty and to U.S. attempts to impose boundaries favorable to its own plans for expansion were so effective that the United States had to reverse itself. After 1786, the federal government began treaty negotiations anew on the basis of a recognition of Indian land rights and acquisition by purchase. Until the mid-1790s, the Indians of the South and the Old Northwest were able to keep enough pressure on the United States to preserve a favorable bargaining position. When they lost that position, it was as much through events in Europe as in the United States. The renewal of large-scale war on the Continent led Spain and Great Britain to settle their long-standing differences with the United States to free themselves for their war efforts, and they withdrew from active involvement in the North American backcountry.

Without the encouragement, and, more important, the supplies and military aid they had been receiving from Britain and Spain, the Indians were far more vulnerable to pressures from the United States and far less able to counter with pressures of their own. The end result was that the United States moved into a dominant position and by 1796 was able to set the basic terms of negotiation with the Indians. Since the primary U.S. goal in regard to the Indians was the acquisition of land, that became the major reason for negotiation. The Indians quickly found themselves in a position where, with Good Peter, they could say, "It seems to us that we are not really free men."

There was little doubt about it. By 1796 the eastern Indians had been caught in the treaty system that for the next seventy-five years systematically and legally relieved them and, later, the western Indians, of their land. The events, the decisions, and the conditions that led to the establishment of that system are explored in more detail in the pages that follow, beginning with a look at the international community of 1763. How was that community viewed by those who concerned themselves with such matters? How closely did their views conform to actual conditions? What significance did that have for American Indian nations?

International Perspectives

At the core of eighteenth-century thought about the international system was Europe itself. There was a rich heritage of thought for intellectuals to draw upon, for the problems of that continent had absorbed the attention of generations of political thinkers. To refine that heritage and relate it to the struggles among the emerging nation-states became the primary task of those in the eighteenth century who took what they called the universal view. They addressed themselves to such subjects as the laws of nature and of nations, the rights and obligations of independent states, and the conditions that made for independence.

The subjects of inquiry were indeed universal, but the examples and answers were almost entirely European. As Georg Friederich von Martens remarked in his *Précis du droit des gens* (1788), the law of nations arose from the practice of civilized people, that is, of Europeans.[6] Having with this brief reference dismissed the bulk of mankind, Martens turned back to Europe with its tangle of political forms and relationships that stemmed from a feudal past. How were these to be reconciled with the increasing claims and power of the nation-states? Did an alliance of protection disqualify a nation from freedom and sovereignty? Did vassalage or tribute? Martens cited his instances: the king of Naples, the Order of Malta, the principalities of Monaco, Moldavia, and Wallachia.

He concluded that neither protection, tribute, nor vassalage could prevent a state from being considered fully sovereign and "occupying its usual place on the great theatre of Europe."[7]

It was a happy phrase. In the eighteenth century, the great theater of Europe provided the central drama for those who concerned themselves with politics on a large scale. Absorbed in this play, they failed to note the subtle shift throughout the eighteenth century from a European theater to a theater of the world. They were not wholly unaware of Europe's increasing contacts with the world. In an appendix to his study of the law of nations, Martens included "A List of the Principal Treaties concluded since the year 1748 down to the present time." His list of 209 treaties included two with North American Indian groups, as well as treaties with rulers in the Barbary states, the Philippines, and South Asian Indian states. Martens's seven-volume master work, *Recueil des principaux traités*, long one of the standard collections of printed treaties, contained even more evidence of European involvement with the world, including treaties with Persia, China, and Ceylon.[8] Awareness of the rest of the world did not, however, mean a desire to integrate it into an intellectual system in which Europe and its thought were paramount.

Europe had not always been so intellectually parochial. In the sixteenth century, Spanish theologians such as Las Casas, Sepulveda, and Vitoria had vigorously debated the nature and rights of American Indian groups and their relationship to the Christian God and to European states.[9] For a number of reasons, including the secularization of political thought, this was not the central concern of eighteenth-century political thinkers. Nor did they take up the leads provided in the seventeenth century by Hugo Grotius, whose emphasis was on the conduct of a just war.[10]

By the eighteenth century, intellectual priorities had changed. Political thinkers who looked beyond the domestic scene were chiefly concerned with finding out just what the law of nations consisted of, and how or if this positive law was related to the natural law that had concerned thinkers in the past. Thus, Emmerich de Vattel, who addressed himself briefly to the question of aboriginal land rights, was most deeply concerned with the problem of making natural law the basis for the practice of states, and not just a theoretical statement of their moral rights and duties. Vattel's major work, *Le droit des gens* (1758), was an extended investigation of this problem.[11]

Martens, a professor of jurisprudence at Göttingen University, was also interested in this problem. He collected the treaties of the world not simply for the convenience of statesmen but so that these modifications of the simple law of nature could be studied and the true positive law discovered. In his view, a general positive law of nations consisted of "certain principles, that have been almost universally adopted by all the powers that have made treaties on the same subject. . . . [Positive law] is the aggregate of the rights and obligations established among the nations of Europe (or the majority of them), whether by particular but uniform treaties, by local convention, or by custom."[12]

It was Europe that, for Martens, set the universal standards. The rest of the world, while admittedly there, existed in a kind of intellectual limbo. The customs, conventions, and treaties of the Iroquois League in North America, or the Mogul Empire in India, or the rulers of Mataram in Indonesia, or the Kombaung dynasty in Burma were simply not seen by eighteenth-century European philosophers as germane to their concerns.

Meanwhile, throughout the century, a change was occurring that would eventually force European thinkers to pay more attention to the rest of the world. A convenient marking point for this change is the Treaty of Paris of 1763. Like the earlier treaties of Aix-la-Chapelle (1748) and Utrecht (1713), it was a European agreement about problems that were chiefly European. But the 1763 treaty was more than that. It proved to be one of the first effective worldwide partition treaties. Later events, especially in India and North America, can be dated from the Partition of 1763, a dividing point in world history as well as in the history of Europe.[13]

In a broad and very general way the shift in attention from Europe to the world can be seen in the subsequent rise of Great Britain, a sea-based power, and the decline in world influence of France, with its superior land and population resources. But the shift can be seen in more specific terms through close analysis of two different treaty systems that were created in the twelve years following the Partition of 1763: the European treaty system, in which Europeans dealt with each other, and the extended treaty system, in which they dealt with the world. The latter system will be seen as more than a measure of European expansion. It will also show the extent and intricacy of the involvement of North American Indian groups in the world of the eighteenth century. The dates 1763 to 1774 are used for analysis because 1775 marks a cutoff date in North America, when the growing importance of the peripheries was made dramatically evident in the English colonies' War for Independence.

The European Treaty System

The long dominance of France in European affairs is evident in the one hundred treaties that were negotiated between European powers from 1763 through 1774. Sixty-nine of the one hundred were recorded in French (see table 1).[14]

Table 1   Language of Printed Treaties in the European Treaty System, 1763–74

Language of Treaties	No. of Treaties
French	69
German	17
Italian	6
Spanish	3
Latin	3
Swedish	1
Portuguese	1
Total	100

SOURCE: Clive Parry, ed., *The Consolidated Treaty Series*, 175 vols. (Dobbs Ferry, N.Y.: Oceana Publications, 1969), vols. 42–45.

Despite France's defeat in the Seven Years War, French was still the language of European diplomacy. The fact was an ever-present reminder that for many years all European arrangements, whether they included France or not, had had to be made with an eye to French interests and desires. And France itself was still an active participant in the postwar European treaty system. Of the one hundred treaties negotiated between European powers, France signed thirty-nine, more than twice as many as the next two most active participants, Austria-Hungary and Russia (see table 2).[15]

Poland is the special case that enforces caution in equating participation with influence. Poland's participation during this period was largely involuntary, and reflected internal divisions and weakness as well as the expansionary policies of neighboring states. France was not being dismembered, however, as Poland was. France was a voluntary, active participant in the multitude of arrangements whereby forty-four nation-states, free cities, duchies, principalities, landgravitates, and empires sought the conflicting goals of stability and power. Moreover, French participation was spread evenly throughout the period (see figure 1), instead of being concentrated in periods of crisis or during the tenure of some especially active foreign minister. Figure 1 also shows the relative inactivity of Great Britain in the European treaty system in the interwar period. The situation changed in 1776 when the British signed six European treaties in one year as they hired troops from several German states for the fighting in North America. This was as many European treaties as they had signed in the entire preceding twelve-year period. A comparison with the French activity shown in figure 1 emphasizes again the prominent position of the French in continental European affairs.

Table 2   Major Participants in the European Treaty System, 1763–74

Participants	No. of Treaties
France	39
Austria-Hungary	18
Russia	17
Denmark	14
Prussia	13
Spain	13
Poland	8
Sardinia	8
Great Britain	6
Bavaria	5
The Palatinate	5
Sweden	5
Venice	5
All others (31):	1–5
Total treaties 100	
Total participants 44	

SOURCE: Clive Parry, ed., *The Consolidated Treaty Series,* 175 vols. (Dobbs Ferry, N.Y.: Oceana Publications, 1969), vols. 42–45.

The Extended Treaty System

Elsewhere the situation was different. In the treaty networks that were developing between European outposts and the various groups with which Europeans came in contact around the world, Great Britain, not France, was the prominent power. Figure 2 shows the activity of the two nations after the Seven Years War. Activity here is measured by the number of treaties signed by each and reported in the standard treaty collections.

Fig. 1. European treaty system, 1763-1774: participation.

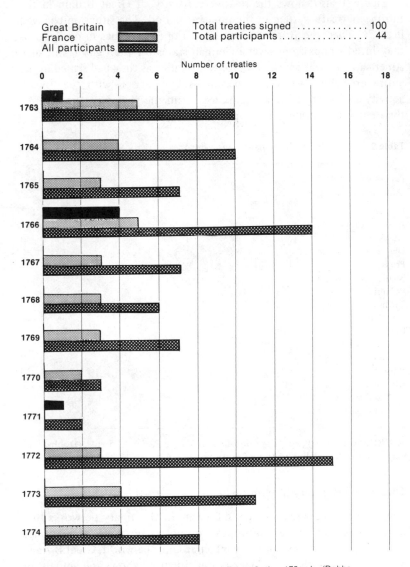

SOURCE: Clive Parry, ed., *The Consolidated Treaty Series*, 175 vols. (Dobbs Ferry, NY: Oceana Publications, 1969), vols. 42-45.

Fig. 2. Extended European treaty system, 1763-1774: major European participation (standard sources).

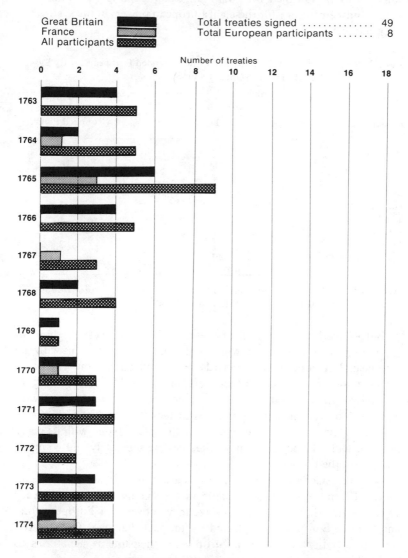

Great Britain
France
All participants

Total treaties signed 49
Total European participants 8

Number of treaties

0　2　4　6　8　10　12　14　16　18

1763
1764
1765
1766
1767
1768
1769
1770
1771
1772
1773
1774

SOURCE: Clive Parry, ed., *The Consolidated Treaty Series*, 175 vols. (Dobbs Ferry. NY: Oceana Publications. 1969). vols. 42-45.

The positions in figure 1 have been reversed. In fact, Great Britain was even more active in the extended system, proportionate to the total number of treaties signed, than was France on the European continent.[16] Totals and percentages for the eight European powers in the system are given in table 3.

Table 3   European Participation in the Extended European Treaty System, 1763–74 (Standard Sources)

Participants	No. of Treaties	% of Total (Rounded Figures)
Great Britain	29	60
France	8	16
Portugal	4	8
Sweden	2	4
Denmark	2	4
The Netherlands	2	4
Russia	1	2
Spain	1	2
Total	49	

SOURCE: Clive Parry, ed., *The Consolidated Treaty Series,* 175 vols. (Dobbs Ferry, N.Y.: Oceana Publications, 1969), vols. 42–45.

But what of the other half of the extended treaty system, those indigenous peoples around the world who were coming to terms with the Europeans? According to standard treaty collections, the two most active non-European participants were India and Morocco (see figure 3). Activity here is not a measure of power but of involvement with Europe. Morocco, in second place, is included in the figure chiefly to emphasize the intensive involvement of first-place India, with its many political and religious units and rulers dealing separately and competitively with the Europeans.

With the standard treaty collections again used as sources, a breakdown of non-European participants in the extended European treaty system is given in table 4. (The discrepancy between the European total and the non-European is explained by the fact that two of the treaties were trilateral, with two non-European participants as signatories to each. The total number of treaties is still forty-nine.)

A regional grouping of non-European participants (see table 5) demonstrates that, according to standard sources, the area of the world most

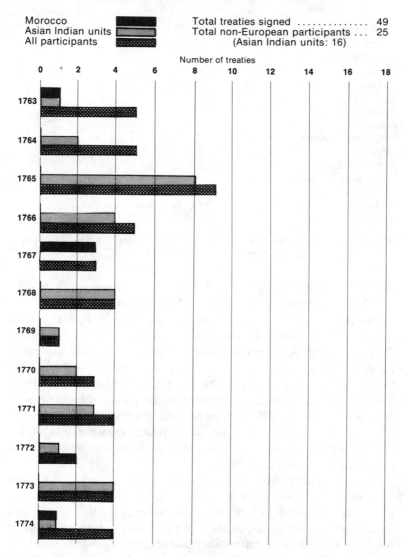

Fig. 3. Extended European treaty system, 1763-1774: major non-European participation (standard sources).

Morocco
Asian Indian units
All participants

Total treaties signed 49
Total non-European participants . . . 25
(Asian Indian units: 16)

SOURCE: Clive Parry, ed., *The Consolidated Treaty Series*, 175 vols. (Dobbs Ferry, NY: Oceana Publications, 1969), vols. 42-45.

Table 4   Non-European Participation in the Extended European Treaty
System, 1763–74 (Standard Sources)

Participants	No. of Treaties	% of Total (Rounded Figures)
India (16 units)	31	63
Morocco	5	10
Algiers	3	6
Tunis	3	6
Tripoli	2	4
Persia (Iran)	2	4
Sulu (the Philippines)	2	4
China	1	2
Kandy (Sri Lanka)	1	2
Seneca Indian Nation (North America)	1	2
Total	51 (49)	

SOURCE: Clive Parry, ed., *The Consolidated Treaty Series,* 175 vols. (Dobbs
Ferry, N.Y.: Oceana Publications, 1969), vols. 42–45.

heavily involved with Europe in this period was South and West Asia,
with North Africa in second place, and North America last.

The picture is not a true one, however. It is distorted by the standard
sources, where North American–British treaties are underrepresented.
Only one North American treaty of the period found its way into a
standard treaty collection: the Seneca peace treaty of 1764.[17] That
treaty was one of five treaties that were negotiated in the single year
1764 between Great Britain and various Indian groups in former French
or Spanish territories. (Some of the Senecas had fought with the French;
it was with that faction that the peace treaty was signed.) In all, between twenty-six and thirty Anglo-Amerindian treaties were signed in
the period from 1763 to 1774.

The uncertainty about the total arises from the fact that it is not
clear from the records whether a formal treaty was actually signed at
four critical meetings in 1765. At those meetings the British bargained
with several Indian groups to allow British forces to take possession of
the forts in the Illinois country they had presumably already won from
the French.[18] The need for the British to bargain at all is indicative of
the many levels of diplomacy being conducted throughout this period,
as diplomats in Europe disposed of the world to their satisfaction, leav-

ing it to men like George Croghan at Ouiatenon on the Wabash River to negotiate with those in actual possession of the ground.[19]

The Great War for the Empire, as Lawrence Gipson has so aptly styled the worldwide conflicts of the 1750s and 1760s, began in the North American backcountry two years before fighting broke out in Europe, and did not end in North America until the general treaty of peace signed in August 1765 at Detroit—some two years after the February 1763 Treaty of Paris had supposedly brought hostilities to a close. The extended European treaty system had a different timetable than the strictly European system. It depended more on the realities of the power commanded by non-Europeans and less on official statements of policy. In the figures and table below, the four agreements regarding British possession of the forts in the Illinois country have been included as formal treaties. If further investigation should show that they were not, the general description of the treaty network binding Great Britain and some twenty-two North American Indian groups will not be greatly changed.

Table 5   Regional Non-European Participation in the Extended European Treaty System, 1763–74 (Standard Sources)

Participants	No. of Treaties, Regional Units	No. of Treaties by Regions
South and West Asia		34
India	31	
Persia	2	
Kandy	1	
North Africa		13
Morocco	5	
Algiers	3	
Tunis	3	
Tripoli	2	
East and Southeast Asia		3
Sulu	2	
China	1	
North America		1
Seneca	1	
Total	51 (49)	51

SOURCE: Clive Parry, ed., *The Consolidated Treaty Series*, 175 vols. (Dobbs Ferry, N.Y.: Oceana Publications, 1969), vols. 42–45.

When the Anglo-Amerindian treaties of 1763-74 are added to the
treaties drawn from standard sources, and adjustments are made to eliminate overlap, North American Indian groups are seen to be almost as
deeply involved in the extended European treaty system as were the
various groups in India. North American Indians were signatories to
thirty treaties, or 39 percent of the total number of treaties (revised
total: seventy-seven), and Asian Indians to thirty-one treaties, or 40
percent of the total (see figure 4).

Even this does not give a clear enough picture, however. A further
breakdown is necessary. Neither North America nor India existed as a
single political unit in this period, although the Iroquois in North America, like the Marathas or the Mogul emperors on the Indian subcontinent,
claimed to speak for those far beyond the areas they could actually
control. A breakdown into the major signatory units (see table 6),
shows the participants with the deepest involvements in the extended
European treaty system.[20]

All of this does not give a complete picture of the relationships involved in the treaties, of course. Nor does it even hint at the complexities that were caused by the different concepts and goals that the participants brought to their treaty relationships. What the charts and
tables do demonstrate, with the vividness of specific figures, is the

Table 6   Major Non-European Participation in the Extended European
                    Treaty System, 1763-74, (Revised Figures)

Participants	No. of Treaties	% of Total (rounded figures)
Creek Confederacy (North America)	8	10
Cherokee Nation (North America)	8	9
Bengal (India)	6	8
Morocco (North Africa)	5	6
Wyandot (North America)	5	6
The Mogul Empire (India)	4	5
Iroquois Confederacy (North America)	4	5
Otawa (North America)	4	5
Total treaties 77		
Total non-European units 46		

SOURCE: Clive Parry, ed., *The Consolidated Treaty Series,* 175 vols. (Dobbs
Ferry, N.Y.: Oceana Publications, 1969), vols. 42-45; various documentary material (see Appendix A).

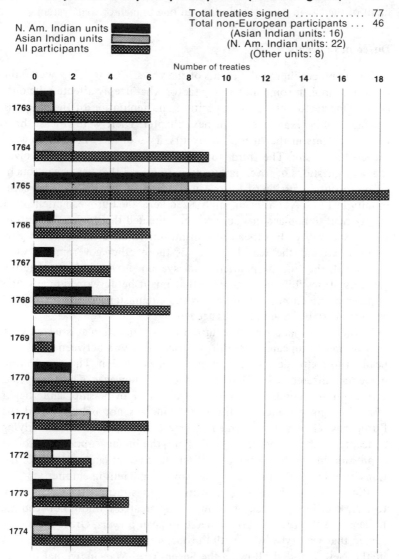

Fig. 4. Extended European treaty system, 1763-1774: major non-European participation (revised figures).

Total treaties signed 77
Total non-European participants ... 46
(Asian Indian units: 16)
(N. Am. Indian units: 22)
(Other units: 8)

N. Am. Indian units
Asian Indian units
All participants

Number of treaties

SOURCES: Clive Parry, ed., *The Consolidated Treaty Series*, 175 vols. (Dobbs Ferry, NY: Oceana Publications, 1969), vols. 42-45; various documentary material. see Appendix A.

worldwide nature of the extended treaty system that was developing throughout the eighteenth century. They also show the deep involvement of the North American Indians in one branch of that system.

Different Concepts

Before proceeding to the events of the years 1763 to 1796, we would do well to look at some underlying factors that deeply affected the outcome. One factor—the unique position and reputation of the Iroquois League—will be examined in the next chapter. There were at least three other constants in the turmoil of events. Two of these have to do with ownership of land. The third, to which the other two are tied, involves the very questions of sovereignty and nationhood that have been touched on in this discussion of European concepts of the international community in 1763. As has been emphasized here, the European intellectual engagement took place in a context that directed the thinkers' attention to the survivals of European feudalism, not to different forms of government around the world. So far as those other governments were concerned, the European intellectual system provided chiefly alternative sets of possibilities, potentials that might be developed in any of a number of directions, depending on the circumstances—the ideological buttressing to be added later, as needed.

Ownership of land was, of course, the basic question at issue between Indians and Europeans in North America, as it was between the Europeans who contended with each other for possession. There was a fundamental difference in these two contests, however. The Europeans agreed on the conditions and prerogatives of ownership, and fought over the right to exercise them. The Indians not only opposed the Europeans' efforts, they denied utterly the validity of the underlying concepts. In the period under study here, the Indians' opposition found expression in conflicts over two different issues of land ownership: the transfer of territorial rights, and the powers inherent in empire.

Right from the beginning of British administration of the backcountry, these differing concepts of ownership created tensions between the Indians and the British. Like other European powers, Great Britain assumed that victory in wars with European rivals gave it territorial rights in the New World. Following the Seven Years War, individual Indians repudiated this assumption in statements that were so widespread, numerous, and similar as to make it obvious that the Indians, in general, had a clear understanding of European concepts of territory and of how those concepts might affect them. Over and over again they denied that France had the right to transfer any Indian territory to Great Britain. Some of the Indians pointed out that even the land on which French forts were built had only been lent to France, not given.[21]

In the South, Great Britain managed to avoid outright confrontation over the issue by returning some French forts to the Indians and concentrating negotiations on trade and the boundary. North of the Ohio, war broke out before negotiations could defuse the situation. There the Indians fought rather than accept the idea that a transfer of title between Europeans was sufficient to effect any change in the ownership of Indian land. Not until the northern Indians were defeated was it possible to try to contain this basic conceptual conflict in the accommodation treaty system that was being put together in the period 1763–68. Then temporary containment was made possible by the device of a comprehensive boundary that reduced the frictions caused by different concepts.

The issue of land ownership surfaced again in a conflict over the powers inherent in empire, and this conflict proved too much for the accommodation treaty system to contain. So far as Europeans were concerned, the imperial relationship conferred the right of land transfer on the dominant power. Again, the Indians denied the validity of the conception, but this time not all the Indians denied it. Disastrous consequences spread out from that small ideological fault.

The question, in general terms, was what constituted an empire. The specific application of the question was to the Iroquois League and to the widespread net of Iroquois relationships as they existed when the League was at the height of its power in the mid-seventeenth and early eighteenth centuries. Iroquois hegemony was not based on territorial domination so much as on mutually acknowledged rights and obligations of varying degrees by which Indian nations over a wide area furnished tribute and warriors. The Iroquois, in turn, functioned as intermediaries between the British and the Indians of the hinterland.[22]

The British, however, interpreted empire in territorial terms and assumed that the Iroquois League had the right to convey the land of its dependents. By about the middle of the eighteenth century, the Iroquois had themselves adopted this territorial conception and had several times sold land where tributaries had long resided.[23] The vigorous resistance of other Indians, especially the Shawnees and Delawares, to this conception of empire, played a strong part in the transformation and destruction of the accommodation treaty system.

European concepts of land-transfer rights and of the nature of empires had the tremendous power and rigidity of implicit assumptions
which, because they are unexamined, are simply not open for negotiation. Paradoxically, European concepts of sovereignty and nationhood
were more flexible precisely because those who had studied them had
to consider alternatives. Presented with different kinds of political arrangements from Europe's feudal past, philosophers had been forced
to compare, consider, define. The result was a blend of natural and
positive "law" at a very high level of abstraction. The level was high
enough to accommodate the variety of European forms of government.
Practical possibilities were thus left open. If non-Europeans were not
included—because they were scarcely considered—there still was little
in eighteenth-century political theory that would automatically bar them
from the family of nations that was the staple of the philosophers'
thought.

For example, Vattel's definition of a nation could have included all
the diverse peoples with whom Europeans were in contact: "Nations
or states are political bodies, societies of men who have united together
and combined their forces, in order to procure their mutual welfare and
security."[24]

In another passage, Vattel brought all people within the law he was
seeking to discover and to relate to practice: "we deduce a natural society existing among all men. The general law of this society is that each
member should assist the others in all their needs, as far as he can do so
without neglecting his duties to himself."[25]

It can be seen that membership in Vattel's natural society was open
to all, regardless of location or social organization. So far as European
theory was concerned, the American Indian nations could qualify for
membership. The practical effect of this theoretical flexibility was that
the Indians were free to make whatever place they could for themselves
in the world that pressed in upon them after 1763. The Indians were
not the only groups for which this was true. That was the actual situation for all nations in the eighteenth century, even those European
nations that fit all the specifically European conditions and had unar-
guable theoretical rights to sovereignty and territorial dominion. Neither
theory, nor Christian status, nor long-established existence saved Poland
from dismemberment at the hands of her neighbors. What counted for
Poland was the disparity of power.[26]

It would be the same for the Indian nations of North America.

2   Iroquois Mystique

In the prolonged struggles that led to the partition of eastern North America among Europeans, alliances with the Indian nations were of primary importance. Competition was keen for the favor and fighting men of various Indian groups, and for none was it keener than for members of the Iroquois League.[1] The Iroquois understood power, possessed it for more than a hundred years, and were skilled in the uses to which power may be put. Moreover, they shared an image of themselves as a people destined for leadership, and this added the intangible qualities of dedication and belief to their formidable military strength.

Iroquois power rested on location, numbers, and political organization. When Europeans first came in contact with them, the Iroquois lived in an area that extended south and west from Lake Champlain to the Genesee River. This strategic crescent was at the center of their power. From it they could command the Lake George and Lake Champlain access routes to the St. Lawrence River, as well as the upper Hudson and Mohawk River passage to Lakes Ontario and Erie and the transmontane West. From it, in the early 1600s, they embarked on wars of expansion and trade control, armed with guns they had procured from the Europeans. By the early 1700s they dominated the area from the Ottawa River (north of the St. Lawrence), west to Lake Huron, and south to the banks of the Tennessee River. On occasion they raided farther west and south, so that the Iroquois presence was felt throughout the entire area of what became the Northwest Territory as well as south of the Ohio River and north into lower Canada.[2]

The extent of their control in this area was a matter of dispute at the time, and is a matter of dispute today. Opinions range from Lewis Henry Morgan's admiring description of a vast tributary empire, to Francis Jennings's skeptical detailing of the weakness of specific relationships

21

at specific periods.[3] It seems clear that what the Iroquois did create during their period of expansion was a reputation for ferocity and power that, in itself, became one of their sources of strength.

All of this was accomplished by a people whose number is not known for sure, but who may have reached sixteen thousand at their most populous, sometime in the mid-1600s.[4] The question of how many Iroquois there were at any given time is a part of the ongoing scholarly controversy about Indian population in the New World, which one scholar has called "la Polémica" because of the passions it has involved.[5] Briefly, the arguments are as follows:

The population of the two Americas before contact with Europeans was much greater than formerly supposed, possibly 100 million, in contrast to the former estimate of 8.4 million. For North America the former estimate was 1.1 million. Estimates today range from 9.8 million to 2.1 million.

Early in contact times, the Indian populations were swept by European diseases for which they had no immunity. These diseases, chiefly influenza, measles, and smallpox, killed unknown millions of Indians.[6]

When European settlers arrived in the New York they were actually resettling lands that had been all but emptied of their inhabitants by a demographic catastrophe. The best-known example of this in North America is the English settlement at Plymouth, where the Pilgrims found themselves heir to the cleared fields and empty cabins of their Massachusetts and Wampanoag predecessors who had died by the thousands before the Pilgrims ever arrived.

To this point the arguments over aboriginal population consist of fairly straightforward disputes over types of evidence, the weight to give to contemporary estimates, and the method of projecting estimates from the slender evidence that is available. Passions become involved when the charge of racism is leveled against those who disagree with the current estimates or against those scholars whose early estimates were low. The charge is made that an unconscious racism predisposed those scholars to accept lower population figures, whenever their sources offered a choice, because they operated on the unstated assumption that the Indians, especially of North America, did not have the political and social skills necessary to maintain large populations.[7]

There can be little question of the political and social skills of the Iroquois, even though there is a question of how many people were involved in the confederacy that they formed and in the area of influence that they fought to create. They sometimes incurred heavy losses in battle, but they made up the losses by adopting prisoners from their defeated enemies. (Adoption was a personal right, exercised frequently enough and on a wide enough scale that it became, in effect, a League policy.)[8] Some losses they were not able to overcome. Internal divisions were a persistent problem for the Iroquois, and they were not able to secure the return of groups that broke away in the mid-1600s and moved north to locations on the St. Lawrence. By 1763, the population of the main part of the League was estimated at between nine and eleven thousand.[9] This was enough to assure them the respectful attention of European and colonial authorities. Moreover, the concentration of this population in the relatively small area of the Mohawk Valley and western New York and Pennsylvania made the Iroquois far more conspicuous than, say the Ottawas and Chippewas who were scattered from the Ottawa River west to Lake Superior.

The organizational skill of the Iroquois is evident in the structure and longevity of their confederacy. Confederation was a common political form throughout eastern North America at least as far south as the James River. Long before the coming of the Europeans, the Indians of the area were forming themselves into confederacies of varying size, strength, cohesion, and formality in a constantly shifting pattern of alliances and conquests. The names of some that existed at the time of European contact have been preserved in the words and understanding of the Europeans who encountered them: the Powhatan Confederacy (Virginia); the Nanticoke Confederacy (Maryland); the Delaware Confederacy (New Jersey, eastern Pennsylvania, and New York); the Wappinger Confederacy (what is now Manhattan and the Bronx); the Mahican Confederacy (on the Hudson River); the Illinois Confederacy; and others. The Iroquois contribution was to take this form, which in practice often had little practical effect, and make it a source of domestic strength as well as a weapon of conquest.[10]

The exact date of the founding of the Iroquois League is not known. Estimates range from about 1390 to about 1570.[11] Scholars today believe that the Iroquois population was growing when the League was founded. There was increasing pressure on resources, and an increase in the number of personal and tribal contacts. In a society where vision quests, moral imperatives, and revenge obligations were intensely personal, increased contacts meant increased opportunities for friction and bloodshed. The League was an attempt to suppress in-group hostilities and turn them outward against the world of those who did not belong. By and large, the attempt was successful.[12]

Originally, five Indian nations were members of the Iroquois League: Seneca, Cayuga, Onondaga, Oneida, and Mohawk. In the 1720s the Tuscaroras were admitted, or what was left of the nation after repeated wars with white settlers drove them from their homes in North Carolina. Other refugee groups also were granted asylum and protection by the League: the Nanticoke and Conoy from Maryland, and the Saponi and Tutelo from Virginia. Still other groups were taken in by conquest: the Huron, Tobacco, Neutral, and Erie, to name only the major conquests of the seventeenth century. Despite these additions, however, the League was commonly known as the Five Nations until after the incorporation of the Tuscaroras in the 1720s. Then it was usually referred to as the Six Nations.

The basic political structure of the Iroquois League, from the village level to the confederacy level, was that of leadership councils chosen from among prescribed groups by methods that allowed the people of the villages a say in the choices. The League Council was the village council writ large. Fifty chiefs, or sachems, made up the League Council which met at least once a year in formal session at Onondaga, the central nation of the five original members of the League.[13]

But the strength of the Iroquois did not lie in political structure alone. That was only the skeleton of their League. Surrounding that was a body of history, legend, feeling, and purpose that was given vivid life in ceremony and song, and reinforced with every new Iroquois conquest. The power of the Iroquois cannot be understood without an attempt to see the League from the Iroquois point of view. Other Indian confederacies had risen and taken in nations by conquest. The Iroquois had more in mind than that. They believed themselves destined to conquer because they had a mission to take in all nations. In their own eyes they were not simply part of a powerful political confederacy. They were nothing less than agents of universal peace.

The Iroquois View

At the core of Iroquois thought about the world was their own League. Before its founding there had been terror and disorder as the Five Nations fought against each other. After the nations had been brought together under the one roof of the Kanonsionni, the Longhouse (of the League), they began to seek the way of reason, righteousness, and peace as explained by Deganawidah, the founder of the League, and by Hiawatha, Deganawidah's messenger.

Degenawidah took one arrow from each of the Five Nations and bound them together, showing the strength that comes through unity. He gave the Longhouse the strong supporting rafters of the Law. He also planted a white pine, the Tree of the Great Peace, which was to spread until all nations could shelter under its branches.

This, in brief, was the founding tradition of the League, stripped of most of the metaphorical expressions that shaped it and gave it meaning to an individual Iroquois—expressions that, in the usual English translations, are reminiscent of Longfellow at his most turgid. The metaphorical expressions were an integral part of the world outlook of a Mohawk or Cayuga, of a Seneca, Oneida, or Onondaga of the seventeenth and eighteenth centuries. Their concrete imagery could move easily from the law as rafters of the Longhouse to the law as a great white mat under the tree of peace: "the soft white feathery down of the globe thistle," as one version of the League's founding has it.[14]

Those whose acquaintance with metaphor was limited to the drawing room or the library quickly discovered its multitude of uses in the Iroquois world. It was an effective vehicle for negotiations. It expressed pride. It bound members of the League into an emotional unity with evocations of their deepest common memories and their highest aspirations. It was a part of ordinary life, as well as of high ceremonial occasions. The individual Iroquois found on every hand reminders of the League, its history, and its eventual destiny.

When the League Council met at Onondaga, all individual members of the League were encouraged to attend. The prayer that opened the council was not only a prayer of thanksgiving but also a recollection of the first council of the League when Deganawidah laid down the procedures that were to be followed thereafter. At the council, songs were sung to commemorate the founding of the League. The very names of the councillors sounded the note of destiny. They were the same names as those of the League's founders at the first council, handed down through the generations as a tangible link with the time when the Five Nations had accepted Deganawidah's good news of peace and power.[15]

There was nothing metaphorical about the business of the councils. The councillors, with their ancient titles, were concerned with contemporary problems of policy that bore on the lives of all those around them, not just on those of the members of the League. In the late seventeenth century they might, for example, convene a council to receive a deputation from the New England colonies. Hard-pressed by a war with the Indians of New England, the English colonists turned often to the League with requests for military aid. Or, on the early eighteenth century, the council might meet to decide on a leader for one of the nations it had settled in the Susquehannah region to the south as a buffer between the Iroquois and the Cherokees and other southern Indians. Whatever the issue, the Iroquois dealt with the present in terminology that recalled the past when they had been given a charter for greatness.[16]

On one other special occasion, the individual Iroquois would be given a vivid reminder of the founding and purpose of the League. That was when death created a vacancy on the League Council and a new sachem was installed. Through the condolence ceremony, the grief of the deceased leader's moiety (a social division comprising roughly half the League's members) was ritually eased and dispersed, and the new leader was invested with the antlers of office and given a charge for future conduct. The light of high destiny shines throughout this condolence ceremony, which might involve hundreds of individuals in a prescribed pattern of chants, dances, hymns, and recitations. Grief and the fear of death intensified the emotional impact of this celebration of the League.[17]

The founders' names were told again, although they were familiar to all. The League's laws were recited by an orator who walked to and fro in the longhouse, which was, itself, a symbol of the League. The new sachem was charged to join the other council members in planting the great tree of peace, the roots of which would grow in the four directions of the compass, strengthening the tree and enabling it to spread and and shelter all the nations. And if other nations did not want to join the great peace, Iroquois law made provision for that. There could be alliances between the Iroquois and other nations. Or the Iroquois could take other nations under their protection, as they had with the client groups to the south and west of their homeland. But if a nation refused both protective status and an alliance of equals, then the law provided that that nation might be destroyed. No nation could hold itself outside the way of justice, righteousness, and peace that had been revealed to the League for all people everywhere.[18]

All this was part of the Iroquois world view. For individual men and women, the very houses they lived in, the trees they passed on their way to the field or the council house were affirmations of destiny. Theirs was the pride not only of accomplishment but of heritage. *Who they were,* gave them standing in their own eyes, as much as what they did. To a remarkable degree they were able to impose this view on others.

The high esteem in which the Iroquois were held by the British can be seen in the emphasis that was placed on them both before and after the French and Indian War. At Albany in 1754 and again in the years following the war, British policymakers frequently acted on the assumption that the way to a solution of the problems of the continent lay through the narrow gateway of the League of the Six Nations.

Albany, 1754

Several lines of historical circumstances came together at Albany in 1754. One was the long-standing rivalry between France and England, a rivalry that periodically broke out in open warfare on the European continent, on the sea, and at the outposts of European empire around the world. Another was made up of the tensions within the Iroquois League and the extent to which the League was or was not an empire that could be controlled from the central longhouse at Onondaga. A third line of circumstance that would assume ever greater importance in the years ahead, was the colonial line. In 1754 it was beginning to diverge markedly from the European-imperial line, and to take a course based on needs and purposes that were perceived differently in the colonies than at Whitehall.[19]

In the years preceding the Albany Congress, the French had announced their intention of driving the English out of the Ohio region, and they had begun the construction of forts in a great arc back of the British settlements in an attempt to contain the British and to connect their own settlements in Canada and Louisiana. By the time the colonial commissioners gathered at Albany in late June of 1754, the situation in the Ohio country had moved from confrontation to warfare. That spring, French troops captured a Virginia-built fort near the forks of the Ohio after first making a formal announcement to the commander that the presence of the British was contrary to the Treaty of Aix-la-Chapelle.[20]

Nothing is more indicative of the way that Europeans took their quarrels with them on their travels than this solumn appeal in the North American backcountry to the 1748 Treaty of Aix-la-Chapelle with its complicated and fragile arrangements stemming from Prussia's seizure of Silesia, the ambitions of the Spanish queen, and difficulties over the Austrian and British royal successions. Only the utmost seriousness could have sustained these quarrels half a world away at a small frontier stockade where the most numerous witnesses were the surrounding trees. The seriousness was sufficient, however. Not only were the European quarrels sustained, they were explanded into eleven more years of fighting.[21]

Where the Iroquois stood in this rivalry was a matter of great concern to the British, both in the colonies and in London. For some time prior to the outbreak of fighting, information about the Iroquois had been disturbing to those policymakers who were relying on the long Iroquois-British friendship to protect the northern flank of the colonies from French attack and to check the French advance of the Ohio valley. By the early 1750s, the French had succeeded in winning allies among the Senecas, the westernmost nation of the confederacy. There were reports of French gains among the Cayugas, Onondagas, Tuscaroras, and Oneidas just south of the St. Lawrence-Ontario waterway to the interior.[22] Further, in 1753, the Mohawks had formally renounced their alliance with the British and had threatened to wreck the special Iroquois-British relationship that had developed through years of negotiation with separate English colonies.

At a meeting at Fort George in June 1753, Hendrick, the Mohawk spokesman, detailed Mohawk complaints about usurpation of their land and about lack of British support and protection for those Indians who had fought the French at the request of the British. He then informed the New York governor, George Clinton, and the members of the provincial council that the Mohawks were breaking the covenant chain that had for so long bound them to the British in New York. Hendrick rejected Clinton's attempts to refer the matter to Albany for future study and action and told him that none of the Iroquois nations would be coming to Albany anymore:

> Brother. By & By you will expect to see the Nations down [at Albany], which you shall not see, for as soon as we come home we will send up a Belt of Wampum to our Brothers the 5 Nations to acquaint them the Covenant Chain is broken between you and us. So brother you are not to expect to hear of me any more, and Brother we desire to hear no more of you.[23]

British policymakers could not afford to ignore these developments. In September 1753, the Lords Commissioners for Trade and Plantations (the Board of Trade) gave orders for the intercolonial meeting that came to be known as the Albany Congress. A later emphasis on national history has obscured the extent to which the congress was an international one, stimulated by and concerned with matters of international influence and power. Among these concerns, French influence among the Iroquois was high on the list.

In the September directive, the lords comissioners emphasized their concern, and spoke of "how great consequence the friendship and alliance of the Six Nations is to all His Majesty's Colonies and Plantations in America."[24] The following summer, in a letter written to the lieutenant governor of New York, they made even more explicit their assessment of the Iroquois alliance:

> The preserving and securing the friendship of these Indians is in
> the present situation of affairs an object of the greatest importance.
> It is from the steady adherence of these Indians to the British Inter-
> est that not only New York but all the other Northern Colonys have
> hitherto been secured from the fatal effects of the encroachments
> of a foreign power, and without their friendship and assistance all
> our efforts to check and disappoint the present view of this power
> may prove ineffectual.[25]

The outbreak of hostilities in the spring of 1754 gave special urgency to the meeting at Albany in June. About 150 Iroquois representatives met with representatives from Massachusetts, New Hampshire, Connecticut, Rhode Island, Pennsylvania, Maryland, and New York. The colonial commissioners were disappointed at the size of the Iroquois delegation and suspected French influence:

> It is a melancholy consideration that not more than 150 Men of all
> the several Nations have attended this Treaty, although they had
> notice that all the Governors would be here by their Commissioners,
> and that a large present would be given.[26]

The disappointment of the colonial commissioners is a measure both of the importance that was attached to the Iroquois alliance and of the extent to which the Six Nations had put their stamp on negotiations with the British. The commissioners were aware that policy decisions among the Iroquois had to rest on a broad consensus. Matters that concerned the League were thoroughly discussed at the village level before being taken up for consideration by the League Council, and individuals were encouraged to attend the meetings of the League Council, whether at Onondaga or Albany.[27] The more individual Iroquois who were present and involved in negotiations, the greater the likelihood of reaching an agreement that would be binding on the League. The British groaned at the expense that was involved, but they continued to provide food, clothing, hunting supplies, sometimes shelter, and often transportation to and from the treaty councils, because that was the Iroquois way of doing business.[28]

The Iroquois stamp could be seen, too, on the formal ceremony with which the negotiations opened. Before any business began or could begin, Lieutenant Governor James DeLancey of New York, on behalf of the British, expressed sympathy for whatever losses the Iroquois had suffered since the last meeting between the two peoples and attempted to remove the obstacles that continued grief might place in the path of negotiation.[29] The figures of speech that were used by the lieutenant governor, the gestures, the whole ritual of condolence extended and received, were all a part of what might be called the export version of the Iroquois condolence ceremony, which they performed at greater length on the occasion of the death of one of the sachems of the League Council.

Their success in getting the ceremony accepted as an obligatory part of any negotiation between themselves and Europeans meant that every such council opened with a part of the ceremony that was one long glorification of the League and that was, in their own eyes, an affirmation of their high destiny. Iroquois influence ran so far in the seventeenth and eighteenth centuries that the condolence ceremony, in its shortened form, became the opening in many European councils with northern Indians where the Iroquois were not even present.[30]

After DeLancey had exchanged the expected condolences with the Iroquois, he moved quickly to the business of the meeting. He spoke of the covenant chain relationship between the Indians and the British, and of the need to strengthen the chain. This complex system of alliances and protectorates, possibly dating back to the early 1600s, was in a perpetual state of change that reflected the strengths, weaknesses, and varying policies of the many white and Indian groups that were involved at one time or another. By the mid-eighteenth century, New York on the one hand, and the Iroquois League on the other, were center links of a chain that was beginning to come apart among the Indians as the Iroquois turned it to their own uses.[31] The British, however, were not so concerned about the intra-Indian relationships in the chain as about their own position vis-à-vis the Iroquois. They needed Indian help to halt the French advance in the Ohio Valley. A prerequisite was to get the Iroquois to reaffirm the ancient covenant chain relationship with the northern and middle colonies, and possibly to include Virginia as well.

The British also attempted to put pressure on the Iroquois to make good some of their claims to empire. If the Iroquois were indeed the head of an empire embracing most of North America east of the Mississippi and north of the Ohio, then they presumably could answer for whatever happened there. DeLancey took that to be the case, at least for purposes of negotiation, when he made the Iroquois responsible for the very presence of the French at the head of the Ohio, an area well within the domain that was claimed by the Iroquois. DeLancey demanded to know why it was that the French were building forts there on Iroquois land. Had the Iroquois given the French permission to build? Had they sold the land to the French?[32]

Following a two-day recess for the Iroquois to meet privately together and compose a reply, they responded that the French had invited themselves onto Iroquois land. No one had invited them, or sold them the land. The Iroquois then went on the diplomatic attack and demanded in their turn why it was that Virginia had built a fort west of the mountains without first sending to the Great Council at Onondaga and getting permission. They also noted that the French were generous with the Indians, while the British were not, and that the French were building new forts and getting stronger every day while the British did not even have a fort at Albany to protect it from the French in Canada. Finally—a point that was slipped in between others with seeming casualness—they pointed out that the quarrel that was beginning over the land west of the mountains was over land that belonged not to France, or to Britain, but to the Iroquois.[33]

This reply was delivered by Hendrick, the Mohawk spokesman who, one year earlier, had broken off negotiations with New York's Governor Clinton, dissolved the Mohawk-British alliance, and threatened to use Mohawk influence to persuade the rest of the Six Nations to do likewise. With the Iroquois back at Albany, Hendrick was back also, fulfilling the traditional Mohawk role as one of the elder nations of the confederacy, a speaker for the League in negotiations with the outside world. Hendrick was one of those Indians who were emerging as spokesmen in many of the Indian nations. He had been to England. He knew white ways at first hand, and from childhood he had been steeped in the ways of the Iroquois. He stands out as a competent spokesman for Indian interests, in this case by carrying the diplomatic attack to the British and pressing it as far as possible.[34]

The British did not know how strong Hendrick's position was, or how far the Iroquois could or would go in defense of the high ground

Hendrick had taken on their behalf. Perhaps the Iroquois who were at Albany themselves did not know. At any rate, the commissioners' reply, delivered the day after Hendrick spoke, went to the unacknowledged heart of the matter: the extent of Iroquois influence in the Ohio Valley.

With great care, the commissioners pointed out that as long ago as 1750 the king had been concerned about growing French influence on the Ohio, and had sent a large present to be given to the Indians there where the French were most active. When asked, through their council at Onondaga, to come to that meeting, the Six Nations had not replied. So, eventually, the king's gifts were given to the Ohio Indians, and at the same time the governor of Virginia proposed to them that a fort be built on the Monongahela to protect them from the French and to insure a supply of British goods. The Ohio Indians agreed, and said they would send to the Six Nations and discuss the proposal. But again nothing was heard from the Six Nations. The fort was therefore built at the request of the Ohio Indians, and then was taken by the French when they invaded the Ohio country.[35]

The Indians' thrust had been turned against them. If they admitted that the Ohio Indians—in this instance, Delawares and Shawnees—had acted without the advice and consent of the Great Council of the Six Nations at Onondaga, they would be admitting that their authority did not fit their claim. They were not likely to make that admission, as the British knew. More specifically, Conrad Weiser and William Johnson knew it.

These two men were among Britian's most experienced Iroquois hands. Weiser was at the meeting as interpreter for Pennsylvania's private and separate negotiations with the Iroquois. Johnson was acting as general adviser for the colonial commissioners, and from his close knowledge of Iroquois affairs could tell the commissioners exactly where to give way and where to stand firm. Johnson was an archetype of those world-ranging Britons who made the early moves toward empire. In 1754 his career was about to take off from its beginning in the Indian trade. Within a year he would be created a baronet, and a year later would be made British Superintendent of Indian Affairs in the Northern Department. In the years after Albany his style and scale of living would come to be like that of early British administrators among Asian Indians on the other side of the world, before the Mutiny and the tightening of the color line. Johnson's Iroquois connections were with the Mohawks. His most enduring link would be through Molly Brant, who would share with him at Johnson Hall the family life that was sometimes possible between whites and Indians in border America.[36]

The connections spin out almost endlessly into the future. Molly's brother Joseph would take a leading part in the American War for Independence, fighting against the rebelling colonists, and in the 1790s, after moving to Canada, he would try to take a leading part in the continuation of the war by the Indians of the Ohio country—those same Ohio Indians who in 1754 were testing the Iroquois hold on them. The Iroquois present at Albany chose to smooth over the challenge, at least in the presence of the whites. After meeting together for two more days, they gave the commissioners their answer. The counterthrust about the Ohio Indians was turned aside by a bland self-assurance, and a presumption that all was well in the Iroquois domain. There was no hint of dissatisfaction over messages that had been received at Onondaga, or not received, or about supplies that had been distributed to others and not to themselves. So the king's gift had been sent by the governor of Virginia to the Indians on the Ohio? "We thank the Governor of Virginia for assisting the Indians at the Ohio, who are our Brethren and Allies."[37]

Whether they were brethren and allies by choice or by coercion was not discussed at Albany. Nor was there discussion of whether, if force should become necessary, the Iroquois could wield it effectively enough to make them the key to relations in the New World that the British thought they were in 1754. There were practical reasons for the British to maintain this position. Support of Iroquois claims in the West strengthened the British denial of French claims in the same area. At the same time, it opened the way for Great Britain to call on the Iroquois for military aid in the war with France. European powers never lost sight of the economies to be achieved by using native allies instead of their own troops in their wars with each other around the world.

Continuation of the Mystique

A twentieth-century observer can grant that the British assumption of Iroquois dominance served British interests, and still wonder at the persistence of the assumption. The British maintained the same position after the war that drove the French not just from the Ohio Valley but from all of eastern North America. They continued to maintain that position after the gap between League promises and League performance had proved disastrous to British policy. By the time that happened, British expansionists were in control of British policy and found it convenient to maintain the myth of Iroquois dominance. The myth made it easier to acquire western lands belonging to the "brethren and allies" of the Iroquois, through negotiation with and manipulation of the League.[38]

But this will not serve as a complete explanation of the Iroquois reputation, which I have here called the Iroquois mystique. The same reputation existed both earlier and later than the short period during the early 1770s when British expansionists dominated the Board of Trade. As Richard R. Johnson has shown, the mystique was strong in New England during the seventeenth century. It continued strong even though warriors from the Mohawk or other League nations never fought for the New England colonists in sufficient number to play the part of *"Maqua ex machina"* that myth assigned to them.[39]

The mystique continued after the American War for Independence and affected the thinking of American policymakers. Their bent was largely expansionist, but unlike British expansionists they did not see a strong Iroquois confederacy as a convenient means of acquiring land from allied or dependent Indians in the West. They saw it rather as a threat to the new American nation. For American officials, the unanswered question throughout the 1780s and early 1790s was, how real was the threat?[40]

The whole subject deserves further investigation. The most that can be done here is to point out the existence of the Iroquois mystique and to suggest that some of the reasons for its persistence lay not just in European conceptions and goals but also in Iroquois history and self-perception. The Iroquois themselves were among the most enthusiastic propagators of the idea of Iroquois dominance. At treaty negotiations with the Americans in 1784, the Mohawk speaker Captain Aaron Hill claimed that the Six Nations could speak for twelve other Indian nations, including not only the western nations of the Great Lakes and the Ohio Valley, but also such southern Indians as the Choctaws of the lower Mississippi Valley.[41] Even when the specific claims of the Iroquois were denied, as the American negotiators denied them in 1784,[42] the idea of an undefined, possibly formidable strength persisted. Thus, in 1791, Secretary of War Henry Knox sent Timothy Pickering on a special mission to the Iroquois to reassure them about United States intentions, and to secure their promise not to join the western Indian nations, then at war with the United States. Since the League was closer to the settled areas of the United States than were the western nations, its reputation and disposition were matters of particular concern to U.S. officials.[43]

There was another important element in the Iroquois mystique. To a remarkable degree, the Iroquois were able to make themselves the standard of Indianness for Europeans and Americans. A comment made by Emisteseguo, a leader of the Creek Confederacy south of the Ohio, will illustrate the point. Speaking to British negotiators in May 1765, he remarked:

> I observe that amongst the white people Friendship is compared to a chain which links people together. In our Nation friendship is compared to a Grape Vine, which tho' Slender and Weak when Young, grows Stronger as it grows Older.[44]

In 1765 the Creek Confederacy had between fifteen thousand and eighteen thousand people, half again as many as the Iroquois League. In the years that followed, the confederacy proved to be a more formidable obstacle to British and American expansion than the League. Yet League terminology prevailed in the thinking of British and American officials. It was never the Grape Vine of Friendship that they wanted to renew with the Indians, both south and north, but always the Chain of Friendship or the Covenant Chain. And at the historical center of the Covenant Chain was the Iroquois League. Having displaced their predecessors in the Chain, and coerced their contemporaries,[45] the Iroquois then captured the terminology of those who would in turn coerce them. Even in decline, the Iroquois retained the center of the stage, if only in the thinking of those who were consolidating the hold of colonialism in North America.

3   Separation in the South 1763-68

During the period from 1763 to 1768, when the basic lines of British policy toward the Indian nations in North America were being laid down and implemented, no less than five different ministries held office in London. The rapid succession of ruling cliques, led in turn by Lord Bute, George Grenville, the marquis of Rockingham, the earl of Chatham (William Pitt the elder), and the duke of Grafton, was more revealing of the British political scene than it was of Indian policy. The policy itself was determined by needs and conditions that were independent of the personal feuds and alliances that swept British ministries into and out of power, and it had a continuity that did not depend on the individual holders of high office. What was true of Indian policy was true of other aspects of British overseas policy as well. Resting solidly on the labors of undersecretaries, clerks, and the substitutes hired by titled officeholders, the government continued to function during this period of rapid ministerial change, and to concentrate on what eighteenth-century Englishmen considered the primary role of government: the conduct of foreign affairs.[1]

By almost any measure, Great Britain had been the victor in the Seven Years War. The colonial power of France had been curtailed everywhere, and in North America it had been broken. Spain, too, was on the defensive. Having given up both East and West Florida to the British, the Spanish had retired beyond the Mississippi River. The war had been an expensive one, however, and the fruits of victory promised to cost still more. War's end found the British government deeply in debt and with increased administrative responsibilities in India, West Africa, and, especially, in North America.[2]

Given these circumstances, the primary needs of the British were, first, peace, and then the establishment of effective and orderly governing procedures lest they lose by administrative default the territories

36

they had won by arms. In the postwar years, successive British administrations were able to concentrate on these goals in North America because the diplomatic situation in Europe was relatively stable, and because the Spanish in New Orleans and on the west bank of the Mississippi seemed content with the status quo.[3] British officials could give their full attention to relations with the Indian nations in the territory that had been transferred to Great Britain at European conference tables by France and Spain.

As with many later European partitions of the world, the problem for the victor was to take possession of the areas assigned by treaty, or at least to establish enough of a presence there that the inhabitants would acknowledge it and consent to make the victor their primary European patron. The British moved with caution in this matter. They had been warned by William Johnson that the Indians in his department north of the Ohio River were extremely uneasy at the defeat of the French, and that there were many rumors of a continuation of hostilities.[4] The situation in the Southern Department was not so immediately menacing, and the first concern of British officials was to preserve the opportunities for peace that seemed to exist south of the Ohio.[5] Because the southern Indians did remain at peace with the British during the whole of this period, it was in the area south of the Ohio that the British were able to move immediately to implement their Indian policy. In the end their emphasis on the Iroquois would undo the achievements of that policy in the South as well as in the North, but the disastrous ending should not obscure the accomplishments that came before. It was in the South that the stated goals of British policy in the immediate postwar period received their test.

The administrative division of British relations with the Indians into two departments, the northern and the southern, had been made in the mid-1750s. At that time there was a general centralization of authority by the British government, in part as a response to the deepening crisis with France, and in part as an attempt to make policy implementation more consistent and efficient.[6] Attainment of the goal in the Northern Department was aided by the strong personality and long tenure of William Johnson (appointed 1756), who served as superintendent until his death in mid-1774. During approximately the same period, the Southern Department had two superintendents: Edmond Atkin (appointed 1756, died 1761), and John Stuart (appointed 1763, died 1779). Neither man lived as close to the Indians as Johnson did, and neither developed the broad network of personal relationships that served Johnson so well in the highly personalized Indian societies. Consequently, neither Atkin nor Stuart functioned with the strength and authority that made Johnson such an effective diplomat.

The division of Indian affairs into northern and southern departments was more than just a device for greater administrative efficiency, however. It was also a reflection of the setting in which policy would have to be carried out. The Ohio River, which was the jurisdictional boundary between the two departments, was also the dividing line between Indian political systems. North of the Ohio was the Iroquois satellite system. Despite the unresolved questions about internal relationships and strengths, the system still functioned effectively enough in the early 1760s to make it a working center for British negotiations with the northern Indians. There was nothing comparable south of the Ohio. What system there was consisted of innumerable units orbiting around strong individual leaders. In the 1780s and 1790s the Creek Confederacy would achieve a brief preeminence, but in 1763 there was no effective center.

This fact determined the methods used by the British to try to achieve their twin goals of peace and administrative efficiency south of the Ohio River. Because there was not even a nominal center of Indian political power which the British could recognize and strengthen, as they did north of the Ohio, they dealt with the Indians on a group-by-group basis. Instead of one center for British administration, as there was in the North at Johnson Hall, William Johnson's estate, there were several regional centers: Mobile, Pensacola, Augusta, Charleston. Much of Superintendent John Stuart's time and strength was spent in traveling to various locations to meet with the Indians.[7]

Officials in London made one early attempt to centralize the implementation of Indian policy in the South. In March 1763, a little more than a month after the signing of the treaty that ended the Seven Years War, Stuart and the governors of the four established southern colonies, were directed to call a grand congress at which they could meet with representatives of the southern Indians and explain what His Britannic Majesty planned to do now that he had won the war against France. The message came from Lord Egremont who, as secretary of state for the Southern Department, was the London official chiefly responsible for affairs in the colonies. The Indians were to be assembled, he said, and told "in the most prudent and delicate Manner of the Change which is going to take place."[8] Some of the difficulties inherent in Egremont's directive can best be understood by first looking more closely at the

Indians who were to be assembled and briefed on the purposes of Britain's King George III.

The Southern Indians

The concern of British policymakers centered on four Indian groups in the South. The group with the most extensive contact with the whites in 1763 was the Cherokee Nation. Cherokee settlements clustered in three major areas at the southern end of the Appalachians, chiefly in present-day Tennessee and North Carolina, but also in Virginia, South Carolina, Georgia, and Alabama. The three residence-locations became the most common means of identification on the part of the whites, and Cherokees in general were known to whites by whether they came from the Lower Cherokee settlements, the Middle, or the Overhill settlements.[9]

Whatever validity this division into settlement-areas may have had for the intragroup relations of the Cherokees—and there is some evidence of early linguistic, ecological, and political congruence—the three geographic divisions had come to have functional validity in diplomacy. In their relations with other groups, the divisions often operated independently of each other. This is well illustrated in the various campaigns of the Anglo-Cherokee War of 1760–61 and in the peace settlement worked out by the Overhills on the basis of a cession of lands belonging to the Lower Towns.[10] Still, there was broad agreement among the Cherokees on the general goals to be pursued by the nation, as became evident at Augusta in 1763 and in the years immediately following.

South and west of the Cherokee settlements were the lands belonging to the Creek Confederacy. The confederacy had two major geopolitical divisions: the Upper Creek, with towns along the Coosa and Tallapoosa rivers, and the Lower Creek, with towns on the lower Chattahoochee and Ocmulgee rivers.[11] The location of their towns in relation to British settlement as of 1763 meant that the focus of Creek-British diplomacy was Georgia. As British ambitions grew for East and West Florida, these, too, became areas for British-Creek negotiations.

Situated as they were, the Creeks had long had ready access to the outposts of the three major European contenders in the South: Spain, France, and Great Britain. They had turned this to their own advantage by maintaining good relations with all the Europeans and allying themselves with none. The effect of this policy had been noted by Edmond

Atkin in a report on Indian affairs for the Board of Trade. The report was made in 1755, the year before Atkin was appointed the first superintendent of the Southern Department. He pointed out that since the Creeks did not choose sides among Europeans, they were courted by all and received presents from all. "The Conduct of the Creeks conformable to those Principles (which was eminent during the last War) hath rendered them of Superior Weight among the Southern Nations, as holding the Ballance between their European Neighbours, and esteemed or feared by the rest of the red People."[12]

One of the major questions for the British at the close of the Seven Years War was how much influence the Creeks would be able to maintain after the withdrawal of the Spanish and French. They had the requisite skills for leadership. Atkin had thought them "the most refined and Political" of the Indians.[13] John Stuart also respected their political ability, and feared it would work to Britain's disadvantage. The Creeks' location in the middle portion of the southern Indian country gave them the potential to affect British relationships with all the other Indians in the area. That, plus their past reputation, plus their feeling of involvement in all Indian affairs, made them a matter of deep concern to Stuart. He recommended that British policy be directed toward preventing the Creeks from achieving an Iroquois-type hegemony in the South.[14]

The westernmost Indians among those in the South who were of major concern to the British were the Choctaws and Chickasaws. Both groups lived in present-day Mississippi, the Chickasaws in the north and the Choctaws in the southeast. Their influence went beyond their home settlements into present-day Alabama, much of which was controlled by the Choctaws, and into present-day Tennessee and Kentucky where the Chickasaws drove out Indians from other groups who attempted to settle there. Although the Choctaws and Chickasaws were frequently mentioned together in British reports, and were invited to attend the same treaty councils, they had no joint political organization and no institutions to express a common purpose. They were often at war with each other, in varying degrees of formality and participation, and they warred as well against the three European groups with which they had had contact.[15]

Several other southern Indian groups occasionally engaged the attention of the British. There were the Small Tribes or Small Nations on the east bank of the lower Mississippi. Their diplomatic importance lay in their potential to obstruct the movement of troops or supplies along the Mississippi, and in the fact that they were close to, first, the French, and then the Spanish on the west bank of the river. At the opposite end of the southern superintendency from the Small Nations were the Seminoles. An offshoot of the Creek Confederacy, the Seminoles during this period were settling in several locations in the northern part of the Florida peninsula. They were objects of increasing British concern as they grew both in numbers and in independence from the Creek Confederacy. Finally there were the Catawbas, remnant of a once-populous and powerful group. These few survivors of disease and prolonged warfare were gathered on fifteen square miles of land in South Carolina, objects of British protection rather than a cause for worry.[16]

John Stuart's estimates of the Indian population of the South in 1764 show the major focus of British concern. Stuart's figures for each group were for the number of fighting men that might be brought into the field against British forces (see table 7).

From these figures an estimate of total population can be made by multiplying by either four or five. Both figures have been used in the table, giving a range for total population of the major groups of from 47,000 to 59,000. Smaller groups, such as the Catawbas, the Five Small Nations, and the Seminoles, might add 1,000 to 2,000, giving an approximate upper total of from 60,000 to 61,000 Indians in the area south of the Ohio in the early 1760s. In the light of modern scholarship, Stuart's estimate is a conservative one.

The geographical difficulties of assembling southern Indian representatives in one location for a joint congress, as Lord Egremont directed in 1763, are apparent from this indication of their widespread locations.

Table 7   Estimate of the Indian Population South of the Ohio and East of the Mississippi Rivers, 1764

Indian Group	Fighting Men	Total Population (Col. 1 × 4)	Total Population (Col. 1 × 5)
Cherokee Nation	2,750	11,000	13,750
Creek Confederacy	3,600	14,400	18,000
Choctaw Nation	5,000	20,000	25,000
Chickasaw Nation	450	1,800	2,250
Total	11,800	47,200	59,000

Based on Indian Superintendent John Stuart's estimates given in Louis DeVorsey, Jr., *The Indian Boundary in the Southern Colonies, 1763–1775* (Chapel Hill: University of North Carolina Press, 1961), pp. 19–23.

Other difficulties lay in Egremont's assumption that the administrative convenience of the British corresponded to the political realities of the Indians. Enough has been said to suggest the different backgrounds of the Indian groups and their complex, sometimes hostile relationships with each other. For a Choctaw delegation to make its way through Creek country to Augusta, was equivalent to a party of Austrians traveling through the Ottoman Empire to seek possible allies and trading partners in Russia. There was a long tradition of enmity, no protection along the way, and no guarantees on arrival. Few cared to take the risk. In fact, both the Choctaw and Chickasaw delegations at Augusta were small, and were long on the road because of the distance involved and hostilities encountered.[17] The Congress of Augusta should not be judged a complete failure, however. To see why not, it will be necessary to look more closely at the congress and the context in which it occurred.

The Congress of Augusta, November 1763

The primary purpose of the British at Augusta in November 1763 was to secure peace with the Indians, many of whom had fought against them in the wars with France. Their conspicuous success in this aim can be contrasted with their conspicuous failure to achieve the same goal in regard to the Indians north of the Ohio. The general peace treaty that was signed at Augusta between the Indians and the British held good for eleven years. That was a long time in an area that had been one of the cockpits of North America. Furthermore, when the peace was broken by the Creeks in 1774, it was as a result of pressures that originated in diplomacy north of the Ohio.[18]

Related closely to the establishment and maintenance of peace between the British and the Indians was the fact that the British used the congress as a showcase for British goods and a demonstration of their ability to provide them in abundance to their friends. They spent between £4,000 and £5,000 on goods for the congress,[19] a measure of the importance that London officials attached to the meeting at Augusta. It was also a measure of their understanding of the centrality of European manufactures in relations with the Indians. In the instructions that Lord Egremont sent to Superintendent Stuart and the four southern colonial governors, he emphasized that the Indians were to be told that the British could provide ample supplies of goods in trade, enough for all their needs.[20]

Governor James Wright of Georgia was even more open in his use of
the promise of British goods as a tool of British diplomacy. In a message
sent to the Creeks at the close of the war with France, Wright pointed
out that neither France nor Spain could supply the Indians any longer.
Great Britain's king, however, stood ready with the horn of plenty:

> The great King George's orders are that you should have a plentiful
> Trade from us if you behave well to his Subjects and not otherwise;
> and that we should live like Brothers and have but one Fire; and we
> can pour in Goods upon you like the floods of a great River when it
> overflows; We bestow our Favours on our friends heartily and with-
> out Reserve.[21]

The goods sent by the British to Augusta for delivery to the Indians
at the congress were performing triple duty there. Wilbur R. Jacobs has
studied the role of gifts in European-Indian diplomacy and their absolute necessity by 1763 if a European nation wanted to conduct any
negotiation with the Indians. Gifts had had symbolic significance in
Indian societies prior to European contact. Mourners were comforted,
children were named, mates were chosen, bargains were struck and
sealed partly through the symbolic language of an exchange of gifts,
which had for the participants a meaning that went beyond words. So,
too, the negotiations between whites and Indians had to be "signed,"
as it were, by an exchange of goods. The long competition between
France and England for alliances with the Indians had skewed the balance of the exchange, until it had come to be a one-sided affair, with
the Europeans providing all the goods and the Indians expecting them
to do so.[22]

British gifts at Augusta served yet another purpose. Besides their
symbolic significance in negotiations with the Indians, and the fact that
the diplomacy of prior years had created a demand that had to be met
if business were to be done, the gifts at Augusta served to validate Great
Britain's credentials as a patron and trading partner. In the context of
1763, when some of the southern Indians still had the choice of trading
with other Europeans, this validation was necessary. No matter how
carefully the French or the Spanish kept the terms of the Paris Peace
Treaty of 1763, if they continued to trade with the Indians they would,
in British thinking, continue to influence the Indians. As late as December 1766 John Stuart was complaining that the Five Small Nations on
the lower Mississippi were always open to French traders and "their
mechinations."[23]

As it turned out, the French did not hand New Orleans to the Spanish until early in 1767, and St. Louis remained in French hands until 1769.[24] Thus the French, as well as the Spanish, maintained a presence of which the British were always aware. It was important, therefore, that Great Britain not only inform the Indians of British victory and secure a pledge of peace but also prove the availability of British goods as a source of supplies for the future. Economics lay close to the surface of European-Indian diplomacy in this period and would soon emerge to fill almost the whole framework of British-Indian negotiations.

For the Indians, the Congress of Augusta offered an opportunity to replenish some of their stocks of European goods at British expense. More than that, the congress offered them the chance of stating their views to a number of British officials from four different colonies, and to the superintendent of Indian affairs in the South. From the Indians' talks at Augusta, and from their words and actions both before and after the Congress, it is possible to reconstruct the main themes of their point of view. The Indians wanted:

- An assured source of supplies of European manufactured goods.
- A fixed boundary between their lands and those of the whites.
- Effective maintenance of the boundary as a barrier to white settlement.
- Acknowledgment of their independent status, and of their right to control the disposition of their lands.

These were the common concerns of the southern Indians as they expressed them at Augusta and at other meetings throughout the South. It should be emphasized that, although their situation was similar and their concerns were common, the southern Indians had no joint policy or institution through which to express a combined initiative or response. Furthermore, different groups emphasized different aspects of their common concerns at different times so that, for example, the Cherokee spokesmen at Augusta concentrated on a source of supplies while the Lower Creeks negotiated part of their boundary with the whites.[25] Underlying these independent initiatives, however, was a consistency of purpose that makes it possible to speak of the general views and goals of southern Indians in this period, even though no joint statement was ever issued and no multilateral agreement was signed after the peace treaty of Augusta.

Since the British had called the meeting at Augusta, they naturally looked on it as an occasion for presenting the British point of view. Of most interest here is the shift of emphasis that had occurred between March 1763, when Egremont directed that the meeting be held, and November, when Indians and whites finally gathered at Augusta. The shift is a demonstration of the way that British policy was influenced by the Indians as well as by other factors. British relations with the settler colonies, British politics, and changes in British conceptions of empire all helped to shape British policy, but these factors cannot completely account for the increased British emphasis on a general Indian-white boundary. In March Egremont did not think the boundary important enough to mention. In November, the boundary was a major subject of discussion at Augusta.[26]

Between Egremont's first directive and the meeting at Augusta, war had resumed north of the Ohio. While British officials welcomed the southern Indians to Augusta, the British at Detroit lay under siege by northern Indians who refused to accept the European partition of their lands. Detroit had been under siege since May, when the Indians began a campaign in which they captured other British outposts and swept the northern frontier of British troops. Partly in response to the resumption of warfare by the northern Indians, George III had, in October, issued the Proclamation of 1763, establishing the land beyond the Appalachians as Indian country and forbidding English settlement there. Thus, when the deliberations at Augusta began, there had been articulated as part of British policy the idea of a general Indian-white boundary.[27]

In his study of British colonial policy in this period, Jack M. Sosin has pointed out that the Proclamation of 1763 was not a departure from past British policy but, rather, an extension and elaboration of what had been done in the past. One of the lessons learned by the British in the Seven Years War was that peace with the Indians could only be preserved by guaranteeing them possession of their land. Sosin argues that land beyond the mountains was already, in effect, guaranteed to the Indians by the 1758 Treaty of Easton, which prohibited white settlement west of the Alleghenies; by Colonel Henry Bouquet's interpretations of that treaty; and by the Privy Council order of 3 December 1761 in which officials of the royal colonies were forbidden to make grants or encourage settlement on Indian lands. The Proclamation of 1763, in this interpretation, simply confirmed and made general a policy that was already in effect.[28]

Other scholars have been concerned with the origins of the proclamation in reports that were made to the Board of Trade in the months preceding issuance of the document. The reports offered suggestions for the governance of the territory Britain had acquired from France, not only in North America but elsewhere in the world. This research has been conveniently summarized by Francis Prucha, who has also called attention to some of the consequences of the fact that the proclamation was in many respects an emergency measure, issued in haste to strengthen the hand of British officials in their dealings with the Indians. In regard to the boundary between Indian and white land, the most serious consequence was that the Proclamation Line along the Appalachian watershed did not conform to the actual situation of either whites or Indians. The Iroquois, the Cherokees, and the Creeks had lands and settlements east of the line, and white settlers from Virginia had lands and settlements west of it. But the idea that was embodied in this inaccurate line, that there should be a general Indian-white boundary and an area set aside and defined as "Indian Country," was, according to Prucha, "a great departure from the past," a "new turn in Indian policy."[29]

Whether the idea of a general Indian-white boundary was a continuation of practices already in effect, or a great departure from the past, is not so important for the purposes of this study as what happened after the Proclamation of 1763 had been issued. Answers to the questions posed by conflicting interpretations would seem to turn on evaluations of the scope and effectiveness of the Treaties of Easton (there was more than one), a task that would require a separate study in itself. If, however, the focus is on policy results rather than policy origins, then the Proclamation of 1763 is set in a different context. Certainly, prohibitions against private purchase of Indian land were nothing new. As Lord Halifax commented in October 1763, the king had been issuing royal orders to that effect for a long time.[30] What *was* new was the sustained effort that was made following the Congress of Augusta to work out one, general, mutually satisfactory boundary to separate land belonging to the colonies from Indian land.

In the light of this effort, the Proclamation of 1763 can be seen, first, as a statement of policy principle that became, in fact, a program for action, and, second, as an expression of a newly self-conscious British imperial view. The long-standing concern of British officials that expansion of white settlements might stimulate manufactures that would compete with those of Great Britain did not disappear, but it was increasingly subordinated to the realization that continued white expansion not only might but would exasperate the Indians into renewed fighting.[31] The proclamation was a policy statement on a grand scale, concerned not just with particular Indians who were disturbing the peace that the

British thought they had won, but with Indians in general in an imperial domain.

The long wars with France had helped to create this imperial outlook. Just as important, the wars had helped to create the administrative means for carrying out imperial policy. For a few years, circumstances favored the efforts of British officials at Whitehall to use these means to coordinate British policy toward the Indians. So far as the boundary was concerned, their efforts were particularly successful in the South, where Virginia alone, of the four established colonies and the two newly established Florida provinces, contested imperial direction of the British side of Indian-white boundary negotiations.[32]

This period of unprecedented imperial activity and accomplishment opened at Augusta on 5 November 1763. Present for the British were Indian superintendent John Stuart, Governor James Wright of Georgia, Governor Thomas Boone of South Carolina, Governor Arthur Dobbs of North Carolina, and Lieutenant Governor Francis Fauquier of Virginia. Colonel Ayres spoke (in English) for the Catawbas, Pia Matta for the Chickasaws, and Red Shoes for the Choctaws. Cherokee spokesmen were some of their most influential leaders, including Attakullaculla (the Little Carpenter), who was instrumental in the negotiation of the major peace treaty of 1761, the Prince of Chota, and Osteneco (Jud's Friend), who had been a member of the semiofficial Cherokee delegation that visited England at the conclusion of the Anglo-Cherokee War. Creek leaders included Captain Aleck, Mustisiqua, and Mico Hatkee of Coweta. Conspicuously absent were the Upper Creek leaders Yakatastanage (the Mortar) and the Gun Merchant, and the Cherokee leader Oconostota (the Great Warrior).[33]

These latter were Indians who would have been called militant nationalists if they had been living at a later period. Their absence, while conspicuous at the congress, was not as serious for the outcome of British-Indian negotiations as might at first seem, since all of them eventually became involved in negotiations for various segments of the Indian-white boundary. It was left to another Cherokee leader, Dragging Canoe, to focus anti-British feeling in the 1770s and split off the more militant among the Cherokees into an independent guerrilla band that came to be known as the Chickamaugas. Dragging Canoe and his band represent the extremist element that every leader, white and Indian, had to keep in mind when they met to talk of peace and accommodation.[34]

The Congress of Augusta did not open with the condolence ceremony, since the writ of the Iroquois did not run so far. On November 5, Superintendent Stuart made the opening statement, and, after a one-day recess, the Indians gave their replies. On November 10, signatures were put to "A Treaty for the Preservation and continuance of a firm and perfect Peace and Friendship"[35] between the British and the Indians represented at the congress. In the five days of formal and informal contacts, the various groups maneuvered for advantage, and, incidentally, prefigured the future in the goals that they stated, goals they attempted to reach in the years ahead.

To a certain extent the British were still fighting the war just past. Stuart was at pains to reassure the Indians that—despite what they may have been told—King George was not compelling the French and Spanish to withdraw across the Mississippi in order to leave the British a free hand to despoil the Indians. Quite the contary. French and Spanish withdrawal was demanded so that the British and the Indians could live in peace, untroubled by the lies that had in the past led some of the Indians to think the British their enemies. The past was past, Stuart told the Indians. There would be no retaliation. Far from wanting to exterminate the Indians, the British wanted their friendship and sought alliances with them.[36]

Of the Indians' major goals, three were discussed at the congress. These were the establishment of a boundary, maintenance of the boundary, and an ample and regular supply of European goods. The fourth goal, an acknowledgment of the Indians' independence and control over their land, was dealt with obliquely at Augusta by the care that was taken not to give offense in that regard. The British were aware that there was resentment among the Indians at the transfer of French and Spanish forts to the British on the basis of arrangements made by the Europeans among themselves. The preceding spring, when British troops had landed at Pensacola and Mobile to take over the forts from the Spanish and the French, respectively, the Creeks had immediately sent to the British and demanded an explanation. They wanted to know why the land was not being returned to the Indians, and pointed out that they had only lent the land to the French and Spanish, they had not given it to them. How was it, the Creeks asked, that "People can give away Land that does not belong to them?"[37]

That this concern was not confined to one group and one protest can be seen in the instructions that Egremont issued for the congress before this particular demand had been received from the Creeks. Following Egremont's instructions, Stuart brought up the subject of the forts in his talks with the Indians at Augusta, and in particular the forts of Albama, Tombigbe, and Loudon in the heart of the Indian country. Stuart gave the Indians Egremont's assurance that the British would use the forts only for the Indians' protection and for the maintenance of the trade that was so important to their well-being. If, however, they were still uneasy at the British presence, they might petition the king to withdraw his troops and close the forts, and Stuart (relying on Egremont) could promise them that their petitions would be favorably received.[38]

The British did not offer to return Mobile or Pensacola, and the whole question of the European right to transfer possession of the forts without permission of the Indians was by-passed for an argument that British possession was to the Indians' advantage. The British were aware that the Indians' sense of their own independence was strong and that great care must be taken in negotiation with them. Egremont had warned that nothing was to be said at the congress to suggest to the Indians that they were now dependent on Great Britain.[39] This care was extended to the provisions of the treaty as well. Peace was to obtain between "His Majesty King George the Third and all his subjects and the several Nations and Tribes of Indians herein mentioned," and in the future "The Subjects of the Great King George and the aforesaid several Nations of Indians shall forever hereafter be looked upon as one People."[40] It was, however, nowhere suggested that the Indians were subjects of King George, nor did the Indians place themselves under British protection.

The Treaty of Augusta included a provision for only one segment of the general Indian-white boundary, that between Georgia and the Lower Creeks. The negotiations for that segment were typical of the methods that had to be used in the South to work out the location of a comprehensive, unbroken boundary between Indians and Europeans. Scattered here and there in the southern backcountry in 1763 were disconnected boundary lines, the outcomes of various wars and negotiations in the past. The task for the British and the Indians in the years after 1763 was to rationalize these segments and fit them into the large-scale plans of the postwar period. Negotiations had to be held between the British and each Indian group that was involved, and the boundary had to be put together piece by piece until the segments fit together into a connected whole. The first segment of what became the general boundary was agreed on at Augusta.

The Creeks at the congress brought up the matter, thus following up a concern they had expressed earlier about some illegal white settlements north of the Savannah River. A new boundary was agreed on, the difference from the past being that this Georgia-Creek line was seen not just as an isolated and temporary palliative but as part of the more enduring and comprehensive line that was the goal of both the British and the Indians. One feature of the negotiations was the same as in the past, however. In a pattern that was as old as European-Indian negotiations over land, the new boundary involved a cession of Indian land. The Creeks had been uneasy about attending the congress at Augusta, since some Creeks were still engaged in hostilities against the British. They were apparently willing to trade some land for assurances that no official retaliation would be taken, and also for the boundary guarantee that was written into the treaty.[41]

Other records make it clear that boundary discussions at Augusta were far broader than would be suggested by this one treaty provision for the Creek-Georgia boundary. In his report to North Carolina legislators, Governor Arthur Dobbs said that the boundary between Indian land and the colonies of Virginia, North and South Carolina, and Georgia had been "settled."[42] That they were at least discussed in detail is borne out by the later statements of some Cherokee leaders. In the midst of boundary negotiations in 1767, Osteneco spoke of the line to be run between Indian land and that of the colonies, and of the fact that when he was in England the king had spoken of his desire to have such a line run. It was talked of at Augusta also, said Osteneco, and "I have not forgot nor ever shall."[43]

In 1770, when the Cherokees were being asked to renegotiate their boundary with Virginia, they referred again to the boundary discussions seven years earlier at Augusta. "Several years ago the talk begun at Augusta," said Oconostota. Attakullaculla agreed. "It is a great while since this talk was begun, now we are come young and old to conclude it. When you all met at Augusta at the great congress, I believe you may remember what passed, and it is now continued."[44]

Another discussion that was begun at Augusta and continued later was the Creek-East Florida segment of the boundary.[45] When these comments and later developments are taken all together, it becomes clear that discussions of a comprehensive Indian-white boundary were one of the major items of business at Augusta in 1763, even though only one segment of the boundary was formalized in the treaty that was signed there.[46]

The remaining goal of the Indians, an abundant supply of goods, was the subject of the Cherokees' talks at Augusta. Their usual sources of supply had been cut off or severely curtailed by the Anglo-Cherokee

War. South Carolina had forbidden Carolina traders to go to the Cherokee towns, as they had done before the war, and had established a fixed
trading center at Keowee. Traders from Virginia were wary about risk-
ing themselves and their goods in the Cherokee country. At this period
there was little trade out of North Carolina with the Indians, but Georgians were becoming more active. Six months before the Augusta congress opened, Oconostota had tried to interest Georgians in the Cherokee trade. He sent a message to that effect to Governor James Wright,
saying "And as you have every Thing that is necessary for Us, and we
have nothing, I design to talk with you about a Trade."[47]

At Augusta, with the governors of Georgia and the Carolinas in attend-
ance, along with the lieutenant governor of Virginia, the Cherokees
talked almost exclusively about trade. Osteneco and Attakullaculla
carried the burden of these presentations, but others spoke as well.
They all hammered away at the same theme: their need for European
goods. They wanted traders to come to their towns again. Keowee was
too far away. Let the South Carolina traders come to the Cherokee
towns, as in the old days. Let the Virginia traders come, and the Georgians.[48] The unspoken accompaniment to these requests was the Cherokee desire to have again a choice of outlets for the deerskins that were
their chief exchangeable resource, and to reap some of the benefits of a
competitive market.[49]

The Catawbas at Augusta wanted and got a confirmation of the land
reserved to them in South Carolina. The single Choctaw speaker confined
himself to general expressions of goodwill, on behalf (though this was
not stated) of the British faction that he represented. The Chickasaws,
like the Cherokees, spoke of trade, and emphasized the fact that they
wanted traders in their towns so that supplies would be close at hand.[50]
With more expressions of goodwill all around, the Congress closed.

There were some discordant notes. The Creeks and Cherokees seemed
on the verge of war, and the Chickasaws warned privately that the Creeks
could not be trusted. But these were the normal frictions of competing
groups. More disturbing for the future of the policies of both the British
and the Indians at Augusta were the comments made by Superintendent
Stuart and the four southern governors in their report to Egremont. After
noting the successful outcome of the congress, the officials pointed out
that the British promise of continued abundant supplies would be a
hard one to redeem in the future:

> And we beg leave to observe to your Lordship on this Head and
> that the general Promise of Goods which we have made by the Kings

orders to the respective Indians requires such a performance as it is impossible circumstanced as we are to be answerable for we have no coercive Power over Traders.

Your lordship will pardon us for suggesting that there never was a time more seasonable for the establishing the Commerce with Indians upon a general safe equitable footing and which we are afraid will never be done by respective Provinces.[51]

The assessment of difficulties was both accurate and prophetic, but imperial control of trade with the Indians was one of the positions that the forces of continuity and order had to abandon. From 1763 to 1768 the battle was fought, and in 1768 control of trade was turned back to the colonies.[52] During the period of control, or of attempts to control trade as part of one coordinated policy toward the Indians, the Indian-white boundary was established in the South. The two facts are connected. Attempts at control, even if inadequate, bespoke an imperial outlook that was willing to act to carry out as well as to coordinate policy. The Board of Trade, its two superintendents in the field, and their deputies, did so act, and this, in connection with actions by the Indians, saw the boundary established by 1768.

Completion of the Southern Boundary

The board made clear its intention in the summer of 1764 when it proposed a general plan for the management of Indian affairs and sent copies of the plan to Superintendents Johnson and Stuart for their advice and recommendations. The Indian-white boundary was part of the plan. The board proposed:

> That proper measures be taken with the consent and concurrence of the Indians to ascertain and define the precise and exact boundary and limits of the lands which it may be proper to reserve to them and where no settlement whatever will be allowed.[53]

That same summer and fall John Stuart set out on a general tour to explain Britain's policies to such Indian Groups as the Seminoles, who had not been represented at Augusta. It was the first of many trips he would make over the next four years as bit by bit and group by group the various segments of the Indian-white boundary were agreed upon and fitted together. In all, eight different treaties were needed (see table 8) to establish one general boundary that extended from the lower Mississippi River east above the Gulf Coast and north to the Ohio river.[54]

Table 8   Treaties Establishing the Indian-White Boundary South of the
Ohio River, 1763–68

Date	Place	Boundary Established
10 November 1763	Augusta	Creek-Georgia
10 September 1764	Pensacola	Creek-West Florida (preliminary)
26 March 1765	Mobile	Choctaw-West Florida Chickasaw-West Florida
28 May 1765	Pensacola	Creek-West Florida
19 October 1765	Fort Prince George (South Carolina)	Cherokee-South Carolina
18 November 1765	Fort Picolata (East Florida)	Creek-East Florida
1 June 1767	Tiger River (in present South Carolina)	Cherokee-North Carolina
14 October 1768	Hard Labor (South Carolina)	Cherokee-Virginia

SOURCE: Various documentary sources (see Appendix A).

Table 8 shows the steps through which the boundary between Indians and whites was worked out in the South. The proceedings of the meetings reveal the consistency with which the goal was pursued by the British and by the Indians. They reveal as well the mixture of needs and desires that went into the pursuit. British desires for peace and administrative efficiency have already been mentioned. There was also the ever-present desire for land. The difference between those officials whose chief concern was orderly administration and continuity of policy, and those whose chief concern was the acquisition of land for settlement and speculation, was a difference in timing and in method. Land was still a focus of desire.

What the boundary negotiations of 1763–68 provided for the British in the South was an acceptable means through which the desires for peace, for order and continuity, *and* for land could all be met. This happy harmonization of conflicting aims was expressed by the Board of Trade in March 1768 in a report that summed up the accomplishments of the preceding five years:

Your Majesty will be pleased to observe that altho on the one hand the Settlements in the new established Colonies to the South are confined to very narrow limits; yet on the other hand the middle Colonies (whose state of population requires a greater extent) have room to spread much beyond what they have hitherto been allow'd and that upon the whole one uniform and complete line will be formed between the Indians and those antient Colonies, whose Limits not being confined to the Westward has occasioned that extensive settlement which being made without the consent of the Indians, and before any line was settled, produced the evil complained of.[55]

The Indians' concerns have already been discussed. The complex way in which they were sometimes mixed in the boundary negotiations can be seen in the statements and actions of one prominent Creek leader, Yakatastanage (the Mortar). Yakatastanage's concern for Indian sovereignty and land rights was evident in the controversy over British occupation of French and Spanish forts. He was joint author of the protest that the land ought to be turned back to the Indians because they had only lent it to the Spanish and French, not given it to them. He noted that it made the Indians angry to see their land given away without their permission, and went on to say (in a passage that has often been quoted): "we love our Lands a great deal . . . the Wood is our Fire, and the Grass is our Bed, and our Physic when we are sick."[56]

Passionate attachment to the land, amounting almost to an identification with it, was one of the factors in the negotiations of these years, an incalculable but pervasive influence in the Indians' actions. So, too, was the independence and the outrage also expressed by Yakatastanage when he said that he and his family were "Masters of all the Land, and they own no Masters but the Master of their Breath." They were outraged because it seemed that "the White People intend to stop all their Breaths by their settling all around them."[57]

Two years after making that statement, Yakatastanage met with British officials in Pensacola and put his signature to a boundary treaty that involved a large cession of Creek land. By so doing he confirmed an unauthorized boundary agreement that had been signed eight months earlier by minor Creek leaders and a small party of British troops. Not only did he confirm the cession of land involved in that boundary agreement, he agreed to enlarge it considerably.[58]

One explanation of this apparent contradiction is that Yakatastanage did not know what he was doing, but there is no evidence for that. He never repudiated the treaty. He did not claim that the whites had misled him or that he had drunk too much rum and did not know what he was signing. His statements, both at the treaty council and later, show that his goals for the Creeks were a source of supply of European goods and favorable terms of trade. The terms of trade that were written into the treaty were, according to Superintendent John Stuart, terms that Yakatastanage and other Creek leaders had specified. Stuart warned them that the terms were too favorable to the Creeks, that the profits on goods procured and traded at those rates of exchange would be so low that no traders would bother. But the Creeks would not sign without them.[59]

The Choctaws and Chickasaws also had European goods in mind in their boundary negotiations with the British. The boundary treaty that they signed in Mobile in March 1765 contains the rates of exchange for thirty-three separate items of European manufacture they wanted to get from the British. Even a partial listing of the items gives an idea of the broad range of goods that was desired. Guns, flints, gunpowder, and lead might be expected, but there were also shirts, handkerchiefs, blankets, saddles, bridles, cooking kettles, scissors, knives, razors, buttons, jewelry, and fabric of various kinds from silk to strouding (a coarse material used for breechcloths and leggings). For the Choctaws, this was a relatively unknown source. They had been accustomed to getting their supplies from the French. As one of their leaders, Alibamo Mingo, remarked, "We have used French guns for 80 years. I wish I was young enough to go out & hunt & try English guns & powder." He added that he did not think the Indians should be worried about the whites' desire for land and settlement. With the British close to the Indians, "they can more easily supply our wants."[60]

The plaintive note of later years is almost wholly missing from the comments made by southern Indian leaders in the first five years of British administration. It is obvious that they saw themselves as actively pursuing policies that would benefit whatever group—immediate family, kin group, age cohort, village, nation—that claimed their highest loyalty. While the Creeks, Choctaws, and Chickasaws concerned themselves chiefly with supplies of European goods during this period, with the establishment of a boundary being a secondary goal, the Cherokees concentrated their efforts on the boundary. Surviving evidence indicates that they took the initiative in working out a boundary between their lands and those of the whites. In the three-year period from mid-October 1765 to mid-October 1768 they negotiated three separate treaties that established their boundaries with South Carolina, North Carolina, and Virginia. "It is a Point which greatly concerns them and to which they are extremely attentive," John Stuart reported to London.[61]

Cherokee attentiveness to the task can be seen in their initiatives. After the Augusta Congress they did not wait for Stuart to act but worked out their boundary with South Carolina officials on their own at a meeting at Fort Prince George in October 1765. At that meeting they also made a proposal for their boundary with North Carolina. This was not a general suggestion but a detailed proposal for a specific line. The proposal became the basis for negotiations with North Carolina.[62]

In the spring of 1766, the Cherokee-South Carolina boundary was marked by a mixed commission appointed for that purpose by the whites and the Indians. According to Stuart's deputy, Alexander Cameron, who accompanied the boundary-marking commission, the Cherokee members "blazed the Trees as we went, and made the boundary very clear and strong as they term it."[63]

By the fall of that year, the Cherokees were negotiating with North Carolina and working on arrangements with Virginia. They postponed a fall meeting with officials of North Carolina in the hope that by spring they could complete the boundary with North Carolina and Virginia at the same time: "so as to make a final conclusion of the whole at once . . . it is troublesome to be always going about it."[64]

There were to be more delays, however, before the Cherokee-Virginia boundary was agreed on in mid-October 1768. Before that time the Cherokees had completed their arrangements with North Carolina and had helped to mark the Cherokee-North Carolina boundary. Evidence of Cherokee seriousness can be seen in the formal quitclaim procedure by which they gave up title to the land on the North Carolina side of the boundary in 1767.

Osteneco was the Cherokee commissioner who performed the ceremony. First he praised the land that was being ceded to obtain a boundary. "The land is very good land, it affords good water, good timber and other good things, but I will not love it." Then on behalf of the Cherokees he gave it up, that the boundary might be run. "I am now done talking, the land is given when the line is run and I quit all pretensions to it." To close the procedure, Osteneco laid down a string of beads on the ground in the course the boundary line was to run.[65]

With the signing of the Treaty of Hard Labor in October 1768, the Cherokee-Virginia segment of the boundary was determined and the Indian-white boundary was complete in the South. It had been a long-continued task. As the Board of Trade noted in its revised plan for the management of Indian affairs, issued in the spring of 1768 before the Treaty of Hard Labor was signed:

> In a plan for the management of Indian Affairs prepared by this Board in 1764, the fixing of a Boundary between the Settlements of your Majesty's Subjects and the Indian Country was proposed to be established by compact with the Indians, as essentially necessary to the gaining of their good will and affection, and to preserving the tranquility of the Colonies.
>
> This Plan having been communicated to the Superintendents they have in the consequences thereof, made the proposition of such a boundary line an object of their particular attention, & of negotiation and discussion with the several Tribes of Indians interested therein.
>
> In the Southern district a Boundary line has not only been established by actual Treaties with the Creeks, Cherokees and Chactaws, but has also, as far as relates to the Provinces of North and South Carolina, been marked out by actual Surveys, and has had the happy effect to restore Peace and Quiet to those Colonies.[66]

What the Board of Trade did not say was that the establishment of the Indian-white boundary in the South had been a joint Indian and white effort. The effort had involved not only Superintendent John Stuart and his deputies, and British officials in all the southern colonies, but hundreds of Indians as well. Choctaws, Chickasaws, Creeks, and Cherokees had attended the congresses, negotiated terms, signed treaties, and—in the case of the Cherokees—helped locate the line and mark it so it would be "strong." What this might entail can be glimpsed through a comment made in 1769 by John Stuart that in places the Cherokee boundary with the Carolinas "is marked at least 50 feet wide the Trees within which Space are blazed on both sides."[67]

While this was being accomplished in the South, events north of the Ohio were giving British-Indian relations there a completely different tenor and outcome.

4   Northern Negotiations
       1763-68

Not until 1765 were the British north of the Ohio River able to proceed with their plans for orderly administration of the territory that had been transferred to them by the peace treaty of February 1763. When the terms of the treaty, with its European partition of North America, became known to the northern Indians, there was a widespread outbreak of fighting. Indians led by Pontiac, Guyasuta, Shingas, and others overran and destroyed outlying settlements and military posts, and bottled up British forces at Detroit and Fort Pitt. Even after the long siege of Detroit was lifted in August 1764, and the Indians in the upper Ohio Valley were brought to terms in November of that same year, the lower Ohio Valley and the whole of the Illinois country were beyond British reach. Finally, in the fall of 1765, British forces managed to establish enough of a presence in the Illinois country to take possession of the forts they had "won" from the French more than two years before.[1]

At the outset, then, British administration north of the Ohio was not only affected by the Indian setting in which it had to function, it was largely determined by that setting. The policy of financial retrenchment, which the British had been following in the North since their capture of Montreal in 1760, had to be dropped. Money had to be found not only for expeditions against the warring Indians but also for negotiations with other Indians—those Indians who had not taken to the field but who had made clear their concern over the terms of the European peace treaty. More than two thousand Indians from nine different nations, including the Pawnee from west of the Mississippi, gathered at Niagara in July of 1764 to hear Sir William Johnson's explanation of British policy.[2] This council was typical of the prolonged, multilateral negotiations that came to characterize British-Indian diplomacy north of the Ohio. It was a pattern that carried over into the early years of American administration of the area.

Several factors contributed to the emergence of this pattern. One was the persistent effort of the northern Indians throughout this period to coordinate their actions. The effort led to many joint meetings, both with and without Europeans, and to cooperative ventures in which Indians of different nations and languages learned to work together. Another was the British policy of centralizing the direction of Indian relations in the offices of the Superintendents of Indian Affairs. The policy was facilitated by the strong personality of Sir William Johnson, who consistently maintained that he and he alone could conclude treaties on behalf of His Britannic Majesty. It was not an empty claim. Treaties concluded by Colonel John Bradstreet in the late summer and fall of 1764, as he moved to the relief of Detroit, were disavowed by General Thomas Gage, commander of British forces in North America, at least partly on the grounds that Bradstreet had usurped Johnson's authority. Negotiations with the northern Indians thus came to be conducted at large councils, like the peace council of 1766, where delegates from several Indian nations gathered at Oswego to deal with Johnson, the only man who had the right to commit the British to the terms of the final treaty of peace.[3]

Another factor that made multilateral negotiations the norm north of the Ohio, was British support for the pretensions of the Iroquois. What Johnson was for British policy, the Iroquois League was assumed to be for Indian policy. Theirs was the necessary final word. For that reason, League delegates were present at the Oswego peace negotiations, although the League had not, as a whole, participated in the Anglo-Indian War of 1763–65. (A few individuals had fought on the side of the British, and a group of Senecas had fought against them, but the Senecas had already made their peace in two separate treaties signed in 1764.) The League was involved at Oswego because it concerned itself with whatever went on in the territory north of the Ohio, and because the British backed Iroquois claims to dominance there.

This dual evaluation of Iroquois importance meant further pressure on other Indians to gather for multilateral negotiations. They could come to final terms with the British through Johnson, and they could at the same time receive the imprimatur of the Iroquois on what had been done. The western Indians at Oswego in 1766 included Pontiac, the famous Ottawa leader, and delegations from those Ottawas, Chippewas, Potawatomis, and Wyandots who had fought the British and who had, during the summer and fall of 1763, wrested from the British the control of the Great Lakes and the upper Ohio Valley. Their independent actions and their early successes did not give them the final word after they had been forced to sue for peace and to work out what terms they could with the British at Oswego. The last word there was reserved for the Iroquois delegates. And they did not hesitate to assume a high stance. They admonished the western Indians, and called on them to keep the peace and honor the terms of the treaty that had been signed.[4]

The key to British policy north of the Ohio can be discerned in this small incident at Oswego. Neither Johnson nor the Iroquois found anything strange in this assumption of authority. The assumption was based on a high evaluation of the Iroquois that was held consistently throughout the period of British administration. The boundary negotiations that began in 1765 and concluded in 1768 were based on this evaluation, but it was just as high when the boundary, with its concomitant land cession, was not involved—as at Oswego in 1766. To understand the boundary negotiations, it is necessary first to examine the assumptions held by the British and the Iroquois, and then to look at some of the Indians the Iroquois felt free to admonish in 1766.

The Iroquois: Past and Present

What the Iroquois had been in the past, they still were in the present. That, in brief, was the position assumed by Iroquois spokesmen in the 1760s and by William Johnson. Past eminence was so great that, in Johnson's opinion, it could have made all the French wars unnecessary. If the British had only given the Iroquois proper arms and support at the close of the seventeenth century, the French would have been driven completely out of Canada. The whole imperial contest could have been decided right then, saving the bloodshed and expense of the protracted wars of the eighteenth century.

Johnson did not express any doubt of Iroquois claims of conquest in the past, and his doubts about the effective reach of their power in the period after the withdrawal of the French were limited to the area of the northern Great Lakes. In a report made to the Board of Trade in the fall of 1763, Johnson attached the Shawnees, Delawares, and Wyandots of Ohio firmly to the Iroquois Confederacy, and noted that during the past century the Iroquois had conquered all the Ohio Indians, as well as the Miamis, and the "western Indians so far as lakes Michigan and Superior, received them into an alliance, allowed them the possession of the Lands they occupied, and have ever since been at peace with the greatest part of them."[5]

Johnson's understanding of what this meant can be seen in the fact that he put the Iroquois conquests in a territorial frame of reference. It was a frame of reference that grew out of the European experience, one in which wealth and position depended on the possession of land and wars were frequently fought over the location of geographical boundaries. Increasingly in the Europe of the eighteenth century, sovereignty was territorially based, and it was in these terms that Johnson defined the Iroquois conquests. The outcome of this interpretation of conquest was so important for the future of Great Britain in North America, that Johnson's words are worth quoting at length:

> As Original proprietors, this Confederacy claim the Country of their residence, South of Lake Ontario to the great Ridge of the Blew Mountains, with all the Western part of the province of New York towards Hudsons River, west of the Caats Kill, thence to Lake Champlain, and from Regioghne a Rock at the East side of said lake to Osswegatche on La Gattell on the River St. Lawrence (having long since ceded their claim North of said line in favour of the Canada Indians as Hunting ground) thence up the River St. Lawrence and along the South side of Lake Ontario to Niagara.
>
> In right of conquest, they claim all the Country (comprehending the Ohio) along the great Ridge of Blew Mountains at the back of Virginia, thence to the head of the Kentucke River, and down the same to the Ohio above the Rifts, thence Northerly to the South end of Lake Michigan, then along the eastern shore of said lake to Missillimackinac, thence easterly across the North end of Lake Huron to the great Ottawa River (including the Chippawae or Mississagcy Country) and down the said River to the Island of Montreal.—However, these more distant claims being possessed by many powerful Nations, the Inhabitants have long began to render themselves independent by the assistance of the French, and the great decrease of the Six Nations; but their claim to the Ohio, and thence to the Lakes is not in the least disputed by the Shawanese Delawares ettc, who never transacted any Sales of Land or other matters without their consent, and who sent Deputys to the grand Council at Onondaga on all important occasions.[6]

In the 1760s the Iroquois did not disagree with this interpretation of conquest. Years later one of them was to say that Indians did not wage war for land but for "bodies," that is, for prisoners, who would increase their numbers,[7] a statement that offers a possible clue to understanding the early Iroquois "empire" and what conquest might once have meant. The extent and effectiveness of that kind of empire would need to be seen in terms of the personal relationships that were central in Indian societies, so that power at any one time might be defined as what services could be claimed from what groups and rendered as an acknowledged due. This is far from a territorial empire with subject or dependent nations who have lost the right of control and disposition of their land.

This is also sheer speculation, based partly on the fact of Shawnee and Delaware resistance to the territorial interpretation of conquest and their concurrent acknowledgment of some sort of Iroquois claim upon them.[8] It is an attempt to get back of sources that are based on European understandings, and recover a world that was ordered in non-European terms. By the 1760s that world had changed out of all recognition as thousands of Indians made individual adjustments to the circumstances of their lives. Among the changes, discernible in varying degrees in different Indian groups, was an increased awareness of territorial limits, especially in relation to a people with wholly different ways of life and with a territorially based sense of property and sovereignty. The care with which the Cherokees worked out their boundaries with the southern colonies is evidence of this change in their perceptions.

So, too, is the Iroquois emphasis in the 1760s on the land and people they had conquered. On the basis of a territorial interpretation of Iroquois conquests, a boundary was worked out in the negotiations of 1765 and 1768 to divide Indian from British land north of the Ohio. Within six years, the location of the boundary had helped to undo British policy in the entire backcountry. This is explainable in purely territorial terms. The boundary that was drawn put on the British side of the line a vast area used mainly by the Shawnees and Delawares of the upper Ohio Valley, and by a breakaway group from the Iroquois Confederacy, the Six Nations of the Ohio, known also as Mingoes. They denied the right of the Iroquois to bargain away this land, and fought to prevent the British from taking possession.[9]

But more than that can be seen in their actions. Among the Delawares in 1762 had arisen the Prophet who gave voice to the Indians' sense of spiritual loss in their rapidly changing world. In the years to come another prophet would arise among the Shawnees who, with his brother Tecumseh, would seek to mobilize spiritual unease for political and military ends.[10] The suggestion is made here that when these groups fought against the 1768 boundary arrangements they were doing more than denying the assumption of Iroquois dominance held by William Johnson and by the Iroquois themselves. They were denying the very frame of reference in which the assumption had any meaning, and they were seeking to regain the Indianness of a world that repeatedly slipped away from their attempts to hold it fast.

The Northern Indians

In 1763 there were perhaps fifty or sixty thousand Indians in the area that the British termed the Northern Department (see table 9). These figures represent a broad range of uncertainty that will be explained when the source for the figures is examined more closely, after we look at the area where the Indians lived.

The Northern Department was bounded roughly by the Ohio and Mississippi rivers on the south and west, and by the Great Lakes and the St. Lawrence River on the north. The eastern boundary varied throughout the period of Johnson's superintendency. In theory the boundary was simply to include the Six Nations and allied and dependent Indians. In practice the boundary was moved about, sometimes by public treaty, sometimes by private agreement, sometimes according to the assertiveness of either whites or Indians, as when the Susquehanna Delawares in 1755–58 forced the revocation of a 1754 treaty and secured the retrocession of land in western Pennsylvania and acknowledgment of a line along the Alleghenies.[11] At no time did responsible leaders of the Iroquois, the western Indian nations, the imperial administration in London and New York, and the colonial administrations in Virginia, Pennsylvania, New York, and Connecticut agree on the exact location of the eastern boundary of the Northern Department. The boundary of 1768 was, among other things, an attempt to settle on a line that would be acceptable to all the interested parties.

Population figures for the northern Indians in 1763 are subject to the qualifications usual for such figures, gathered as they were under difficult circumstances and often based on little more than hearsay. These particular figures have an even wider range of uncertainty than usual for two reasons. First, Johnson, in his zeal to uphold and strengthen the Iroquois, may well have overestimated the League figures and underestimated some of the western nations, particularly in the Indiana-Illinois area. Second, many of the Indians of the upper Great Lakes were lumped together by Johnson under the general heading of "Ottawas, Chipeweighs, ettc." Johnson's population estimates, like those of Superintendent John Stuart in the Southern Department were confined to an estimate of fighting men. In table 9 this base figure has been multiplied

Table 9   Estimate of the Indian Population North of the Ohio and
East of the Mississippi Rivers, 1763

Indian Population	Fighting Men	Total Population (Col. 1 × 4)	Total Population (Col. 1 × 5)
Iroquois Confederacy			
Central Groups			
Mohawk	160	640	800
Oneida	250	1,000	1,250
Tuscarora	140	560	700
Onondaga	150	600	750
Cayuga	200	800	1,000
Seneca	1,050	4,200	5,250
Iroquois of Oswegatchie	80	320	400
Nanticoke, Tutelo and other Susquehanna affiliates	200	800	1,000
Total	2,230	8,920	11,150
Canadian Groups			
Caghnawaga	300	1,200	1,500
Canadasaga, Adirondack, and Algonquian of Montreal	150	600	750
Abnaki (scattered)	100	400	500
Nipissing of Three Rivers	40	160	200
Wyandot (Huron) of Loretto	40	160	200
Total	630	2,520	3,150
Ohio Groups			
Shawnee	300	1,200	1,500
Delaware	600	2,400	3,000
Wyandot (Huron) of Sandusky	200	800	1,000
Total	1,100	4,400	5,500
Iroquois Confederacy Totals	3,960	15,840	19,800

Source: Adapted from William Johnson to the Board of Trade, 18 November 1763, ed. O'Callaghan, *New York Colonial Documents* 7: 582–84.

[a]From F. W. Hodge, ed., *Handbook of American Indians* 1: 598.

Indian Population	Fighting Men	Total Population (Col. 1 × 4)	Total Population (Col. 1 × 5)
Western Nations			
Great Lakes Groups			
Wyandot (Huron)			
of Detroit	250	1,000	1,250
Potawatomi of			
Detroit	150	600	750
Potawatomi of			
St. Joseph	200	800	1,000
Ottawa of Detroit	300	1,200	1,500
Ottawa of			
Michilimackinac	250	1,000	1,250
Ottawa of St. Joseph	150	600	750
Ojibwa (Chippewa)			
of Detroit	320	1,280	1,600
Ojibwa of			
Michilimackinac	400	1,600	2,000
Menominee	220	880	1,100
Winnebago	360	1,440	1,800
Sac	300	1,200	1,500
Fox	320	1,280	1,600
Ottawa, Ojibwa, and others throughout upper Great Lakes country	4,000(?)	16,000	20,000
Total	7,220	28,880	36,100
Illinois and Indiana Groups			
Miami	230	920	1,150
Kickapoo	180	720	900
Mascouten (Potawatomi?)	90	360	450
Piankeshaw	100	400	500
Wea	200	800	1,000
Illinois Confederacy	400[a]	1,600	2,000
Total	1,200	4,800	6,000
Western Nation Totals	4,420 to 8,420	17,680 to 33,680	22,100 to 42,100
Area Totals	8,380 to 12,380	33,520 to 49,520	41,900 to 61,900

by four and by five to give the bounds within which the actual population total might lie.

Johnson estimated the fighting men of the upper Great Lakes Indians at four thousand, and explained his estimate by saying, "This is the most exact computation which can be made of these numerous people, who are scattered throughout the Northern Parts, and who having few places of fixed residence, subsisting entirely by Hunting, cannot be ascertained as those of their confederacy residing near the out Forts."[12]

Because of this uncertainty, population totals in the table have been given as a range, the first total without the "Ottawa, etc." figure, the second with that figure included. The large number of fighting men attributed to that group makes a great difference in the estimates. Certainly there were many Ottawas, Ojibwas, Crees, and other Indians around the upper Great Lakes who had little contact with the British in 1763, so the chief practical effect of giving such a broad population range in the table is to call attention to a degree of uncertainty that is greater than usual.

The Sioux (Dakota) of the Minnesota country are not included in these estimates, although they sent a delegation to at least one of the councils held by Johnson in 1764, and population figures for them were included in Johnson's report.[13] In this period the Sioux were not deeply involved in British-Indian negotiations, and were not a significant factor in developments in the Northern Department.

The most striking characteristic of the remaining Indians in the Northern Department is that in 1763 many of them were refugees. The five original nations of the Iroquois League—the Mohawk, Oneida, Onondaga, Cayuga, and Seneca—were among the few northern nations still living on ancestral land. Religious rivalries, imperial competition, outbreaks of disease, inter-Indian trade wars, had set the nations in motion all along the eastern seaboard and along trade routes deep into the interior. The Iroquois League itself had divided, with some Catholic converts going to Canada and some establishing their own separate village at Oswegatchie.[14]

The Tuscaroras, the Nanticokes, the Tuteloes, the Ottawas near Detroit and St. Joseph, the Shawnees, the Delawares, the Wyandots (Hurons) of Loretto, Sandusky, and Detroit were remnant peoples. The Ottawas and Wyandots had been smashed and scattered by the Iroquois during the trade wars of the seventeenth century. The Tuscaroras had been decimated by slave raids and warfare, and had fled their homes in

North Carolina, finding refuge, finally, with the Iroquois. The Shawnees, too, had come from the South, the eastern division from South Carolina and the western branch from the Cumberland Valley in Tennessee. Prolonged warfare with the Catawbas, the Cherokees, and the Chickasaws had eventually driven them north into the Wyoming Valley of the Susquehanna River and along the north bank of the Ohio from the Allegheny to the Scioto. In their northern homes, the Shawnees were occasional allies of the Delawares, another people who were scattered and on the move. The original homes of the Delawares were in New Jersey, Delaware, and eastern Pennsylvania. The process of dispersal before the advance of white settlement was hastened for the Delawares by the Iroquois. In the mid-eighteenth century the Iroquois made the Delawares a protectorate, assumed control of their external affairs, and sold Delaware land to the whites.[15]

In his 1763 report, William Johnson categorized these remnant Indians partly on the basis of location: the Wyandots of Detroit, the Ottawas of St. Joseph, and so on. This was an accurate reflection of their political fragmentation, or, to look at it in another light, of their independence of action. Either way, what this meant in diplomacy was difficulty in presenting a unified front. The Ottawas of Michigan did not join the 1763–65 war against the English; the Ottawas of Detroit and St. Joseph did. The Wyandots of Detroit were leaders in the war; the Wyandots of Loretto remained neutral. And so throughout the whole area.

If the Indian population of the Northern Department were computed on the basis of density per square mile, the area would seem all but deserted. A traveler might go for days without hearing any shot but that of his own gun, or seeing any smoke but that of his own fire. The country was not settled in the European meaning of the term, but neither was it open to settlement nor even to travel unless the Indians permitted. Speaking of the British difficulty in taking possession of French forts in the Illinois country, William Johnson said that the British would never get there without first obtaining the friendship and permission of the Indians in between: the Shawnees, Delawares, Six Nations of the Ohio, Miamis, Kickapoos, Potawatomis, Piankeshaws, Weas, and then the members of the Illinois Confederacy.[16]

The Indians' power was not one of numbers, although Johnson estimated they could have put eight to twelve thousand men in the field. Rather, their power rested on their mobility, their ability to live off the country, and the fact that they held the transportation routes. The straits, the passes, the navigable rivers, the shores of the lakes were, for the most part, in Indian hands.[17]

Beyond all that was the communications network by which messages were passed from one end of the Indian Country to the other. The network antedated the coming of the whites and functioned effectively enough so that, for example, an invitation from William Johnson at Johnson Hall could be passed along well-established trade routes from New York to Green Bay on the western shore of Lake Michigan, there to be discussed by the Menominees, who might or might not decide to go and meet Johnson at a specified time and place.[18] The hypothetical traveler of the 1760s would find that his passage through the interior did not go unmarked, and that his reputation ran ahead of him. He moved through a close web of Indian relationships so that what he said to the Delawares on the lower Muskingum would affect his reception by the Wyandots at Sandusky, and that, in turn, would determine whether he could even go on to the Ottawa settlement below Detroit.[19]

He would find also that his hosts, the Delawares or Wyandots or whomever, would be full of news as to what the French in New Orleans were going to do, or of questions about the proceedings of a council at Fort Pitt. Rumors, allegations, wishful thinking traveled the communications network mixed in with accurate news, and a great deal of time and effort was spent by both whites and Indians in sorting one from the other. No story was commoner during this period than that of a united Indian front that would at the least be able to force acceptance of the Indians' demands and, at the most, would drive all whites from the continent. The story was never true, but, until the defeat of the western nations at Fallen Timbers in 1794, it was the dream of the Indians and the dread of the colonizing whites that it might be so.[20]

Years of Warfare, 1763–65

The first two years of British administration were spent largely in coping with the war launched by the northern Indians at several different locations in the spring and summer of 1763. At one time it was thought that the attacks were all planned and coordinated by the Ottawa leader Pontiac. Francis Parkman thought so. Two volumes in his multivolume history of the French and English struggle in North America are on "the conspiracy of Pontiac." William Johnson, however, who was writing in the fall of 1763 when reports of British losses were coming in almost daily, did not credit Pontiac with such sweeping power. He merely noted that "Pondiac" was the head of a "flying camp" of raiders made up of Detroit-based Wyandots, Potawatomis, and Ottawas.[21]

Pontiac's role in the war has been carefully examined by Howard Peckham, who has concluded that Parkman was incorrect. There was not a single conspiracy but a mass uprising sparked, perhaps, by the Ottawa leader's laying siege to Detroit in the spring of 1763.

In 1761 and again in 1762 there had been widespread rumors that the Indians were planning concerted attacks on the British forts. War messages were circulated throughout the entire Great Lakes-Ohio-Mississippi country, and repeated calls were made for united Indian action. The messages came from several different centers: Pontiac's "flying camp" of Ottawas, Wyandots, and Potawatomis; the Shawnee and Delaware towns in the Muskingum country; the Wyandots at Sandusky on Lake Erie; the Senecas in western New York. Even before the terms of the European peace treaty became known, the Senecas were ready for war and were trying to secure enough allies for a concerted drive against the British. When Pontiac made formal peace with the British in 1766 and promised to call in the war messages he had sent to the far Indian nations, he remarked that only some of the messages were his. Most of the rest of them had been sent by the Senecas, he said.[22]

The necessary preoccupation of the British during the first years of their administration north of the Ohio can be seen in the peace treaties that were the chief subjects of negotiation with the Indians during those years (see table 10). In the table the treaties have been classified as formal and informal to distinguish those negotiated by William Johnson in full-dress council, with formal diplomatic procedures, from those negotiated by other British officials under more informal conditions in the field. In some cases, the informal field treaties were the key to future British actions, as when, in two separate treaties in the summer of 1765, George Croghan, Johnson's deputy superintendent, secured the consent of several Wabash and Illinois Indian nations to British freedom of passage to the Illinois country. The two treaties negotiated by Colonel John Bradstreet in August and September 1764 are included in the table as informal treaties. Although Gage initially disavowed the treaties, and Johnson denounced them, they were later accepted by Gage and by some leaders of the Iroquois League. In later negotiations, the Iroquois tried to use one of Bradstreet's treaties to beat down objections that the Shawnees were making to the British presence in the Ohio country.[23]

The cause usually given for the Anglo-Indian War of 1763–65 is an economic one. Both Peckham and Randolph Downes have stated that the Indians reacted to trade cuts and the British policy of stringent econ-

Table 10   British-Indian Treaties of Peace, the Northern Department, 1763–1766

	Date	Place	Indian Nation	Type
1.	3 April 1764	Johnson Hall	Seneca	Formal
2.	18 July 1764	Niagara	Wyandot of Detroit	Formal
3.	6 August 1764	Niagara	Seneca	Formal
4.	12 August 1764	Presque Isle	Delaware	Informal
			Shawnee	
			Wyandot of Sandusky	
5.	7 September 1764	Detroit	Ottawa	Informal
			Ojibwa	
			Potawatomi	
			Wyandot of Detroit	
			Miami	
			Sac	
6.	8 May 1765	Johnson Hall	Delaware of	Formal
			Susquehanna	
			Delaware of Ohio	
7.	11 May 1765	Fort Pitt	Shawnee	Informal
			Delaware of Ohio	
			Six Nations of Ohio	
8.	8 July 1765	Ouiatenon on the	Kickapoo	Informal
		Wabash River	Miami	
			Wea	
			Piankeshaw	
			Mascouten (Prairie	
			Potawatomi?)	
9.	18 July 1765	Ouiatenon	Ottawa	Informal
			Illinois Confederacy	
10.	28 August 1765	Detroit	Wyandot	Informal
			Ottawa	
			Ojibwa	
			Potawatomi	
			Miami	
			Wea	
			Piankeshaw	
			Kickapoo	
			Mascouten	
11.	31 July 1766	Oswego	Ottawa	Formal
			Potawatomi	
			Wyandot	
			Ojibwa	
			Iroquois Confederacy	

SOURCE: See Appendix A.

omy by taking up arms against the British.[24] It is beyond question that the northern Indians were outraged by a policy that was almost the equivalent of a blockade of the supplies that they needed in order to survive. This was especially true after 1760, when French sources became informal and irregular. But to make this scarcity the only cause of the war is to miss the point of the Indians' own statements. It also obscures the Indians' clear perception of the European emphasis upon territory and what that might mean for the people who happened to be living on territory that the Europeans coveted.

There were in 1763 two separate but related territorial challenges to the western Indian nations north of the Ohio. The first, as has been mentioned, came from the Iroquois League which, by 1763, had wholeheartedly adopted the European conception of empire with its assumption of the right to dispose of the land of imperial dependents. The Iroquois challenge had the backing of British officials who, for reasons of their own, found an Iroquois partnership useful, and it was resisted chiefly by those Indian groups most immediately threatened, the Shawnees and Delawares of the upper Ohio. It is in their resistance to the Iroquois-British threat that there are occasional haunting glimpses of a denial of the whole territorial frame of reference as translated into terms of Iroquois empire.

The more general and widespread territorial challenge to the Indian nations north of the Ohio threatened the Iroquois as well as the western Indian nations throughout the entire area. The Indians' understanding of this challenge is highlighted in their repeated and widespread denials that the French and the British could, between themselves, dispose of the Indians' land. Vis-à-vis the Europeans, the Indians had clear and definite ideas about the ownership of land. As early as 1761, after the French had conceded Canada to the English, some Indians were making explicit statements that their policies were independent of those of their European ally. When the English trader Alexander Henry arrived at the post of Michilimackinac in the fall of 1761, he was lectured by the Chippewa leader Minivavana:

> Englishman, although you have conquered the French, you have not yet conquered us. We are not your slaves. These lakes, these woods and mountains, were left to us by our ancestors. They are our inheritance; and we will part with them to none.[25]

Minavavana's statement was only one of many similar statements made by Indian leaders throughout these years of uncertainty and warfare as the Indians sought British acknowledgment of their position.

During the siege of Fort Pitt in the summer of 1763, Shingas, a Delaware leader, expressed the reason the Indians had gone to war against the British:

> Brothers you have Towns & places of your own; you know this
> is our Country & that your having Possession of it must be offensive
> to all Nations therefore it would be proper, that you were in your own
> Country where our friendship might always remain undisturbed.[26]

The Indians were sometimes bitter, sometimes cynical, and frequently outspoken about the European assumption that unceded Indian land could be bartered back and forth at European conference tables. Sir William Johnson noted that the northern Indians had allowed French and British settlements in their country only for "the conveniency of trade," and that this had nothing to do with dominion over them since neither the French nor the British had ever conquered them, and since the Indians had "all along considered the Northern parts of North America as their sole property from the beginning.[27]

Johnson said that at several conferences the Indians had told him:

> they were amused by both parties [the French and the British] with
> stories of their upright intentions, and that they made War for the
> protection of the Indians Rights, but that they plainly found it was
> carried on to see who would become masters of what was the property of neither the one nor the other.[28]

At a meeting with Johnson in the spring of 1765, the Onondaga speaker for the Iroquois Confederacy expressed the same sentiment even more clearly:

> we hear from the French that you had designs upon us, and we
> heard from you that they had the same, but of late we find you
> both had the like Motives.[29]

The western nations of Indians shared these opinions. When the European terms of the peace became known in the West, there was an immediate reaction. George Croghan reported in the spring of 1763 that the Indians around Fort Pitt insisted that "the French had no Right to give away their Country; as, they say, they never were Conquered by any nation." That same spring, forty-seven Shawnee villages sent a message to French officials who had remained in the area for the formal transfer of administration, and demanded an explanation: "The English come and say that the land belongs to them, that the French have sold it to them." A group of Missouri, Osage, and Illinois leaders told other French officials frankly that they would continue the war rather than allow the English on their lands. The substance of their talk was simple: these lands are ours, they belong to no one else, let no one else lay a claim to them, not even other Indians.[30]

A less defiant but no less explicit declaration of the position of the western Indian nations was made to Croghan during the summer of 1765 when he was negotiating with several Wabash River Indian groups to obtain for the English the right of passage through the Wabash country. The European assumption of the right of transfer was here politely and firmly denied. The Indians pointed out that the French had no rights in the land whatsoever, except those the Indians had granted them:

> we have been informed that the English, wherever they settle, make the Country their own, and you tell us, that when you Conquered the French, they gave you this Country. That no difference may happen hereafter, we tell you now the French never conquered, neither did they purchase a foot of our Country, nor have [they a right] to give it to you, we gave them liberty to settle for which they always rewarded us and treated us with great Civility.[31]

These explicit statements of the northern Indians' concern for sovereignty and land rights come from widely scattered sources, and are, perhaps, more accessible to later scholarship than to British officials in the 1760s. But British policymakers in London did not have to depend on these scattered sources to tell them what the northern Indians were saying. No one expressed the Indians' position on sovereignty and land-ownership more clearly and consistently than Superintendent William Johnson. In report after report, Johnson conveyed the message. The Indians, he said, "have been represented as calling themselves subjects, altho the very word would have startled them had it even been pronounced by any Interpreter; they desire to be considered as Allies and Friends." And again: "I must beg leave to observe that the Six Nations, Western Nations, etc., having never been conquered, either by the English or French, nor subject to Laws, consider themselves as a free people."[32]

There were, of course, British officials to contest the Indians' claims. Jeffrey Amherst, commander in chief of British forces in North America in the early 1760s, responded with disdain to Croghan's warnings of Indian unrest: "Whatever Idle notions they may Entertain, in regard to the Cessions made by the French Crown, can be of very little Consequence, as it is in their Interest to Behave Peaceably."[33] But Amherst was an exception, and his disdain was not shared at Whitehall, particularly after the renewal of hostilities. British policy came to be one of nonconfrontation and accommodation to the Indians' position. This can be seen in the Proclamation of 1763 and in the negotiations to create a comprehensive Indian-white boundary. The acknowledgment cannot be taken as an espousal of the Indians' cause or as a willingness to withdraw jurisdictional claims so far as other European powers were concerned. Rather, the acknowledgment was a recognition of the limits of the possible in British administration of the backcountry. In the setting of those limits, Indian words and actions were an important influence.

British policy thus came to be based on British perceptions of their own needs and interests, as constrained by estimates of what the Indians would do to protect *their* needs and interests. This was the usual context of diplomatic negotiations, but the Indians' role in these matters has been underplayed so consistently that in this instance it is worth emphasizing the obvious.[34] As has been seen, British perceptions of their own needs and interests were not, in themselves, simple matters. Beyond the usual conflicts of attachments and purposes, was the widening rift between the settler colonies and the metropole. A divergence of interests had existed from the first, but after the Seven Years War the divergence widened and deepened as officials in London took an ever more imperial view of affairs that the colonists were beginning to see as strictly domestic. All of these elements were part of the context in which negotiations for the northern portion of the Indian-British boundary took place in 1765 and 1768.

Multilateral proceedings, an emphasis on Iroquois dominance, assertions of Indian sovereignty carried to the point of warfare, and an imperial point of view in opposition to a settler point of view, meant that an extraordinarily large number of conflicting interests had to be reconciled or pushed to one side in the boundary negotiations. Another interest was also involved—as it turned out, a decisive one. That was the interest of those whose ambitions and futures were tied to speculation in land. Land as a commodity on the futures market, land to be acquired cheap and sold dear like any other article of commerce, was a view that transcended the imperial-colonist dichotomy. Entrepreneurial ambition stirred on both sides of the Atlantic. There was a broad range in the trading practices of these entrepreneurs, from the secret, unscrupulous maneuvers of Connecticut speculators at the Albany Congress of 1754 to George Washington's open purchases of Virginia military grants in the transmontane country. It was a business where prudence today might well mean profit tomorrow. Hence, Benjamin Franklin's low-profile interest in land that he thought had become available as a result of northern boundary negotiations.[35]

An equally broad range in scale existed, from the homestead grant sought by an individual trader from Indians who were in his debt, to the imperial domains requested from the British Crown by aristocratic merchant bankers whose capital—they hoped—would be the land that was granted. The decisive influence of these land merchants was not felt in Indian affairs until 1770 and after, but the beginnings can be seen in the early 1760s in the long and complicated negotiations over an Indian-British boundary in the Northern Department.[36]

Boundary Negotiations, 1765–68

There were two distinct stages in boundary negotiations north of the Ohio. The first occurred during the spring and summer of 1765 when preliminary discussions were held with the Six Nations of the Iroquois and with the western nations most affected by the boundary. At that time agreements in principle were worked out. The second stage was in the fall of 1768 when the final boundary location was determined and the defining Treaty of Fort Stanwix was signed.

Scholarly attention has centered on the Fort Stanwix negotiations, but those were, in fact, only the visible proceedings, the public proclamation of decisions that, by and large, had already been reached three and a half years earlier. In May 1765 at meetings held almost simultaneously at Fort Pitt and at Johnson Hall (William Johnson's estate in the Mohawk Valley), and in July 1765 at another meeting at Johnson Hall, the hard bargaining was done. It is at these 1765 meetings that the tangled lines that led to future events can be separated out and seen most clearly. In particular, the way that the northern portion of the boundary was from the first indissolubly joined to the dominance of the Iroquois and to the interests of the land merchants, is made plain in the negotiations of 1765 and in the preliminaries to them.

The views and actions of London officials from 1763 to 1765 have already been discussed in connection with the southern boundary negotiations. By the time of the first northern boundary meetings in May 1765, the boundary principle had been enunciated in the Proclamation of 1763, and had been translated into a directive in the Board of Trade's plan for the management of Indian affairs issued in July 1764.[37] The plan represented a transition from the early and rather vague British hope, expressed the year before by Secretary of State Egremont, of preserving peace by securing the Indians in the possession of their land, rights to which could be acquired "by fair purchase only,"[38] to a commitment to a definite, mutually-agreed-on boundary. The transition was in line with William Johnson's thinking. He had recommended the boundary as early as November 1763.

In the comprehensive report that has been cited here several times, Johnson pointed out that one advantage of such a boundary was that it would allay the fears of both Indians and whites. It would provide a guarantee to the Indians, thus quieting their apprehensions that their land would be taken without their consent. At the same time, the whites would not need to fear that their settlements would be confined to the eastern seaboard forever. The boundary could be moved from time to time as need arose, and as the Indians agreed. In this first explicit statement of the tactic of the moving boundary, Johnson recommended:

> that a certain line should be run at the back of the Northern Colonies, beyond which no settlement should be made, until the whole Six Nations should think proper selling part thereof. . . . I am certain I can at any time hereafter perswade them to cede to His Majesty more land, if it may be found wanting from encrease of people, which is very improbable, there being already more pattented and unsettled than can possibly be well occupied in many years. . . . If such a boundary (having due regard to their hunting grounds) should be thought adviseable, I shall immediately on receiving Your Lordships commands, make the Indians acquainted therewith, and settle the same in such manner, as may prove most to their satisfaction, and the good of the public; and I have no doubt that the Indians, on such determination, and on having their several grievances concerning their lands redressed, will be well satisfied on that score.[39]

In Johnson's recommendation, the official British policy of acquisition of land "by fair purchase only" was linked to the boundary principle, and the whole was placed in the hands of imperial administrators. Officials of the separate colonies might be consulted, but the directing force and the final say were at the supracolonial level. Johnson had his own authority in mind, an authority that was to be exercised as an extension of the authority of the Board of Trade and, ultimately, of the British Crown. Johnson's concern was matched in the South by Stuart's insistence on the preeminence of his office, and in London by the board's concern for the imperial direction of Indian affairs in general.[40] Although not everywhere successful, the administrative structure of command that was implicit in Johnson's 1763 recommendation to the board

came to prevail in the matter of an Indian-British boundary. This may
have been because the boundary was a matter that could be handled
through the central-command structure as it existed. A boundary could
be handled more easily than, for example, Indian trade, the regulation
of which demanded a large number of supervisory personnel that the
imperial administration did not have and would not have been able to
pay for.

However that may be, in the matter of the boundary, imperial centralization prevailed. In the North this meant that imperial policy, as
actually worked out in the field, was wholly dependent on William
Johnson and his staff. Imperial directives were filtered through Johnson's
understanding of events and relationships, and shaped by the power he
could bring to bear in negotiations. His concern for a boundary has already been cited. Equally important is the context in which he recommended action, that of Iroquois dominance. Boundary negotiations
were to be made with the Six Nations, and if in the future more land
were needed and the boundary moved, those negotiations would again
be with the Six Nations. Johnson underestimated the influence of the
land interests when he said he did not think more land would be wanted
in the near future, but it is safe to say that if he had foreseen the pressures his response would still have been the same. The Six Nations would
be the ones who would have to be consulted.

Johnson never wavered from his position that the Iroquois League
held by right of conquest the entire Ohio country, including land south
of the Ohio River from the Blue Ridge Mountains on the east to (at
least) the head of the Kentucky River, and north across the Ohio River
to the north shore of Lake Huron. It followed that the Indians in this
vast area held their land at the pleasure of the Iroquois, and that only
the Iroquois had the right of disposal. Johnson's objections to the Bradstreet treaties of the late summer of 1764 were based on this position.
In the treaties some of the western nations gave up land to the British
Crown. Johnson protested that those nations had no land to give. Their
land belonged to the Six Nations, and while it had been the policy of
the French to try to make the western nations independent of the Six
Nations that policy had not succeeded. In regard to disposal of their
lands, said Johnson, the western nations "never yet would take upon
themselves seriously an affair of that nature."[41]

It is worth noting that when Johnson made this objection to the
purported land cessions by some of the western nations, he was not
yet engaged in boundary negotiations. The close connection of the

northern boundary negotiations with the interests of merchants seeking a grant of land has cast doubt on the good faith of any statements made by the British officials involved. Johnson's insistence on Iroquois supremacy was not, however, invented to serve the needs of the merchants. He not only held this position before boundary negotiations began, he held it before the merchants even tried to get a cession of Indian land.

The business interests involved in the 1765-68 boundary negotiations were chiefly Philadelphia merchants who had suffered losses in the Anglo-Indian War of 1763-65. Large quantities of merchandise had been captured by the Indians, and the merchants were seeking compensation. They did not at first try to get a grant of land from the Indians. They tried to get a reimbursement from the British Treasury. Their agent in this attempt was George Croghan, Indian trader, small-time merchant, and deputy superintendent of Indian affairs in the Northern Department. In January 1764, Croghan was in London to urge the claims of the Philadelphia merchants and to make the proper connections so that the claims might be taken up and urged at a high enough level to gain possible consideration.[42]

While Croghan was in London he also—and separately— urged on the Board of Trade the advantages of drawing a "natural boundary" between Indians and whites in the Northern Department, and he proposed a line "across the frontiers of the British middle Colonies from the heads of the River Delaware to the mouth of the Ohio where it empties into the Mississippi."[43] The proposed line ignored the whole question of the southern Indians, a question that both Johnson and Croghan were inclined to ignore. Croghan, like Johnson, had an Iroquois-centered view of the continent. All the land west of the line proposed by Croghan was to be reserved for the use of "the Six Nations, and of the several Tribes dependent on them."[44] Croghan, whose interests were avowedly commercial, thought that this arrangement would satisfy the Indians and at the same time secure to the British the fur trade of the whole region.

Again, the recommendation for a boundary and the assertion of Iroquois dominance were not made in connection with the merchants' claim—at that time directed to the Treasury. The interest of Croghan and the Philadelphia merchants shifted to a grant of land as reparation for their losses only after it became clear that a special act of Parliament would be required before the Treasury could pay their claims. Then the boundary negotiations became the vehicle through which a reparations grant was sought from the Indians. With the help of Croghan and Johnson, the merchants were successful in getting the Indians' agreement.

The grant of land made by the Indians came to be known as the Indiana grant.[45]

The long and tangled history of the Indiana grant is beyond the bounds of this study. Here it is sufficient to say that as the Philadelphia merchants exerted themselves to have the grant approved in London more and more people became involved at higher and higher levels until the Indiana grant, like the boundary negotiations from which it derived, became the vehicle for purposes not originally intended. During the course of this maneuvering, the two issues became so closely joined that not even the Crown could separate them again. By the time the matter arrived at that level of consideration, the grant had attracted the attention and support of the expansionists among British policymakers and had become part of a full-blown plan for a new western colony, called, eventually, Vandalia.[46]

By that time also, George Croghan was all but squeezed out of the enterprise. The distance between his scrabbling existence of trading trips, debt, and ever-imminent bankruptcy, and the lives of the British peers who became associated with the Indians' reparations grant, was one to be measured only on some exponential social scale. Yet Croghan was the indispensable contact in the field, the man who could go among the western Indians, sit down with them, and discuss indemnity to the merchants as well as the Indian-white boundary that was the policy of the British government.

Croghan and William Johnson were both indispensable—to the merchants, and to policymakers as well. Because they were, British policy became captive to their interests and understanding. The captivity was the more complete because Iroquois interests and goals coincided briefly with those of the two British officials, thus presenting an appearance of harmony. That the harmony was based on the assumption of Iroquois dominance might have served as a warning to London officials, but they were accustomed to considering the Iroquois first in the formulation of policy north of the Ohio. They had had to do so for more than a hundred years. And when they finally did raise a question regarding Iroquois claims, it was in relation to the southern Indians, not to Iroquois "dependents."[47]

William Johnson opened formal negotiations with the northern Indians at Johnson Hall the last of April 1765, and on the eighth of May concluded a treaty that included provisions for both indemnity and a boundary. The treaty was signed by representatives of two groups of Delawares, those who lived east of the Allegheny Mountains on the

Susquehanna River, and those who lived west of the mountains. These last were usually identified as Delawares of the Ohio. The treaty also contained an explicit acknowledgment of the Delawares' subordinate status in relation to the Six Nations of the Iroquois League. The way that these two articles built conflict into the very arrangement that was supposed to eliminate conflict in the future is worth looking at more closely. The articles read:

> That many of the Traders who were plundered and severely treated by the Delawares in 1763, having represented the great distresses to which they are thereby reduced, and prayed relief, the Delawares are therefore to fall immediately on a Method for making them some restitution by a Grant of Lands, provided His Majesty shall approve thereof and the Six Nations first give their approbation thereto.
> That whenever His Majesty shall be pleased to direct that Limits shall be settled between his subjects and the Indians with their consent, the Delawares engage to abide by whatever Limits shall be agreed upon between the English and the Six Nations, and shall never disturb His Majesty's Subjects on that Account.[48]

The Six Nations did not sign the treaty of 8 May 1765, but it was, in fact, their treaty as much as it was William Johnson's. There were nine hundred Indians at the formal council that preceded the signing of the treaty, and the majority of them were members of one or the other of the Six Nations, not of the Delawares. They had much business of their own to conduct with Johnson, and they were also involved in all of the negotiations with the Delawares. The subordinate position for the Delawares that was assumed by both Johnson and the Six Nations can be seen in the way that Johnson handled the subject of the boundary.

Johnson introduced the subject at a special meeting of the chiefs of the Six Nations, saying that it was "the most important Affair I have at this time to mention." He listed Britain's reasons for seeking a boundary. the king's desire to do the Indians strict justice, the wish to "put a final end to disputes between his People and you concerning Lands," and so on. He added frankly that the boundary should "best agree with the extent and increase of each Province."[49]

To this the Six Nations leaders made no objection, merely observing through their Onondaga speaker that a line "will be very necessary provided the White People will abide by it," and that this time the king ought to make his people keep within bounds, "which they have not yet done."[50] They then made their first boundary offer—one that placed many established white settlements on the Indians side of the line—and the bargaining began in earnest. The Delawares were involved only peripherally, yet it was the Delawares who would be asked to make reparations from Delaware land that would be cut off and lie on the white side of the line. The position of the Six Nations and of William Johnson was, of course, that the Delawares only held their land at the pleasure of the Six Nations anyway, and what had been given could also be bargained away.

William Johnson knew that in the past the Susquehanna Delawares had gone to war rather than give up their homes, which the Six Nations had sold to Pennsylvania in 1754. The Delawares had won that struggle, and the land had been returned. In the war just past, however, the Delawares had been defeated, and were at the council to get what terms they could. Johnson reminded the Six Nations of their responsibilities in the matter of the tentative boundary that had been agreed upon:

> since you say you are the owners of all the land you spoke about, I expect never to hear any grumbling about it, & that you will never suffer any other People to sett up a Title to it, for if you do, or if any of you attempt to Evade it hereafter, you cannot be considered as an honest People.[51]

The Onondaga speaker affirmed the Iroquois position that the boundary had been agreed on unanimously by the whole confederacy, and by "our Nephews the Delawares." He then ran through the location of the boundary, point by point, so that there might be no misunderstanding. Further, he said, the Six Nations would send a message to the western nations telling them of Iroquois intentions regarding the boundary. This would be done soon, at a public meeting among the Shawnees "where all the Western Nations often hold their Councils."[52] The Six Nations were sure that the western nations would be reconciled to what the Iroquois intended to do.

What the Iroquois intended could be seen in the boundary that was traced out by the Onondaga speaker. The western portion of the boundary followed the line of the Ohio from Kitanning, about thirty-five miles (fifty-six kilometers) above Fort Pitt, to the mouth of the Tennessee River (called, at that time, the Cherokee River), and up that river to its source.[53] Thus, with casual grandeur, the Iroquois asserted that all of the old Northwest plus most of present-day Kentucky, Tennessee, and West Virginia were part of their domain. This was in addition to land in western Pennsylvania where Delawares, Shawnees, and some smaller affiliated groups were living with Iroquois permission. The boundary, as laid out by the Onondaga speaker in 1765 on behalf of the Iroquois Confederacy, was nothing less than a boast of the League's triumphs at the height of its power, one hundred years in the past. That the Iroquois boast of 1765 would, after 1768, also be used to suit the "extent and increase of each Province," such as the provinces of Virginia and North Carolina, only added to the boundary's potential for the destruction of the policy and authority of both the League and of British imperial government.

George Croghan handled British negotiations with the western nations in the spring of 1765. At the same time that William Johnson and the Iroquois were concluding the May 8 agreement with the Delawares at Johnson Hall, Croghan at Fort Pitt was talking to the Shawnees and to some Delawares and Six Nations of the Ohio. His journal of the negotiations does not mention any discussion of the boundary or of reparations for the Philadelphia merchants. He did bring up the matter of reparations, however, both at Fort Pitt and on his subsequent trip to the Wabash country to secure the right of passage to the former French forts in the Illinois country. This is brought out in a letter he wrote later that year to Benjamin Franklin in London, telling Franklin of his success in getting the western Indians to agree to reparations. Croghan said that in his public and private conferences with "the Shawanese, Delawares and Weyondotts, and the Several other tribes who had robbed and murdered our Traders" he had urged on them the justice of indemnifying the traders for their losses. He said that the Indians told him they had no way of making reparations except by giving up part of their land, which they were willing to do, "and especially of that part which lies on this side of the River Ohio (on the back part of Virginia) as it was now of no use to them for Hunting Ground."[54]

As result of Croghan's May 1765 meetings at Fort Pitt, delegations from the Shawnees, the western Delawares, and the western Six Nations went to Johnson Hall that summer, and on July 13 they acceded to the peace-boundary–reparations treaty that had been signed on May 8 of that year. The articles of the treaty were read and explained to them, and each group "agreed to subscribe to the same & to abide by every Article which might be construed to extend to them."[55]

Looking over the terms of the May 1765 Treaty of Johnson Hall, and the July 1765 accession to that treaty, William Johnson might well be satisfied. Besides implementing the terms of earlier peace treaties and agreements, he had secured the promise of a reparations grant to the

Philadelphia merchants, as well as agreement on the specific location
of a major portion of the general Indian-British boundary north of the
Ohio. From the standpoint of the many British interests, both official
and unofficial, that were involved in the area, more could scarcely be
asked.

But what of Indian interests in the same area? How had they fared?
Enough has been said of Iroquois actions to show their persistent efforts
to assert their ancient dominance, and to have that dominance recognized by both the British and the "dependent" Indians. Their cession
of "Kentucky" lands, which they could not control, and of western
Pennsylvania lands, used chiefly by Delawares and Shawnees, was part
of the same pattern of assertion. In this respect, the 1765 treaties were
an expression of Iroquois general policy. Further, the League was anxious to establish a comprehensive boundary that the whites would respect. Finally, the Iroquois expected to benefit from the presents that
would seal the bargain between them and the British and serve as ratifi-
cation of the final agreement.

This leaves the Shawnees, the Delawares of Ohio and Pennsylvania,
and the Six Nations of the Ohio. It also raises again the persistent and
troubling question of Indian concepts of territory, and how those were
involved in or affected by the 1765 agreements. Since the two agreements were critically important in later years, it is worth looking again
at territorial concepts before turning to consideration of the Indian
groups that were not so well served by the treaties as were (in the short
run) the British and the Iroquois.

At the outset it should be noted that most discussions of Indian concepts of landownership are too general to be useful in an investigation
of this kind.[56] When one is trying to understand the behavior of a specific Indian group as it grapples with the problem of who gets this or
that particular piece of land for which many are contending, general
statements about the sacredness of the earth as "the mother of man"[57]
are not very enlightening. Whether the earth was sacred or profane was
not at issue. Power and prestige were at issue, as well as ownership and
control of certain specific areas of land. In such a contest, what territorial concepts would prevail? Which ones even applied?

To help answer these questions, it will be useful to separate Indian
ideas about land into three categories: intra-Indian, inter-Indian, and
intercultural. The sets of ideas that determined ownership and use of
land within one Indian group were separate from those prevailing in the
relationship of that group with other Indian groups. These, in turn,

were not the same as the ideas governing conduct in negotiations with Europeans, whose market approach to land was totally different from the basically religious orientation of the Indians. Because of the emotional appeal of this religious orientation to writers of today, emphasis needs to be laid on the fact that differences in cultural outlook did not preclude meaningful negotiations. Neither the Indians nor the Europeans were cultural automatons who could not perceive and react to differences in the views of other people.

Little need be said here about intra-Indian ownership and use of land. Evidence for the precontact period is sketchy. What can be said with confidence is that customary procedures changed as the Indians reacted to the changing circumstances of their lives after the invasion of the Europeans. Scholars' opinions have also changed. The old view that "simple" hunting societies, at an early stage of social evolution, had no conception of land ownership but held all land in common, has given way to a new appreciation of the complexity and variety of ideas and usages among the Indians east of the Mississippi. For example, in precontact times, among certain highly stratified Indian groups, such as those in Virginia and New England, choice garden plots along the river were the exclusive property of families of hereditary rulers. In contrast, among the Mahicans in the three-corners area of present-day New York, Vermont, and Massachusetts, the right of usufruct (or use) of river tracts was hereditary in the lineage groups that were the base of Mahican social organization. North and west of the Mahicans, among the precontact Hurons of upper Lake Huron, land was owned and farmed by individuals or by nuclear families, but the right of reversion was retained by the community at large.[58] These few examples suggest the variety of forms that land ownership and use might take in supposedly "simple" societies.

Of more immediate relevance to this study are the concepts of land ownership demonstrated in inter-Indian relations. Here again, evidence for the precontact period is sketchy, but the treaties of 1765 can be analyzed without such evidence. It is not necessary to establish some precontact time of purity from which all else is a falling away. As the anthropologist A. F. C. Wallace has noted, "whatever the source of a culture element, if it is a functional aspect of culture at a given date, it is as much a cultural property of a society as some earlier and perhaps abandoned custom."[59] Long before 1765, observers were recording well-defined territorial limits for the various Indian groups north of the Ohio and east of the Mississippi. Associated with these limits were clear and commonly accepted ideas of trespass, as well as of permissive use by outsiders. This last is of particular interest here, because of its bearing on the 1765 treaties. The Iroquois had agreed to give up land that was used chiefly by other Indians. Under the concepts and usage prevailing among Indians of the Northeast at that time, did the Iroquois have that right? The question requires a closer look at the forms of inter-Indian land use.

There were different categories of permissive use of land by outsiders: short-term hunting rights, for example, or longer-term hunting, passage, and settlement rights as part of a general political alliance, the rights to expire when and if the alliance did. There was also a kind of semipermanent tenure that, by 1765, was well recognized and fairly widespread. It might be called dislocation tenure, since it was granted to (or imposed upon) those Indian groups who for one reason or another had left their territorial homelands. These could be captive groups, forcibly settled on lands belonging to their captors. They might be refugee groups seeking asylum and a place to settle. They might simply be desirable allies invited onto the land to strengthen defenses. Or they might be dependent groups, that little-understood category which in 1765 either did or did not include the Shawnees and Delawares, according to who was doing the categorizing.[60]

It is at this point that power again enters the picture and impinges upon concepts. The clash of territorial concepts took place in a context that was created by relationships of power. Those relationships, in turn, through their successes or failures, changed the very concepts that were at issue. If it turned out that the Iroquois were successful in their cession of "dependents'" land, then in the future this might be seen as one of the possible prerogatives of a landowning group. In 1765, the prerogative was not yet established. Iroquois efforts in that direction, as has been noted here, had had mixed results, and the point was still arguable. The whole concept of territorial dependency-rights was in that elastic stage where it was being shaped by ongoing events. In such a situation, all of the disputants could make a good case that custom as well as justice was on their side. The 1765 treaties, which asserted the Iroquois views, were later repudiated by other Indians—the Shawnees, in particular—who denied the territorial rights asserted there. The whole question was, however, quickly subsumed in the far broader struggle of the western Indian nations, including the Shawnees, to prevent white settlement north of the Ohio.[61]

This leads to the final category of Indian territorial concepts, those in the intercultural realm. By 1765 there were various ways by which

Indian land could legitimately change ownership. Conquest was one means. So was assertion of ownership rights, either by settlement or use, over territory that had been abandoned by others. So was sale to the Europeans.[62] Such sale transactions had been going on for more than a hundred years, and there were innumerable records of sales that were never disputed and never denied. The exceptions, such as the Delaware Walking Purchase, were famous precisely because the conditions of fair sale that had been established were violated in such instances, and the Europeans refused redress. The lack of effective means for the redress of legitimate grievances was one of the factors that turned the whole business of land transfer into a mockery of legitimate transactions. In 1765, the process was beginning to gather speed and intensity for the Iroquois and the western Indian nations. Indian ideas about the conditions of fair sale were clear enough and they were widely held. But, increasingly in the years after 1765, these ideas could not be acted on because of the overwhelming power that was brought to bear against the Indians.

It might be thought that the treaties of 1765 can be dismissed on the grounds that the Delawares and Shawnees did not really know what was in them, or that the Delawares, in particular, were not aware of the terms worked out at the conferences between William Johnson and the leaders of the Six Nations. On this point, the records are clear. Before signing the first treaty on May 8, the leaders of both the Ohio and the Pennsylvania Delawares stood up in full council and repeated the terms of the treaty, word for word. This would, of course, include the articles stipulating that the Delawares would make a reparations grant of land to the Philadelphia merchants, and the article securing their prior agreement to a general Indian-white boundary wherever it might be located by the Iroquois in negotiations with the British. The treaty was discussed again in full council in July before delegates from the Shawnees, the Six Nations of the Ohio, and other Ohio Delawares. As has been mentioned earlier, the delegates acceded to the treaty and agreed to abide by the articles that applied to them.[63]

After the treaty of accession had been signed, the western delegates were lectured by an Onondaga speaker. He warned them not to say, in the future, that they had not understood the terms of what they were signing. Neither should they claim that the agreed-upon terms were really something different. He pointed out that the treaty was written down upon paper, in the fashion of the English, who used such a method of recording for all their contracts, agreements, and treaties. If, in the future, a question should arise, they could easily consult this written copy to determine exactly what had been decided. "Brothers & Allies, We are therefore all resolved & determined to follow literally the Treaty that we have agreed to, & we hope, expect, & we insist on the same from you, as making together but one same spirit and body politick."[64]

If nothing else, the talk by the Onondaga speaker served notice on the western Indians that the Iroquois League and its ally, Great Britain, were determined on the treaties of 1765. The Indians from the Ohio were no more in a position to protest than were the Indians from western Pennsylvania. In the Anglo-Indian War that was still continuing in isolated outbursts of violence, these Indians had fought against the British and they had lost. They were not in a position to stipulate terms. They were suing for peace, and for a resumption of trade so that they could replenish their supplies of European goods. Where need dictated, they followed—but not blindly. The very words of agreement in the treaty of accession left a convenient loophole. Who would decide which of the treaty articles did indeed "extend to them"?[65] The wording left the future open to argument as to the extent of obligation assumed by these groups in relation to the reparations and the boundary. Above all, it left open the question of how far they would be bound by future arrangements worked out by the Iroquois.

After the July meeting at Johnson Hall in 1765, northern negotiations were at a standstill for almost three years while William Johnson awaited further instructions from London. Orders to complete the boundary came in the early part of 1768. The form in which they came, and the circumstances surrounding their transmittal, signalled a change in the environment in which British policy toward the Indians was formulated and carried out.

From the summer of 1767 to the outbreak of war between Great Britain and her Atlantic seaboard colonies, the attention of officials in London was directed more and more to the mounting difficulties of administering those colonies, and less and less to the administration of the backcountry. The ministries of Chatham and Grafton were hard put to finance the everyday operations of government, so the troops, military posts, and negotiating expenses required to maintain a significant British presence in the backcountry came to seem one of the more expendable items in the British budget.

Beginning in the summer of 1767 with the Townshend Acts, British attempts to offset domestic revenue losses and also to assert financial legislative rights in regard to the white settler colonies, set in motion a wave of colonist-protest that mounted until it could not be contained. At the same time, expansionists both within and outside of government circles were urging that the backcountry be opened for white settlement. They argued that new colonies could be formed at Detroit, at the forks of the Ohio, and at the juncture of the Ohio and the Mississippi. Western colonies would help to balance the power of the seaboard colonies and would provide revenue for the Crown, through quit-rents or through increased trade, instead of being a drain on the British Treasury.

These various pressures and needs were taken into account in a plan proposed in September 1767 by Lord Shelburne, secretary of state for the Southern Department. Shelburne suggested that Great Britain cut her losses by abolishing the Indian Service entirely. Three new American colonies would be created (at the locations mentioned), and most British troops could then be withdrawn from the backcountry.[66] Shelburne's drastic plan was not adopted. It was, however, an indication of the power of the forces of expansion at the highest levels of British government.

The short-term effect of Shelburne's proposal was a strengthening of imperial control in regard to the Indian-white boundary. A new cabinet-level office, secretary of state for the colonies, was created, and Lord Hillsborough was appointed to it in January 1768. In view of the threat inherent in such plans as Shelburne's, the boundary became a matter of urgent imperial priority. In January and again in March 1768 William Johnson was directed to complete negotiations on the northern boundary.[67] The instructions were set within a frame of reference that accepted the Iroquois as negotiators for the whole area. It was with the Six Nations that the line was to be settled, "in conformity to what was agreed upon at the Congress in 1765."[68]

The agreements made in 1765 were to be modified, however. This was illustrated by two separate maps sent to Johnson, and by an explanation in a report from the Board of Trade, a copy of which was also sent to him. The western terminus of the boundary was not to be at the mouth of the Tennessee River, as agreed in 1765, but rather at the mouth of the Kanawha River. The Kanawha, almost seven hundred miles (eleven hundred kilometers) up the Ohio from the Tennessee, was the terminus of the Cherokee-Virginia portion of the Indian-white boundary in the South. By making the northern boundary end at the same spot, uniformity would be achieved and possible conflict avoided. Both North and South, then, directed the Board in March 1768, that the "Boundary Line between the Indians and the Settlements of his Majestys subjects (everywhere negociated upon and in many parts settled and ascertained) shall be finally ratified and confirmed."[69]

With this authorization, Johnson moved ahead on northern negotiations. They culminated at Fort Stanwix in upper New York in early November 1768. More than three thousand Indians were present at the proceedings, as well as commissioners from New Jersey, Pennsylvania, and Virginia. The council was the public affirmation of the arrangements that had been worked out in the several meetings of 1765. It was also a moment of power for the Six Nations of Iroquois Confederacy. They were the ones who signed the deed that ceded land to white merchants as reparations for war losses. Two days later, on November 5, 1768, they signed the Treaty of Fort Stanwix. The treaty included a boundary agreement that, among other things, made available for transfer the land that had been ceded to the merchants two days earlier. It also ignored the London directive regarding the Kanawha River. The boundary description noted that the western terminus of the boundary between whites and Indians had been set at the mouth of the Tennessee (Cherokee) River, because "the same is and we do declare it to be our true Bounds with the Southern Indians and that we have an undoubted right to the Country as far South as that River."[70]

It has been suggested that the Tennessee River terminus was the price of a bargain whereby Virginia would drop some of her claims to land around the forks of the Ohio—land that was desired by the Philadelphia merchants, among others—in return for the Iroquois cession of the entire Kentucky region.[71] Given the extent and power of the interests involved in the setting of such a comprehensive boundary, the suggestion is certainly plausible, although not provable. It is not a complete explanation either, for it discounts the Iroquois as active participants in the Stanwix negotiations and reduces them to unwitting pawns. The Stanwix boundary of 1768 was, in fact, in close "conformity to what was agreed upon at the Congress in 1765" from Oswego on the east branch of the Susquehannah, south and west to the mouth of the Tennessee. (Agreement on the line north from Oswego, which could not be worked out in 1765, was obtained in 1768, and the line was extended north to near Fort Stanwix.) In 1765, as well as in 1768, the Iroquois asserted their right to dispose of this whole area, just as, both earlier and later, they asserted their dominance over "dependents" from the mountains to the Mississippi. The Fort Stanwix bargain—if bargain there was—could not have been made outside the Iroquois context that has been detailed in this study.

Part of that context was the Iroquois sense of destiny. Beneath the surface pageantry of the council proceedings at Fort Stanwix, the Six Nations were engaged in their ancient search for power. In the opening paragraphs of the treaty they listed again those nations they had brought under the roof of the Longhouse of the League: "To all to whom These presents shall come or may concern; We the Sachems & Chiefs of the Six Confederate Nations, and of the Shawanoes, Delawares, Mingoes of Ohio and other Dependent Tribes on behalf of ourselves and of the rest of our Several Nations."[72]

The rest of the several nations were not in evidence at Fort Stanwix in November 1768, but the Six Nations were there in strength. To show that the Stanwix decisions were legitimate within the Iroquois frame of reference, and that they had wide popular support, the British carefully listed by name thirty-seven leaders of the various groups present, and then gave the totals attending for each group: more than two hundred Mohawks, four hundred Oneidas, three hundred Tuscaroras, three hundred Onondagas, eight hundred Cayugas, four hundred Senecas, and seven hundred Indians from such affiliates as the Nanticokes and Conoys.[73] If the Iroquois were correct in their assertions of rights and authority, then the Treaty of Fort Stanwix could, indeed, stand on their signatures alone, and the Delawares, Shawnees, and "other Dependent Tribes" would abide by the Stanwix agreements.

The fact that these Iroquois assertions were turned to the eventual benefit of white expansionists has obscured the fact that the Iroquois made similar assertions of authority at other times and places. At Fort Pitt in the spring of 1768, before the Stanwix treaty was signed, they took the Shawnees to task for differing with Iroquois policy. The meeting had been called by George Croghan on behalf of the Crown, and was attended by Pennsylvania commissioners and by representatives from the western Shawnees, Delawares, and Six Nations (Mingoes). The reasons for the meeting were classic in the relations between Indians and whites in North America: unprovoked killings and illegal settlements by whites. The situation was taken so seriously by the Pennsylvania legislature that, in February, it had appropriated £3,000 for condolence gifts to go to the Iroquois of New York and the West in compensation for the killings. The legislature also passed a law forbidding white settlement on what was still Indian land in the Monongahela Valley, and had authorized commissioners to go there and order the white squatters to leave on pain of death.[74]

To this situation, the Indians meeting with Croghan and the Pennsylvania commissioners at Fort Pitt added their own separate concerns. The Shawnees used the occasion to dissent from the general Iroquois policy of accommodation with the British. Speaking through Nymwha, they denied that the British had any right to occupy forts in the Indian country. They protested British intentions to trade directly with the Indians in the Illinois country (thus cutting the nearer tribes out of the lucrative middle-man position). Finally, they took vigorous issue with British assertions of territorial mastery: "you think yourselves Masters of this Country because you have taken it from the French, who you know had no Right to it as it is the Property of us Indians."[75]

Here was a clear divergence from the Iroquois position, and the Iroquois at the meeting rebuked the Shawnees sharply for taking a stand that was at odds with Six Nations' policy. They brought out a copy of the August 1764 treaty that Colonel John Bradstreet had negotiated with some Shawnees and other western nations and pointed out that in it the Shawnees and other had agreed that the British might build and occupy forts, and travel freely to the Illinois country. What, then, were the Shawnees complaining about?[76]

The Shawnees did not maintain their defiance. Later in the meeting they withdrew their complaints, and they asked to be included in the distribution of goods from Pennsylvania. For years, they and some of the other western nations were reluctant to act against the Six Nations of the Iroquois, thus lending credibility to the Six Nations' continued claims of dominance. Even after it became apparent that the Shawnees and Delawares were heavy losers by the Treaty of Fort Stanwix, it was six years before they again went to war to try to secure their own separate rights to land.[77]

No matter what the circumstances, the Iroquois did not yield in their assertions. This can be seen in their attitude toward whites as well as Shawnees. That same spring of 1768 they not only refused to help the Pennsylvania commissioners remove the illegal squatters on the Monongahela, they undercut the commissioners' own efforts to do so. After the commissioners had visited the white settlers and told them that the penalty for failure to move was death, some of the Iroquois went to the settlers and told them that there was no need for them to move, after all. The Six Nations intended to sell that land to the whites, anyway, when it came time to make the final arrangements on the Indian-British boundary. At the Fort Pitt meeting, the commissioners told the Six Nations representatives that they intended to try again to remove the squatters, and they asked the Iroquois to come with them and tell the settlers of the "great Displeasure" of the Six Nations at their settling on Indian land. The Iroquois refused, saying there was no need to make enemies over land that the confederacy was going to sell to the whites.[78] The illegal settlements disturbed the Shawnees and Delawares who lived in that area, and they disturbed the white authorities, who feared an outbreak of hostilities, but the Iroquois were unperturbed. They asserted a right of disposal and maintained it consistently.

This same attitude pervaded the Treaty of Fort Stanwix. Immediate British gains from the treaty were obvious. Thousands of square miles of land passed to the Crown, and the comprehensive Indian-British boundary was carried north of the Ohio nearly as far as the Mohawk River. Separate from that, there was the reparations grant to the merchants. Immediate Iroquois gains were also obvious. Goods and specie valued at more than £10,000 were given out at the close of the treaty proceedings in payment for the land that had been ceded. In addition, the British had publicly reaffirmed their backing of Iroquois claims to dominance. Later developments make clear that the Six Nations took this not just as a symbolic gesture but as a British commitment for military aid when the Iroquois tried to bring their "dependent" nations into line. For their part, the British hoped that the Fort Stanwix agreements would at last put a "final end" to disputes between whites and Indians, as William Johnson had suggested in 1765.

Both the Iroquois and the British were to be disappointed in their expectations.

5   Transformation of the Treaty System 1768-75

By the end of 1768 four areas of common agreement had been defined by British and Indian leaders in the series of formal treaties negotiated between Great Britain and the major North American Indian groups east of the Mississippi River. The major areas were peace, friendship, trade, and a comprehensive Indian-British boundary. The treaties that embodied these mutual interests were in two categories: belligerency treaties, like the early ones between Britain and the northern Indians in which the chief purpose was to mark the end of hostilities by exchanging prisoners and so on; and accommodation treaties, in which terms of coexistence were given formal expression.

From 1763 to 1768, while this treaty system was developing, there were few external pressures from either the international or the domestic scenes to complicate the efforts of policymakers. Colonial agitation over Grenville's Revenue Acts and the Stamp Act had come and gone without seriously affecting imperial-Indian relations in the hinterland. But after 1768 the context in which the system functioned began to change rapidly. Colonial quarrels with the metropole increased in frequency and violence. While the Cherokees met in October 1768 to complete their boundary with the southern colonies, British troops were ordered into Boston to maintain the order that was one of the goals of British policy, whether in the West with the Indians or in the East with white colonists. The very reasons that Bostonians gave for arming themselves—that a war with France was imminent—meant a renewal of disquiet in the West. Nymwha, the leader who spoke for the Shawnees at Fort Pitt in the spring of 1768, commented on the rumor of coming war between France and Great Britain and suggested that, if the two powers were going to fight again, they do it on the other side of the ocean "where you used to fight."[1]

After 1768 there were many pressures on the treaty system of 1763-68. Some were a direct result of colonial-imperial conflicts. The colonists' nonimportation agreements, protesting the revenue-raising Townshend Acts, had, by the end of 1769, reduced imports from Britain by almost one-half. This, in turn, affected the trade that was, from the Indian point of view, the chief reason for a treaty agreement in the first place. "When we first saw the white people and fastened their ship to the great tree," an Onondaga speaker told William Johnson, "the band of our union was a fair trade."[2] The nonimportation agreements of 1768-69 put a severe strain on this band of union. The situation was particularly acute for the Cherokees, since Virginia, one of their chief trading partners, maintained the official ban on British imports until mid-1771, after other colonies had resumed more normal trade.

Other pressures came from those who wanted white settlements to expand into the West. This was one of the constant factors of British imperial policy, but after the 1768 Treaty of Fort Stanwix the pressures became intense. The reparations grant to the Philadelphia merchants and the Iroquois cession of the Cumberland-Kentucky regions seemed to open the whole south-central section of the continent to development. Quite apart from colonial-imperial struggles, the treaty system of 1763-68 contained its own disruptive features. The compromises that had been made, the bargains that had been struck, had the potential to destroy the agreements that were the purpose of the treaties.

The context of 1768-75 helped realize to the full this destructive potential. Subjected to the pressures of those years, the treaty system itself changed and became part of the general destruction. By the end of the period, treaties were no longer public agreements between politically separate and sovereign groups. The authority to make treaties had been usurped by private individuals, both Indians and whites, who transformed treaties into little more than private contracts for the acquisition of land, on the part of the whites, and supplies, on the part of the Indians.

The response of British imperial authorities to the disintegration of the treaty system of 1763-68 was the Quebec Act of 1774. Appearing as it did in the company of the Coercive Acts, the Quebec Act was seen by aroused white colonists as proof that the British ministry was plotting against the freedoms and future development not just of Massachusetts alone but of all the colonies. This loss of British prestige and authority in the white settler colonies was paralleled on the Indian side by the loss of Iroquois prestige and authority among the western Indian nations in the area north of the Ohio and west of Fort Pitt. For obvious reasons, the changes in the relationship between the Iroquois and the western nations are not as well documented as the changes in the relationships between Great Britain and her colonies. It is easy to recover Lord Hillsborough's 1768 instructions to the colonial governors that they should dissolve the provincial assemblies, if necessary, to prevent any endorsement of the Massachusetts Circular Letter. To recover the instructions sent by the Iroquois Confederacy in 1770 to the western nations is another matter since the original messages were destroyed in the wars that swept over all the parties involved.

Yet the purpose of the British and Iroquois messages was apparently the same. Each was an assertion of central authority over dissenting members of the group. In his 1768 directive to the colonial governors, Hillsborough was upholding the principle of the Parliamentary Declaratory Act against colonist declarations on taxation. In their 1770 messages to the western nations, the Iroquois were upholding their right solely to determine policy for the extended confederacy against the efforts of some members to form a rival confederation with its own separate authority and policy. As an indication of the seriousness with which the Iroquois took this threat, they sent one hundred separate message-belts with their embassy to the West. Despite the relative permanence of beaded message-belts, as compared to the parchment or paper used by Hillsborough and British imperial authorities, the belts have not survived.[3] Neither have the details necessary for a full account of the embassy. The problem is persistent in Indian history. Because of the lack of records, the prolonged and bitter struggle among the northern Indians has been little noticed. Yet the indications are that toward the end of the eighteenth century this upheaval in northern Indian relationships was a critical factor in the conflicts from which the new American nation eventually emerged, victorious.

Accomplishments of
the Treaty System of 1763–68

In the four areas of mutual concern—peace, friendship, trade, and an Indian-white boundary—the treaty system of 1763–68 functioned with moderate success. Peace had been general between whites and Indians south of the Ohio since 1763, and north of the Ohio since 1765. There were individual acts of violence that were exceptions to the general condition but no large-scale or widespread violence to give the lie to the treaties of peace. Friendship, too, was general, if friendship is taken in the diplomatic sense to mean a formal political relationship that allows or even encourages more casual exchanges, both personal and economic. Between the Iroquois Confederacy and Great Britain the formal relationship was closer than that. They were friends and allies in a deeper sense that had its roots in shared endeavors, as against the French in the Seven Years War, and they remained so even after the death of Sir William Johnson in 1774.

Trade was a matter on which Indians and whites seldom agreed, but it is difficult to determine if the basis of disagreement was a cultural difference or was due simply to the opposing viewpoints of buyer and seller. Scholars have noted that the economic system prevalent among most Indian societies was wholly unlike the competitive, acquisitive system that was emerging among whites of the eighteenth century. But it is not clear how much of the Indian economic outlook, which was based on shared resources and distribution according to socially determined standards of need, carried over into their dealings with whites.

Statements can be found to suggest that there was a carryover. Yakatastanage (the Mortar), for example, when laying down the trade terms that were a condition for the Creek-British Treaty of Pensacola, 28 May 1765, commented on the Indians' need for European goods. He pointed out that Creek hunters had to go much farther than they once did in order to get deerskins, and even then they could not get enough to supply their wants in trade. Yakatastanage's conclusion was that since the Creeks needed supplies, and since they could not procure enough skins to pay for the supplies, the British ought to lower prices.[4]

Yakatastanage was engaged in hard bargaining at Pensacola in 1765, however. He also pointed out that, if the Indians came down to Pensacola to trade, the British ought to lower prices because they would not have the cost of transporting the goods all the way to the Creek towns—an observation that would not be out of place in the world of Adam Smith.[5] Yakatastanage was a seller in a buyer's market, as well as a Creek Indian with a distinct cultural attitude toward economic exchange, and the difficulty in separating the two in his case is simply an instance of difficulties elsewhere. A clear pattern of cultural economic differences does not emerge from the Indian side of the proceedings when whites and Indians discussed recurrent problems over trade. What does emerge is a widespread, persistent Indian desire to sell more dearly and buy more cheaply.

The record of the treaty system's accomplishments in trade was a mixed one that satisfied neither the whites nor the Indians. British offi- cials knew that one key to peaceful relations with the Indians was abun- dant trade, and, as has been seen, the promise of abundance was held out as an inducement for the Indians to acquiesce in British rather than French patronage. But circumstances made it impossible for the British to carry out their promise of abundance. North of the Ohio the war with the northern Indians intervened, and, as a wartime measure, trade with those Indians was stopped altogether for a time. Not until all pris- oners were returned by the Shawnees, Delawares, and others in the spring of 1765 at Fort Pitt was trade with those nations resumed. Their comments to George Croghan during the Fort Pitt meetings show that the need for supplies was always a controlling factor in their policy.[6]

South of the Ohio, trade relations became complicated in different ways. The attempt to set fixed prices for exchange, as evidenced in the Choctaw-Chickasaw-British Treaty of Mobile of 26 March 1765 and the Creek-British Treaty of Pensacola of 28 May 1765, had the long-range effect of undermining the authority of both British and Indian leaders, and of souring the relations between the two peoples. Independent traders would not do business at the prices incorporated into the treaties. It was a situation that Superintendent John Stuart had fore- seen and had tried without success to forestall. He suggested to home authorities that, perhaps, if the traders themselves were put under strict regulations, the prices might be lowered to those demanded by the Indians. Or perhaps the imperial administration could subsidize the trade since private individuals could not be expected to go among the Indians to trade "merely from Motives of public good." They had to have the prospect of profits equal to their trouble and risk.[7]

Meanwhile, Creek leaders who had insisted on the favorable prices, found their prestige involved in the failure of trade on those terms. They "greatly insist" on the lowering of prices as agreed at Pensacola, John Stuart reported. A message from the Creeks to the governor of West Florida confirmed this. The message was succinct, and vaguely threatening. The Creeks noted some of the specific terms agreed upon— sixty bullets for one pound of leather, and one full bottle of rum for the same price—and said that they expected "the Trade as agreed on at the Meeting at Pensacola." If the whites refused to sell at those prices, then the Creeks would have to decide what steps to take next.[8]

What those other steps might be concerned Superintendent Stuart greatly. Since Pensacola, he said, the Creeks had been "insolent and suspicious." They gave indications of wanting "to form a confederacy of the great Nations of this department." Further, he had heard that they had sent messages to all the major Indian nations to sound them out on their willingness to break completely with the British.[9]

At no time did British officials, whether imperial or colonial, have power for the kind of regulation that John Stuart suggested. A trade subsidy was also out of the question. An administration so pressed for funds that it was willing to risk a rupture with the colonies was not likely to assume the costs of turning the Indian trade into a kind of foreign aid program. The risks of unregulated trade were well understood, but there agreement ended. Arguments arose over who would do the regulating. When Virginia, in 1765, attempted control through a separate colonial monopoly, Indian superintendent Stuart protested to the Board of Trade that Virginia's unilateral establishment of prices and regulations would undercut imperial control. Further, it would create unrest among the Creeks and other Indians who would expect to be supplied with goods at the same prices that Cherokees were paying under the Virginia plan. Was the imperial administration prepared to assume this cost for those provinces that could not afford to match Virginia's prices?[10]

In 1767 the Board of Trade disallowed the Virginia bill that established a public trade with the Cherokees. But that did not end the matter. The whole system of Indian administration was under reexamination in 1767, and needs in that area were set against the apparent need to have troops and resources available for the growing contest with the white colonists. Opposition to imperial control of trade with the Indians had existed from the first. Since British authorities were not willing to underwrite the cost of fully centralized control, they took this opportunity of reducing the points of conflict with colonial merchants. In 1768 control of the Indian trade was returned to the separate colonies.[11]

The effect of this decision was to multiply the points of conflict with the Indians as traders entered their country in increasing numbers and made increasing use of rum to gain the advantage in trade. What the treaty system of 1763–68 accomplished in the matter of trade was chiefly a statement of the preferences of whites at the imperial level and of Indians at the leadership level. Their ideal was a tightly controlled exchange at prices set not by the market but by negotiation. The plan entailed control that neither set of leaders could command, and demanded subsidies that were not available under peacetime conditions.

There were hundreds of miles of unguarded boundary between white and Indian lands, and no imperial regulation could prevent individual whites from slipping across the boundary with a pack-load of goods for illicit trade. Nor could the most comprehensive system of Indian sur-veillance prevent individuals from slipping away into the woods to bar-gain away the winter's harvest of skins for a few bottles of rum.

The greatest success of the treaty system of 1763–68 was the estab-lishment of the Indian-British boundary in the South. By the close of 1768, the boundary there was complete. British settlements on the coastal rim and Indian settlements in the interior were separated by a line that began on the lower Mississippi River, ran east below Choctaw and Creek lands, and turned north to mark the division between the southern settler-colonies and lands belonging to the Creeks and Cher-okees. The boundary intersected the Ohio River at the mouth of the Kanawha River, some 200 miles (320 kilometers) below Fort Pitt. By 1768 the Carolina-Cherokee sections of the line had been run and marked by mixed boundary commissions. The task of marking the lower portion of the line continued in the years after 1768 even while the upper portion of the line was dissolving under the pressures directed against it by the outcome of negotiations for the northern boundary.[12]

North of the Ohio River, by the end of 1768, the agreed-upon line was nearly complete. From the mouth of the Kanawha River below Fort Pitt it proceeded upriver until it swung east above the fort and continued northeast in an irregular course to Canada Creek near the Mohawk River east of Oneida Lake. The incomplete portion of the line north of the Mohawk River was still the subject of negotiation in 1771 when Hillsborough directed William Johnson to see if he could com-plete the line to Canada. Johnson replied that he had been talking to the Iroquois about the matter, and thought that it would be possible to come to an agreement.[13]

This upper portion of the northern boundary line was relatively non-controversial. The lower portion, as has been discussed, followed the Ohio River to the mouth of the Tennessee, a course that drove straight into the heart of the Indian country and threw into uncertainty the status of much of present-day Kentucky, Tennessee, and West Virginia. It put into the hands of the forces of expansion a weapon that proved too strong for the forces of order.

The movement for new colonies in the West might well have been too strong for restraint in any case. What the dangling Ohio section of the Fort Stanwix line did was to direct expansionary pressures toward

the areas that might be presumed to come within the vaguely defined
Iroquois cession, both south and southeast of the Ohio. Before the
period of transformation was at a close in 1775, not even this presumption was needed. Areas north of the Ohio were also bargained for as the
treaty system became the captive of individual, entrepreneurial interests.

The Context of 1768–75,
and the Transformation

The threat that the Fort Stanwix cession posed for the whole central section of the Indian-white boundary line was a matter of concern
for imperial authorities at the time. So was the threat to the British-
Iroquois alliance if the cession were refused. Officials in England could
see the first threat clearly, but were not in a position to evaluate the
second since they did not know how deeply Iroquois pride was involved
in the declaration that their southern boundary was the Tennessee
River. Neither did they know how or if this declaration was involved in
the reparations grant to the Philadelphia merchants. If the original
boundary were to be preserved, the task must somehow be accomplished
while also preserving the good will of the Six Nations of the Iroquois,
and of Sir William Johnson, the man who was Britian's chief contact
with the Six Nations. A letter to Johnson from colonial secretary Hillsborough, written early in January 1769, attempted to achieve all these
goals.

Hillsborough first conveyed the king's commendation for the northern superintendent's zeal in His Majesty's service, and then noted the
king's disquiet about the boundary below the Kanawha River. The king
wished, said Hillsborough, that Johnson had not allowed the Six
Nations to find out that the British had any claim to the country south
of the Ohio as it was this, apparently, and "this alone" that caused
Johnson to depart so far from the instructions he had received from the
Board of Trade.

Aside from its interest as a commentary on what British home officials thought could be kept secret from the Six Nations, the letter re-
veals how Johnson's part in the cession was then being interpreted at
Whitehall. Hillsborough went on to express the concern of the members
of the Board of Trade that the acquisition of so large an additional tract
of land would be "productive only of disadvantage and embarrassment,"
particularly in regard to the Cherokees and the southern boundary.

Among the Cherokees it would produce "Jealousy & Disatisfaction" and it would "throw into confusion" the arrangements already made with them and the other southern Indian nations for their boundary with the whites.

Hillsborough closed the letter with instructions to Johnson to try and persuade the Iroquois to take back the cession they had made south of the Ohio. He noted that it would please the king if Johnson could settle the boundary according to the original instructions, and suggested how Johnson might placate Iroquois pride. Perhaps Johnson could make the Six Nations understand that His Majesty declined the cession only because he was concerned about them and their posterity, and not at all because he doubted their right to those lands.[14]

Hillsborough's opposition to expansion in North America is well known. It is a position that was put to the test a few years after the date of this letter when he resigned his secretaryship over the issue of the new western colony of Vandalia. But there is more in his letter of 1769 than opposition to the expansionary pressures that were being stimulated by the Fort Stanwix consequences. The net of relationships was wide, and included not just the Six Nations, who might be offended if the cession were rejected, and the Cherokees, who might turn against the British if the cession were accepted, but the rest of the southern Indian nations who had agreed to the boundary. Typically, Hillsborough did not express concern about the western Indian nations, although unrest was greatest there. It was a settled article of British faith that those nations were part of the Iroquois empire, and that the Six Nations could speak for them.

Increasingly after 1768, however, those western nations that had been affiliated with the Iroquois Confederacy began to draw away from it and to speak for themselves. The Shawnees, in particular, after their brief open defiance of the Six Nations at Fort Pitt in the spring of 1768, began a quiet campaign to gather support among other Indian nations, not just those of the West but those of the South as well. The first obvious result of their efforts was a large all-Indian congress held at one of the Shawnee towns on the Scioto River in the late summer of 1770. The Six Nations of the Iroquois Confederacy were not invited to the congress, and, like the British, had to depend on the reports of spies to learn the purposes and outcome of the meeting.

The Iroquois were certainly aware of the Shawnees' strong disapproval of the Stanwix cession of lands. But Shawnee opposition did not cause the Six Nations to reconsider the sale. On the contrary. At a meeting held at German Flats (New York) in July 1770, the Iroquois reaffirmed their right to dispose of the land, and by so doing asserted once again their claim of dominance over the Shawnees. In the presence of Sir William Johnson and of a special Shawnee delegation, they publicly confirmed the sale of the land to the British.[15]

It is not known whether this Shawnee delegation returned to the Scioto River in time for the all-Indian congress, bringing word of the confirmation of the Stanwix cession. Whether they did or not, Indians at the congress were chiefly concerned with the wider implications of their relationships with the Iroquois Confederacy, with the British, and with each other. The Shawnees could not hope to interest the more remote Indian nations in their particular grievance over the Six Nations' land cession, except by presenting it as a specific instance of a general situation that threatened all the Indians east of the Mississippi.

A general threat was, apparently, the basis of the appeal for Indian union that was made at the First Scioto Congress in the late summer of 1770. Details of the proposed confederation are lacking, but the purpose was to enable the Indians to take united action against both the British and the Iroquois Confederacy. It was decided at the congress that the first step in strengthening the confederation would be to end the inter-Indian conflicts that would divide and weaken it. These conflicts are not detailed in the sources, but some reasonable guesses can be made. The Shawnees' relations with the Cherokees and Chickasaws were always threatened by a renewal of the hostilities that had driven the Shawnees out of the Cumberland Valley in the early eighteenth century. There was also long-standing enmity between the Chickasaws and the Kickapoos. Farther south, the Creeks and Choctaws were, in 1770, engaged in intermittent warfare that had been waged since 1766. Action against the British and the Iroquois was to be deferred until conflicts such as these could be resolved.[16]

A possible rapprochement between Indians north of the Ohio and those south of the Ohio was a matter of particular concern to British authorities. In October 1770 General Thomas Gage, commander of the British forces in North America, wrote to southern Indian superintendent John Stuart to warn him of the danger:

> The Congress held at Siota by the Shawnese and Western nations . . . has had more effect than our Indian officers thought possible to be brought about. The spies sent thither inform that all the Western tribes over the Lakes and about Lake Michigan as well as

the Oubache Indians had unanimously agreed to make peace with
the Cherokees and other Southern nations. ["Oubache" Indians
were those living on the Wabash River: the Miamis, Weas, Piankeshaws, and one group of Wyandots.] You see that the Shawnee
deputies have not worked in vain, and hope the Creeks will be less
reserved when you next talk to them upon the business of those
deputies in their nation and that Emistisiguo will tell you the drift of
their negotiations as he has promised to do. The scheme of the
Shawnese to form a confederacy of all the Western and Southern
nations is a notable piece of policy, for nothing less would enable
them to withstand the Six Nations and their allies against whom
they have been much exasperated on account of the boundary treaty
held at Fort Stanwix.[17]

Gage concluded by noting that he trusted that Stuart's influence
with the southern Indians would enable him "to defeat the machina-
tions of the Shawnese, whose deputies will not fail to use every endeav-
our to draw them into the combination they have been forming."[18]

Sir William Johnson was also greatly concerned at the possibility of
an alliance between northern and southern Indians. With the memory
of the 1763–65 war with the northern Indians vividly in mind, he pointed out to colonial secretary Hillsborough that a North-South Indian
union

is really a matter of the most serious nature; for if a very small part
of these people have been capable of reducing us to such straits as
we were in a few years since, what may we not expect from such a
formidable alliance as we are threatened with, when at the same time
it is well known that we are not at this time more capable of
defence, if so much, as at the former period?[19]

The Indians had become increasingly alarmed about the British presence, said Johnson, and even though they had a healthy respect for the
strength and resources of the British, "they still believe that it is in their
power to give us such a check as may prevent us from attempting what
they apprehend we have in view. Many will talk, some will think, and a
lesser number will act, but this is nevertheless the true political state of
their sentiments at present."[20]

Johnson did not point to the Fort Stanwix boundary treaty as a
cause of Indian unrest but rather to "the imprudence of our own people" and the Indians' own "natural suspicions." He also cited the presence of the Spanish, and of the French, who acted as Spanish agents.

Representatives of those two nations gained favor with the Indians by giving them presents, and then endeavored to turn the Indians against the British. This was not hard to do, said Johnson, since most of the Indians felt that from the British they had "everything to fear."[21]

Johnson's response to the threat of a union of northern and southern Indians was to back the efforts of the Iroquois to reestablish dominance over the western Indian nations. This backing fell short of the outright military aid that some Iroquois had planned to ask for at German Flats in July 1770. They had wanted to attack the Indians who were defying Iroquois authority in the West, and they had planned to invoke the British-Iroquois alliance as justification for British military aid. The matter never came to a public showdown. Working with some Iroquois leaders who wanted to prevent war and to avoid a British-Iroquois rupture, Johnson had managed to forestall the militants and prevent the demand being made. In his report to Hillsborough, Johnson said that the militants had wanted to make the demand publicly as a test "of the nature of our friendship and the regard we paid to former engagements."[22]

With British troops being withdrawn from the interior because of the increasing seriousness of the quarrels with the white settler-colonies, there was little likelihood of Great Britain's going to war on behalf of the Iroquois. Short of war, however, the Iroquois had Johnson's encouragement and support, since the British had based their policy in the North on the supremacy of the Six Nations. The one-hundred-belt embassy that has been mentioned set out for the western nations following the meeting at German Flats. This was the first of several embassies that were charged with the task of reasserting the preeminence of the Great Council at Onondaga. It is a measure of the respect or fear that the Six Nations could still inspire that their embassies were received at all during this period of turmoil and realignment. Courteous faces were turned toward the Iroquois delegations in council, and they were thanked for their advice—which was then ignored. Still, no one was ready to make an open break until the Shawnees finally did so in the summer of 1774.

The one-hundred-belt embassy left upper New York sometime after July 1770, and arrived back home in January or February 1772. The length of the mission is more than just a commentary on contemporary means of transportation. It is also an indication of the limitations on diplomacy when the task of assembling the Indians for a meeting might sometimes take weeks or even months, depending on seasonal variations in weather and in economic activities. Then, too, this particular embas-

sy, after visiting the western nations on the Scioto River, went deep
into the South as far as Charleston, and embarked from that port for
Philadelphia and home. This southern penetration suggests that the Iroquois and perhaps Johnson as well were trying to counter the Shawnees' bid for southern adherents by gathering southern support for the
Six Nations and the British. At any rate, the Iroquois embassy, led on
its southern swing by Catawba Indians from South Carolina, traveled
through the Cherokee Nation on the way to Charleston, and also had
contact with the Creek Indians. In Iroquois terminology, the embassy
was engaged in opening roads to the Great Council at Onondaga, and
the Creek leader they spoke to "promised to make use of the road they
had opened."[23]

Spokesman for the Iroquois embassy was Thomas King, an Iroquois
praised by Sir William Johnson as having "superior capacity."[24] King
died at Charleston, after having carried out the mission assigned to him.
Beyond the personal tragedy of King's death, is the exemplification of
another aspect of diplomacy among the Indian nations: the difficulty in
maintaining continuity. Hardship, disease, and intermittent warfare
stalked the routes of the embassies that traveled through the forests on
missions for their scattered nations. Negotiations interrupted by death
had to be restarted by another delegation, often while events overtook
and outdated the policy that had been decided upon.

Before he died, however, King led the Iroquois mission to Fort Pitt
where, in December 1770, he informed the Shawnees that he brought
word from the council at Onondaga. Messages were sent to the same nations that had met that summer at Shawnee invitation in the First Congress of Scioto. Sometime in 1771, probably in early summer, the
nations gathered for the Second Congress of Scioto, this one called by
the Iroquois to undo the work of the Shawnees at the first congress.
King and the Iroquois embassy felt confident enough of their position
to rebuke the Shawnees publicly before the assembled Indians. The
charges were two: that the Shawnees were allying themselves with Indians hostile to the Six Nations and the British alliance, and that the
Shawnees had taken up their residence on the Scioto without Iroquois
permission.

If the Iroquois had any sense of a decline in their prestige among the
western Indians, it is not evident in their account of the Second Congress of Scioto. They assumed the power of the confederacy and the
English alliance, saying that those who looked elsewhere for allies
would be punished by those who remained faithful to the alliance.[25]
In 1772 another Iroquois delegation said much the same thing at yet

another Congress of Scioto, again called by the Iroquois in the heart of the Shawnee country since the Shawnees, despite their promises in council, were still trying to form a separate confederation and were still protesting the Fort Stanwix cession of land. At the Third Congress of Scioto, as at the second, the Iroquois were given promises by the western nations, that—again—were not kept. When, back at Johnson Hall, William Johnson urged the Iroquois to more direct and forceful action, the Iroquois replied that they would call one more time on the western nations to come to Onondaga to renew their proper alliances. If the western nations did not come then, the Iroquois would attack them and force them into line. And, in a comment that shows the continued potency of the Iroquois sense of destiny, they added that it was their custom to call three times upon erring nations before they struck.[26]

This was the old Iroquois sense of rightness and mission, and yet there was a significant change. The law as laid down by Deganawidah *did* require the Iroquois to call three times upon a nation before they attacked it, but the purpose of the three calls was to enable all nations to come in, voluntarily if possible, under the branches of the Great Tree of Peace. The words of Iroquois spokesmen after the Fort Stanwix treaty of 1768 show that the Great Tree of Peace had become identified with the British alliance. It was to this alliance that the erring western nations were to be recalled, not to the old Iroquois ideal of a time of peace and brotherhood. "We have already called upon them twice and agreeable to our own ancient customs shall do so the third time before we strike," said Teyawarunte, Onondaga speaker, at the council at Johnson Hall in April 1773, "but should they then neglect us you may be assured we shall fall upon them and show them their folly and our attachment to the English."[27]

Not all the Iroquois so completely identified the interests of the Six Nations with the interests of Great Britain. A group of Senecas, led by Agaustarax, persistently opposed the pro-British alignment of the rest of the confederacy, and championed the cause of the Shawnees by saying that the Iroquois should rescind the Ford Stanwix land cession. In reporting this fact to Whitehall, William Johnson was led to comment on the Shawnees' land claims and on the Fort Stanwix cession in general. In his comments he made a distinction between two different sections of the cession. It is a distinction that is useful to keep in mind when considering the disintegrative effect of the cession on British policy and on the position of the Iroquois.

The Iroquois cession of 1768 can be divided for purposes of analysis at the Kanawha River, the point between the authorized and unauthorized portions of the cession. South and west of the Kanawha lay the whole Cumberland-Tennessee-Kentucky region so productive of future difficulties. North and east of the Kanawha lay the sweep of lands between the Blue Ridge-Allegheny Mountains and the Ohio River, both the river and the mountain chain being, in this area, on a roughly parallel course angling from northeast to southwest. The Indiana grant—the reparations grant to the Philadelphia merchants—lay within this fertile rectangle. In his discussion Johnson did not bring up the matter of the grant, but he did point out that it was this part of the Iroquois cession that the Shawnees were protesting, and that this part was within the area he had been instructed to obtain.[28]

Johnson was, of course, an interested party, but events seem to bear him out. Early Shawnee protests were directed against the cession of land north and east of the Kanawha, and when the Shawnees and some Delawares went to war in 1774, this was the area they fought to keep free of white settlement. The war has been given the name of Lord Dunmore's War, but it might better be called the War of the Stanwix Cession, since that cession was the center of the conflict. After being defeated in that war, the Shawnees, with other western nations, then fought to keep whites from settling the unauthorized portion of the Iroquois cession in Kentucky and Tennessee. The fact of the fighting is well known in American history, but the reasons and the background are not.[29]

The claim of the Shawnees to the land north and east of the Kanawha River is difficult to determine now, since their whole relationship to the Six Nations of the Iroquois Confederacy is unclear. Johnson said that the Shawnees' claim was a "weak pretence" at best, and that even the north side of the Ohio, where they still lived, "is more than they have any title to, having been often moved from place to place by the six Nations and never having any right of soil there." Johnson was still speaking as an interested party, but the view of Iroquois supremacy that he expressed in the midst of Shawnee turmoil over the cession was at least consistent with the one he had expressed in November 1763 before any cession was under discussion.[30]

The Shawnees themselves, in the Second Congress of Scioto in 1771, acknowledged their one-time subordination to the Iroquois Confederacy when they answered the Iroquois charge that they were living on

the Scioto River without Iroquois permission. Not at all, said the Shawnees. They had been so discouraged by Iroquois neglect of them and by
Iroquois failure to give them land between the Ohio and the Lakes as
promised, that they had set out to move west wherever they could find
a home. But the Iroquois would not let them leave. When the Shawnees
tried, they "were stopped (many years since) at the Scioto by the Six
Nations who shook them by the heads and fixed them there, charging
them to live in peace with the English."[31]

Whatever the relation of the Shawnees to the Iroquois League had
been in the past, it is clear that by this period the relationship was
changing, and that the Fort Stanwix cession was an important element
in the change. There were other grievances, however, among them a
basic disagreement over the policy to be pursued toward the British.
During the preliminary negotiations for the Fort Stanwix treaty in
October 1768, secret messages arrived from the Shawnees, and were
taken to Sir William Johnson by Iroquois who favored the British alliance. In the messages, the Shawnees spoke of unrest among the western
nations because of the growing strength of the British. They reminded
the Six Nations of "the old agreement" between the Iroquois and several of the western nations to the effect that they would all unite and
attack the English if the English became so strong as to be a threat to
the Indians. The time had come, said the Shawnees, for them all to
meet to decide on a course of action toward the British. Following hard
on this message from the Shawnees, the Six Nations made the Fort
Stanwix grant to the British.[32]

The sources of Shawnee antagonism thus went beyond the Stanwix
cession, and they also went deeper into the past. At one time the eastern branch of the Shawnees had lived with part of the Delawares in the
Wyoming Valley of the Susquehannah River in Pennsylvania (near present Wilkes-Barre). That land had been sold by some Iroquois at the Albany Congress of 1754. The eastern Shawnees had then joined the western branch on the upper Ohio, chiefly on the north side from the
Allegheny River to the Scioto, but they had made extensive use of the
land south and east of the forks of the Ohio as well, and also had hunted in what is now Kentucky. The Stanwix cession could only have
seemed a deliberate affront to the displaced Shawnees, particularly as
they disagreed with the whole Iroquois policy of a British alliance.
Their claim to the land that had been given up was an uncertain one,
shadowed by the ambiguities of their relationship to the Iroquois, and
of changing Indian concepts of landownership. Their response to the
situation was not at all uncertain. They became leaders in the Indian

resistance to white advance in the Ohio Valley, whether that advance
was by the British or, later, by Americans.

The factors that helped to undo British policy and to dissolve the
remaining ties of the extended Iroquois Confederacy were all present in
the Indian setting before the Treaty of Fort Stanwix was signed. The
treaty provided a focus for long-standing discontents, and a rallying
point for those Indians who were restless under Iroquois direction, exasperated by Iroquois pride, and totally at odds with the Iroquois
policy of alliance with the British. Among whites, the treaty, with its
attendant land cession and reparations grant, provided the legal base
for those expansionist forces that were always present, both in the
colonies and in the metropole. The Stanwix cession was the longed-for
opportunity to expand on a grand scale beyond the mountains onto
land where the Indian title had apparently been quieted.

It was well understood that the land was not yet officially opened
for white settlement. It was also understood that the same had been
true of other land acquired from the Indians in the past, as authorities
had attempted to control colonial development through gradual and
directed expansion. This had not worked well in the older settled areas,
and there was no reason to believe it would work at all in areas that
were farther from centers of authority. What had happened in the past
was very likely to happen again when the broad and ill-defined area of
the Stanwix cession was officially opened for white settlement. Those
who had gone on ahead and made their improvements on the land
would be accorded first opportunity for the letters patent that would
give legal title to the land.[33]

These considerations affected the smallest scale of expansionist
activity, those individual families or groups of families like the Holston
River settlers from Virginia who, upon hearing of the Stanwix cession,
promptly moved farther west to the Watauga River in what is now eastern Tennessee.[34] This group of settlers has a secure niche in American
history because of the compact by which they governed themselves, but
movement on this small a scale was not the most significant expansionist response to the Stanwix cession. The greater ambitions that were
drawn by the cession can be glimpsed in the petitions for land grants
that were made to the Virginia government after 1768.

Some of them were for land in the part of the cession that had been
authorized by the Crown, as: "on the Lower side of little Kanawha at
its Confluence with the River Ohio" (present Parkersburg, West Virginia).
But more were for land in the extended, unauthorized portion of the
cession, below the Kanawha River and south of the Ohio, as: "below

the mouth of Great Guyandott" (present Huntington, West Virginia). These were not individual families wanting to carve homes out of the wilderness. One group asked for 20,000 acres "in the new Country beyond the Alleghany Mountains lately ceded to his Majesty by the Indians," the grant to begin at the mouth of the Cumberland River, far down the Ohio (above present Paducah, Kentucky). Another group requested 60,000 acres to begin at the falls of the Cumberland and extend downriver "in the Territory lately ceded by the Six Nations to his Majesty."[35]

The most ambitious expansionist activity set in motion by the Stanwix cession was, of course, the much-studied movement that culminated in the new colony of Vandalia. In 1769 Samuel Wharton began to draw together the highly placed men who came to be known as the Walpole Group. They organized under the name of the Grand Ohio Company, absorbed smaller claimants, including those involved in Wharton's own Indiana-reparations grant, and went on to near fruition as a proprietary colony before the Quebec Act of 1774 disrupted their plans and put an end to the project. Before that happened, however, the Vandalia movement had become part of the complex of interacting elements that were set in motion by the Fort Stanwix cession, and, as such, it played its part in the transformation of the British-Indian treaty system.

Besides the two factors that have been discussed—the indigenous setting north of the Ohio and white expansionist forces—there was one other major element in the transformation of the treaty system. This element was the Cherokee Nation, south of the Ohio. Cherokee lands adjoined those of Virginia, North and South Carolina, and the northern portion of Georgia. The Cherokees had been the most active of the southern Indians in establishing the Indian-white boundary. They had taken the initiative in negotiations, and when, in October 1768, they signed the definitive Treaty of Hard Labor, which completed the Virginia portion of their boundary and then affirmed the boundary in its entirety, they put the seal on five years of effort. Less than a month later, the British and the Iroquois signed the Treaty of Fort Stanwix, which threw into confusion not only the Virginia section of the Cherokee line but also the status of all the land south of the Ohio to which the Cherokees might lay claim.

Colonial secretary Hillsborough and the Board of Trade had foreseen that the Fort Stanwix cession would bring pressure against the middle section of the Indian-white boundary. They were accurate, too, in their forecast that the Cherokees would be caught up in the agitation to adjust the boundary westward. What they did not foresee was the way that the Cherokees became actively involved in that adjustment, not only at the Stanwix-cession end of the line but also in Georgia at the southern end of the Cherokee section of the boundary. Cherokee policy, if such it was, must be inferred from evidence that is sketchy. If the evidence is put in conjunction with other known factors, however, and set within a context of specific events, the inferences are plausible. All together they at least suggest reasons for the way the Cherokees handled the crisis of 1768–75.

The crisis was a general one throughout the area of British administration, both in the coastal colonies and in the backcountry, and this general unrest fed into and aggravated the Cherokees' own particular crisis. The Cherokee crisis was chiefly economic, but it was diplomatic in part. During these years of economic stress, the Cherokees were also engaged in a realignment of their relations with the Indian nations north of the Ohio. Far from opposing the Fort Stanwix cession, as Hillsborough had feared, the Cherokees supported it, possibly as part of their drive to align themselves with the Six Nations. The Stanwix cession could have come as no surprise to them, since a Cherokee delegation had visited the Iroquois in the spring of the year the Stanwix treaty was signed,[36] and since what the Iroquois were planning was common knowledge anyway. What seems to have happened is that the Cherokees came to look on the cession as a possible diversion for British expansionary pressures, and also as an economic resource to be exploited. This reasoning is conjectural. What is not conjectural is the fact that the Cherokees resold parts of the ceded land (thus relieving for a time the pressures against areas closer to their homes) and secured in exchange a supply of the European goods that had by that time become necessary for their daily existence.

In the period from 1768 to 1775, this need had become critical because the Cherokees were running out of resources to exchange for European goods. Although an agricultural people, they seldom had a surplus to sell. In the past, they had hunted for the market and secured what they needed through an exchange of deerskins. Skins by the hundreds of thousands had been packed out of the Cherokee country to supply Cherokee needs. The skins had gone from inland trading centers to river and seaports for export to the great European trade fairs in a chain of trade that linked Leipzig with Chota, the center of the Cherokee Upper Towns. By the late 1760s the Cherokees were being shut out

of the trade in two ways. Extensive hunting had reduced the numbers
of deer so that skins were harder to obtain. And, increasingly, large
groups of whites were coming into Cherokee country to procure skins
on their own, thus cutting out one payment in the trade chain: that to
the Cherokees. "It is the white hunters that trouble us," said Oconostotah to superintendent John Stuart at a meeting in 1770. "Let them
go over the mountains and not hunt on Holston's River [west of the
mountains in Cherokee country]. But Capt. Guess comes into our
grounds with fifty men and kills our deer and when we tell him of it he
threatens to shoot us down."[37]

In the midst of this Cherokee crisis came the deepening crisis in relations between the settler colonies and the home government. The pressures exerted by the colonies in the nonimportation agreements, particularly those protesting the Townshend Acts, disrupted normal patterns of trade and severely reduced the supply of goods available for
exchange. Even if deerskins had been abundant, the Cherokees would
have continued to feel an economic pinch until mid-1771 when Virginia
finally rescinded its nonimportation agreement. By then, however, the
Cherokees had begun to sell land.

The pattern of Cherokee land cessions can be seen in table 11. These
cessions can be seen simply as Cherokee responses to pressure for land.
Pressure there certainly was, but the responses were not at all simple.
They were highly selective modifications of the Cherokee-white boundary that gave up ground at the very ends of the line and held firm in
the middle. Further, most of the land that was ceded was land where

Table 11   Cherokee Land Cessions, 1721–75

Prior to 1763		1763–69		1770–75	
Date	Square Miles	Date	Square Miles	Date	Square Miles
1721	2,623	1768	850	1770	9,200
1755	8,635			1772	10,917
				1773	1,050
				1775	27,050
Total	11,258		850		48,217

SOURCE: Adapted from Charles C. Royce, *The Cherokee Nation of Indians,* in
Bureau of Ethnology Fifth Annual Report, 1883–1884 (Washington, D.C.: Government Printing Office, 1887), p. 378.

the Cherokee claim was at least doubtful. The three largest cessions of the 1770s fell within the area of the Iroquois-Stanwix cession below the Kanawha. The remaining cession in that period, that of 1773, was of land that belonged as much to the Creeks as to the Cherokees. Beyond that is the fact that in the 1773 cession (a renegotiation of the Cherokee boundary with Georgia), the Cherokees took the initiative as early as February 1771. When an outraged John Stuart tried to exert imperial authority by telling the Cherokees that their projected cession was illegal under the terms of the Proclamation of 1763, the Cherokees replied that the proclamation did not apply to them since they were not subjects of the British Crown.[38]

Stuart was convinced that traders were the moving force behind this particular cession, a fact that, if true, emphasizes the need of the Cherokees for a resource they could exchange for European goods. The Cherokees were determined on the cession, at any rate, since in the spring of 1771 they met with some traders to run the cession's boundaries. This act was wholly independent of colonial and imperial authorities, as well as of the Creeks, who also claimed the land. Stuart managed to delay the proceedings until he could get imperial approval, work out arrangements with Georgia, involve the Creeks, and modify the cession to protect adjoining segments of the Indian-British boundary. The transaction was finally completed in June 1773 in the joint Cherokee-Creek-British Treaty of Augusta, commonly called (from the Georgian point of view) the "New Purchase." The Creek agreement to this treaty was so resented by other Creeks, who were determined that the boundary should stand unchanged and no more land be ceded, that they began a guerrilla war to force the Georgians to stay out of the New Purchase area. The warfare continued until October 1774, when a treaty of peace and friendship was signed at Savannah—partly as a result of a trade embargo against the Creeks.[39]

In this muddle of conflicting authorities and purposes, one feature stands out as having particular interest for the future of the treaty system of 1763–68. That is the apparent attempt on the part of the traders with whom the Cherokees met in the spring of 1771 to acquire land directly from the Cherokees without the approval of any governmental authority. Direct private negotiation was not new—individual traders had been doing it for years, usually on a small scale—but the imperial administration of the British had supposedly put an end to private land-purchases. The timing, the openness, the large scale of the 1771 attempt give it a significance it would not have had in an earlier context. It was an indication of the changes that were taking place in the treaty system.

These changes can be seen in the other three cessions that the Cherokees made in the early 1770s. The Treaty of Lochaber, signed in October 1770, renegotiated the Cherokee boundary with Virginia, adding a large tract of land to Virginia in the process and preserving the mouth of the Kanawha as the northern terminus of the line. Virginia's representatives had boycotted the 1768 Hard Labor negotiations, conducted by John Stuart on behalf of the Crown, at which the Virginia-Cherokee boundary had originally been laid down. Stuart had settled with the Cherokees on the basis of his understanding of Virginia's position as it had been expressed at the Congress of Augusta in 1763. The complaints of Virginia authorities, following the Hard Labor agreement, had finally convinced the imperial authorities that another treaty should be negotiated, and the Treaty of Lochaber was the result. Part of the land ceded by the Cherokees in the Lochaber boundary adjustment contained Virginia settlements—settlements that had been authorized by Virginia before the Proclamation of 1763 but never given any legal recognition by the Crown.[40]

A further modification of the Virginia-Cherokee boundary was made by the Donelson-Attakullaculla agreement of 1772. The agreement was made during the course of the survey of the Lochaber line, and swung the northern portion of that line far west to the head of the Kentucky River and down that river to its junction with the Ohio (between present Cincinnati and Louisville). This was 230 miles (370 kilometers) from the old terminus at the mouth of the Kanawha. Three years later, in the Treaty of Sycamore Shoals, the Cherokees ceded to Richard Henderson and his associates the vast area that become Transylvania and, eventually, Kentucky.[41]

Beyond these circumstantial details of the Cherokee negotiations of the early 1770s stands the fact of significant change. In these few years the treaty-making function was shifted from the public to the private domain. The change is illustrated in the three land cessions just discussed. The 1770 negotiations took place under imperial authorization and were conducted by Superintendent John Stuart on behalf of the British, and by Oconostota and Attakullaculla on behalf of the Cherokees, in the presence of a thousand Cherokees. The 1772 negotiations, although later accepted by the British Crown, took place in private on the initiative of individual whites and Indians, and without prior authorization. The 1775 negotiations were also wholly on private initiative, and the outcome, while still called a treaty, was nothing more than a land sale-and-purchase agreement between the Cherokees and a group of white businessmen. The two earlier negotiations were still tied to the Indian-white boundary that had been the subject of nearly ten years of bargaining, but the third negotiation cut loose from the boundary entirely and simply availed itself of land in the Fort Stanwix cession.[42]

As further evidence of what was happening, in 1772 the settlers who had moved to Watauga Creek after receiving news of the Stanwix cession, discovered that the Lochaber line, the Cherokee-Virginia boundary of 1770, ran to the east of their settlements and left them on Cherokee land. Independent of any authority but their own, they negotiated with the Cherokees and obtained a lease for their land. At the 1775 Sycamore Shoals negotiations, the Wataugans negotiated separately with the Cherokees and bought their land outright. Elsewhere other negotiations were also being conducted by private individuals, and bargains were being struck that ignored both the Indian-British boundary *and* the Fort Stanwix cession. In 1773 William Murray and his associates concluded an agreement with the Illinois Confederacy for a large tract of land north of the Ohio River. And in 1775 Murray joined with a group that included Governor Dunmore of Virginia and negotiated with the Piankeshaw and Wea Indians for a still larger tract on the Wabash River. By 1775 British imperial authorities had lost all control of negotiations, and one suspects that Indian leaders had also.[43]

British officials were appalled at what was happening. Sir Frederick Haldimand, in command of British forces in North America, wrote to William Johnson to protest the "very Extraordinary proceedings of Mr. Murray," and to urge a course of action. First, Johnson was to try to persuade Indian leaders to make a covenant with each other that they would never sell land in the future without the express consent of the Crown, as conveyed through the Indian superintendent. Second, Johnson was to try to get the Indians to annul the sale to Murray. Failing that, perhaps the prior claim of the Six Nations could be invoked. Haldimand approached this cautiously, asking, "whether or not it could not be made to appear that the very lands now sold to Mr. Murray are part of those formerly conquered by the Six Nations, and to which they lay a claim."[44]

Johnson's agreement was prompt and predictable: "The lands you speak of are certainly within the claims of the Six Nations, and the purchase appears to have been made without the Consent and Contrary to the Expressed Sense of government." Johnson then voiced the old

complaint of British administrators against the colonists' habit of going
far into the backcountry to settle—"the Indians Justly observe that we
have not half settled the Country near the sea"—but added that he des-
paired of this ever being stopped unless the king should hit upon "some
vigorous measures."[45] But no measure was vigorous enough to stop the
forces that were then transforming the treaty system and moving all the
participants toward war.

There has been much speculation on the reasons for this surge of
private land-acquisition in the early 1770s. Attention has most often
centered on a British legal opinion issued in 1757 regarding land
acquisition in Asian India. This is commonly called the Camden-Yorke
opinion after its authors, the then solicitor-general, Charles Yorke, and
attorney-general Charles Pratt, later the earl of Camden. In the 1750s
the question had arisen whether the Crown needed to issue letters
patent for lands that had been acquired from the grand mogul of India
or from other Indian princes or governments. Yorke and Pratt advised
that an Indian treaty or grant was sufficient to transfer the rights of soil
without any further royal action, although the grants and the grantees
were, of course, subject to the sovereignty of the Crown and, through
royal charters, to the protection of the Crown. From these facts has
arisen the debate concerning the effect of the Camden-Yorke opinion
on private land-acquisition in North America.

The debate is concerned with the time when the opinion first became known in North America and with the means of its transmission
from one purchaser or would-be purchaser to another. Adding spice to
the debate is the fact that key words regarding the grand mogul of India
were omitted from a copy of the opinion that, in 1773, William Murray
showed to the British commander at Fort Chartres in the Illinois country as justification for the purchase of land from the Illinois Confederacy. Without the grand mogul terminology the opinion seemed to refer
to "Indian Princes and Governments" in general, and thus to apply to
North American as well as South Asian Indians. It is believed also that
Richard Henderson had a copy of the opinion (in its altered form), or
at least knew of it when, in 1775, he purchased the Transylvania area
from the Cherokees in the "treaty" of Sycamore Shoals. The most
recent thorough investigation of the subject is by J. M. Sosin, whose account in an appendix to his study of British administrative policy,
Whitehall and the Wilderness, clears a way through the misconceptions
and partisanship of earlier scholars and, as he says, prepares the ground
for the definitive account when further facts come to light.[46]

But the Camden-Yorke opinion, whatever its influence, was only one of a number of factors affecting land transfers in the early 1770s. More important than the opinion itself was the situation that made it seem relevant, or that gave someone the incentive to lift the opinion from the oblivion of almost twenty years. That situation was the result of the interaction of many different factors, not the least of which was the action of the Indians who sold the land. The whole debate on the Camden-Yorke opinion, and on land acquisition in general, has been carried out as if the Indians existed only to sign the treaties of cession. When Indian policies and relationships are added to the account, as they have been here, there emerges a much fuller picture of the conditions in which the Camden-Yorke opinion could have any impact.

The situation that developed in the North American backcountry following the Iroquois cession and reparations grant at Fort Stanwix in 1768 was reason enough for the movement toward private land-acquisition. The trend was inherent in the conditions, and was not the product of a twenty-year-old legal opinion, altered or otherwise. The opinion is useful, however, as a reminder that Great Britain was, even then, a worldwide power with involvements in the Caribbean, on the west coast of Africa and the Indian subcontinent, as well as in North America, and that this was the broader context of imperial decisions. Beyond that, an illuminating comparison can be made between North America and the India of the Camden-Yorke opinion. The setting of British land-acquisition in India was the decline of the Mogul Empire and the struggles that ensued among many participants, including the English, to perpetuate or replace that power. The setting of British land-acquisition in North America was the similar decline, on a much smaller scale, of the power of the Six Nations of the Iroquois League. The support of the British could not arrest that decline and may actually have hastened it as the western nations became increasingly resentful of the British presence and of the British alliance that the Iroquois tried to force upon them. The actions of the Six Nations as they sought to hold onto power, and of other Indian nations as they tried to replace Iroquois power or to benefit from Iroquois decline, combined with British imperial policy and with white expansionist pressures to create the chaotic conditions of the early 1770s.

As for private land-acquisition under these conditions, the Grand Ohio Company's Vandalia project served as the vital example of what could be done by private initiative in dealing with the Indians. William Johnson had given the proceedings the color of legality, but the initiative, motivation, and rewards were wholly private. Even then, a firm rejection by the Board of Trade might have saved Britain's stated policy of nonexpansion, but expansionary pressures in England became too strong, not only for the board but for the Privy Council and the king. In January 1770 the lords of the Treasury approved the twenty-million-acre grant requested by members of the Grand Ohio Company in the Stanwix cession area. After that, the project cleared one obstacle after another until in August 1772 the Crown gave its approval.[48]

By September, the new secretary for the colonies, the earl of Dartmouth, was writing to Johnson of the plans for a new colony on the Ohio.[49] The new venture was an advertisement of the fact that handsome profits could be made by private enterprise in dealing with the Indians. This simply reinforced the strong bent toward individual initiative that already existed among whites with ambitions toward wealth and standing. Add to this, Cherokee economic need and their willingness after 1768 to dispose of peripheral lands, especially hunting lands, where their claim was disputed by their Indian neighbors, and the situation south of the Ohio develops of itself out of volatile elements beyond the control of any one group, no matter what its intentions. North of the Ohio the Camden-Yorke opinion may have played a greater part in developments, but always there was the Vandalia project as the shining example, and back of Vandalia was the whole complex history of the Iroquois League that had made Vandalia possible.

There is even a sense in which nonexpansionist British policy contributed to its own decline and to the transformation of the treaty system from a set of negotiated agreements on subjects of mutual interest to a means by which whites could acquire land from the Indians. In theory, the line of separation decided on by British policymakers and approved by Indian leaders both North and South should have solved some of the persistent problems of contact. In practice, the emphasis on separation meant that diplomatic attention was focused on the boundary to the virtual exclusion of other concerns. Early in British imperial administration, Indian-British treaties dealt with conditions of peace, trade, and criminal jurisdiction, as well as with the boundary. When control of trade was turned back to the colonies in 1768, the boundary became the raison d'être of the treaties. Since boundary negotiations almost always involved a cession of some Indian land (see table 12), they became, in effect, instruments of cession. This happened even though the imperial administration, with the best of inten-

Table 12   Boundaries and Land Cessions in Treaties Between Great Britain
               and the Southeastern Indians of North America, 1763-74

Date	Boundary Negotiated	Land Cession Involved	Confirmation of Boundary	Further Land Cession Involved
1763	x	x	–	–
1764	x	x	–	–
1765a	x	x	–	–
1765b	x	x	x	x
1765c	–	–	–	–
1765d	x	x	–	–
1765e	x	x	x	x
1767	x	x	–	–
1768a	x	x	–	–
1768b	x	x	x	–
1770	x	x	–	–
1771a	x	x	–	–
1771b	x	x	x	x
1772a	x	x	x	–
1772b	x	x	–	–
1773	x	x	–	–
1774	–	–	–	–
Total	15	15	5	3
Total treaties	17			

SOURCE: Various documentary materials (see Appendix A, treaties marked with
superior b).

tions, wanted to protect the Indians and to limit settler expansion to
moderate and controlled growth behind a slowly moving boundary.

    In the context that has been described here, the step from treaties as
a public instrument of cession to treaties as a private instrument of cession was a very short step, and one easily taken. The general breakdown
of imperial relations quickly followed, and a general war was not far behind.

6   Years of Chaos
       1775-86

With the approach of war, a common world vision began to take
shape among the leaders of the settler colonies. Unlike the Iroquois
world vision, which was of peace, the nascent vision of Americans in
their contest with Great Britain was of righteous struggle. The struggle
was defined in universalistic terms. Not the American cause alone was
at stake in the impending war, but the cause of all of the colonies under
British rule. More than that, the colonists' struggle was also that of
Englishmen themselves, since tyranny, once strengthened through victory overseas, would not confine itself to the colonial possessions.

The Iroquois and other American Indians did not fit well into this
universalistic framework. The framework could be stretched to accommodate the Catholics of Canada, by emphasizing their colonial status
rather than their Catholicism, but the Indians' relations with imperial
Britain fell into a different sphere. That sphere was diplomatic, characterized by give and take between independent entities. In such a situation, the choices for the dissenting colonists were to seek Indian alliances or to try to persuade the Indians to remain neutral. Benjamin
Franklin thought that the colonies ought to make an alliance with the
Six Nations of the Iroquois Confederacy a cornerstone of their own
confederation, but the decision of the Continental Congress was for
neutrality as a first choice, and alliances if they became necessary, or if
Britain used Indian allies. In the end, Great Britain and the United
States both sought alliances with the Indians.

Because of these factors, the universalistic American view of a righteous struggle against tyranny was not expanded to include American
Indians. In the Indians' position of political independence, it could have
little appeal, and it did not address itself to the problem of economic
dependence that underlay Indian political sovereignty. For the
Iroquois, of course, and perhaps for other Indian groups with aspira-

tions for leadership, the American vision had the fatal flaw of making white Americans the leaders in the universal well-being that was to come when the vision was fulfilled.

The war years, besides being years of tragedy for all the peoples east of the Mississippi, were, for many of them, also years of opportunity. Among whites, the upheaval of old relationships meant the establishment of foundations on which a new nation might rise. Among Indians, old relationships were temporarily reestablished as most of the Six Nations and the western nations submerged their differences in a common effort against the Americans. The Delawares tried to use an American alliance to undergird their bid for independence from the Six Nations but were forced by American military weakness in the West to join other Indians in a British alliance. South of the Ohio, the war brought temporary decline to the Cherokees, but a rise in the power and prestige of the Creek Confederacy. Both of these major developments south and north of the Ohio continued into the postwar period, affecting the policies of all concerned.

Indian postwar policy was, in brief, containment of the new American nation behind the Indian-white boundary that had been negotiated with Great Britain. In the North this meant the Fort Stanwix line of 1768. In the far South this meant the Georgia-Creek-Cherokee line negotiated in 1773. North of that section to the Ohio the line was a shambles, with cession after cession extorted by states and individuals from the defeated Cherokees. The Indian policy of containment was aided in the South by the Spanish, once again in possession of East and West Florida, and in the North by the British, still in possession of Canada and maintaining a presence in the Northwest posts on soil over which the Americans claimed sovereignty.

American policy in the immediate postwar years, as distinct from the policies of the separate states, was more complicated than that pursued by any of the other powers in the backcountry. To the central government, such as it was, belonged the initiative in establishing the conditions for peace, expansion, prosperity, justice, and all the other goals of the righteous struggle with Great Britain. In relation to the Indians, these goals were contradictory. Unless the Indians could be brought to agree on expansion—which was, in contemporary thought, a prerequisite for prosperity—there would be no peace. If the Indians did not agree and expansion took place anyway, there would be no justice. American postwar policy was a series of attempts to find a way out of this basic dilemma. The first attempt, that of pressuring the Indians into agreements that would allow for white expansion and at the same time be acknowledged as just and equitable, was, by 1786, clearly a failure.

This was not wholly the fault of the central government, or of the basic contradiction with which United States policymakers struggled. It was equally the fault of those states that pursued independent and conflicting policies. Virginia, North Carolina, and Georgia were vigorously and unilaterally expansionist. New York and Pennsylvania, while bending every effort toward expansion, acknowledged the interest of the new confederation government in their negotiations with the Indians. Out of this acknowledgment came joint efforts that established precedents for state-federal cooperation. That cooperation remained an important element in negotiations with the Indians even after the constitutional assertion of 1789 that such transactions were a national prerogative. The groundwork for these developments was laid in the immediate postwar years.

State-federal cooperation in the South was more difficult to achieve than in the North partly because of the preindependence situation that had helped lead to war. The disintegrative effects of the prewar treaty system of the Indians and the British had created political chaos south of the Ohio. The crisis in authority that had been evident in the multiple, independent negotiations between whites and Indians continued after the war. It was reflected not only in the familiar conflicts between the states and the confederation government, but between the states and their own expansionist communities in the West, and within the Indian nations as well. Severe divisions within the Cherokee nation weakened the consensus that had helped create a boundary. The Choctaws and Chickasaws were divided over allying themselves with Spain or with the United States and signed mutually exclusive treaties with both. The Creeks, too, had their divisions, but for a time their leader, Alexander McGillivray, managed to hold together a large enough following to pursue a consistent and effective policy.

This confusion in authority was repeated north of the Ohio in the western areas beyond the boundaries of New York and Pennsylvania where the western Indian nations in the postwar period pursued several goals. They contended with each other for a leadership position. They also sought to free themselves from the lingering effects of Iroquois prestige. At the same time they tried to secure the cooperation of the Six Nations in presenting a united front to the Americans. In this latter effort they were aided by Great Britain. Given the persistence of political chaos, the new United States government came gradually to the position that the only way to bring order was through the centralization of authority and the reestablishment of a treaty system as a means of public negotiation at the primary level of authority, rather than at the secondary level, or as an instrument in private hands. The Indians north of the Ohio had long since reached the same conclusion. They called for a new, jointly negotiated treaty with the United States and disavowed the first United States-Indian treaties that had done their part in contributing to the general chaos of the years 1775-86.

Emergence of a Vision

One of the first needs of the colonies, as difficulties with Great Britain increased, was to stand well in the eyes of the world. This went beyond a desire for sympathy and understanding; the practicalities of gunpowder and arms—which would have to be procured abroad—and the question of what military forces might be put into the field for or against the colonies were matters of concern. It was with particular urgency, therefore, that the delegates to the First and Second Continental Congresses sought to give larger dimensions to their quarrel with Great Britain. In the fall of 1774 and again in the spring of 1775 they addressed themselves to the various peoples within the Empire and in Great Britain itself, saying, in effect, that the colonists were fighting a battle that concerned them all.

They pointed out that Englishmen in England would be hard put to preserve their rights if Englishmen in the New World lost theirs. They invited Britons in St. John's, Nova Scotia, and East and West Florida to join them in the nonimportation agreements that were the initial economic measures against the North ministry. They condoled with the Irish on their mistreatment by the king's ministers, and asked for Irish good offices in bringing a peaceful resolution to the growing conflict in America. To the Jamaican assembly the delegates gave thanks for Jamaica's favorable petition to the Crown on their behalf, and applauded its understanding that liberty was indivisible. If liberty were destroyed in the mainland colonies, it would inevitably be destroyed in Jamaica also.[1]

One mainland colony, in particular, was of immediate concern. The location and history of Canada (the Province of Quebec) made that colony a potential threat that had to be dealt with immediately by the United Colonies. But the Canadians presented a peculiar problem to a people concerned that their grievances be seen in the larger framework of a fight for the universal values of liberty and justice. The majority of Canadians were Catholic, an affiliation that was galling to the largely Protestant colonies south of the St. Lawrence. The leniency shown toward Canadian Catholics in the Quebec Act of 1774 was, in fact, one of the original grievances of the Protestant colonies. It could, however, scarcely be the grounds of an appeal for Canadian support of the colonists' cause.

Necessity found a way out of the ideological difficulty. A long letter from the Continental Congress to the people of Quebec in the fall of 1774 addressed Canadians not as Catholics but as fellow subjects of the king. The matter of religion was dismissed with the comment that the Quebec Act, despite its professed liberality, had not really bestowed freedom of religious conscience on the Canadians since they had that freedom already from God. What the act had done was take away other rights that they were entitled to now that they were members of the British Empire.

By such means the delegates to the Continental Congress sought to broaden the ideological base of their struggle and enlist support for it as a universal cause. They pointed out to the Canadians that King George's ministers were denying them the inherent rights of British subjects, such as the right to a trial by jury and the right to be governed by a legislative body of their own choosing. The delegates invited the Canadians to express their anger by sending their own delegates to the Continental Congress when it met again in the spring. By the time the Second Continental Congress convened in May 1775, Crown Point and Ticonderoga had been seized by an American force led by Benedict Arnold and Ethan Allen. The delegates hastened to assure the Canadians that the act was not directed against them but was an act of self-preservation. Then the colonists' major theme of universality was sounded again:

> We yet entertain hopes of your uniting with us in the defence of our common liberty, and there is yet reason to believe, that should we join in imploring the attention of our sovereign, to the unmerited and unparalleled oppressions of his American subjects, he will at length be undeceived, and forbid a licentious Ministry any longer to riot in the ruins of the rights of Mankind.[3]

The American Indian nations presented a different kind of problem to the colonists, although there were some points of similarity. The

Indians' location within the borders of the colonies made them a greater potential threat than Canada ever was, and their distinct and separate
cultures made them more alien by far than even the Catholics. Yet the
colonists did not attempt to draw the Indians into the universalist
framework that was being developed to give ideological coherence and
significance to the struggle with Great Britain. In this early period, the
universalist understanding of the colonists ran as far as members of the
British Empire. They made their appeal to the Indians on other
grounds, and their approach was that of one sovereign group to other
sovereign groups.

The question of relationships with the Indians was first raised in the
context of the problem of how to create a government that could not
only prosecute the war that was underway but also secure foreign financial support, form alliances, if possible, and negotiate for territory and
peace. All agreed that, under the circumstances, a united front was
essential. Internally, the colonies might—and did—quarrel with vigor
and frequency. To the outer world, however, they had to display greater solidarity if they were not to be picked off one by one in the preda-
tory world of the eighteenth century. This was a long-standing concern
of one American colonist with much experience of the world, and in
the spring of 1775 Benjamin Franklin set down a plan of cooperation
and union to help the colonies avoid that fate.

The first article of his plan announced the formation of a confederacy of the twelve (later thirteen) colonies whose delegates were then
meeting in Philadelphia: "The name of this confederacy shall
henceforth be: *The United Colonies of North America.*" The last article
set the conditions under which the colonies would "return to their
former Connection and Friendship with Britain." Since King George
and the North ministry were convinced that they had already done all
that reasonable men could do to meet the colonists' demands, those
conditions were not likely to be met. In that case, according to Franklin's plan, "this Confederation is to be perpetual."[4]

Franklin discussed in general terms the external relationships of the
proposed confederation. The authority in such matters was to rest in
the Congress, which alone would have the power to determine war or
peace, enter into alliances, or reconcile the colonies to Great Britain.
He gave more detailed consideration to relationships of two different
kinds: those with other members of the British Empire in North America and those with the Indian nations of North America. The former
could, upon application, join the confederation and be entitled to all

the privileges of the original members. Franklin made specific mention of Quebec (all of Canada plus the backcountry to the Ohio), St. John's (Newfoundland), Nova Scotia, the Bermudas, and East and West Florida.

The Indian nations were to be approached differently. In the first place no offensive war was to be waged by any colony against any nation of Indians without the express consent of Congress after it had determined that such a war was just and necessary.

In the second place:

A perpetual alliance, offensive and defensive, is to be entered into, as soon as may be, with the Six Nations; their limits ascertained, and to be secured to them; their lands not to be encroached on, nor any private or colony purchase to be made of them hereafter to be held good, nor any contract for lands to be made, but between the great council of the Indians at Onondaga and the general Congress.[5]

Franklin's private interest in the Fort Stanwix cession can be seen here, for if any part of the reparations grant or the Vandalia project were to be salvaged, it had to be emphasized that the sole authority for Six Nations land sales was at Onondaga. His awareness of the chaos caused by the transformation of the British-Indian treaty system can also be seen in his attempts to guard against a similar fragmentation of authority. But beyond these considerations was Franklin's judgment that an alliance with the Six Nations of the Iroquois Confederacy was a prime necessity for the proposed colonial confederation.

The pressures of the war effort and internal political maneuvering at the Second Continental Congress delayed consideration of Franklin's proposal or of any plan of confederation until the following spring. The primacy given to working out satisfactory relationships with the Indians can be seen, however, in the fact that these relationships took precedence over the ones with Europe. Before Franklin was appointed to the Committee of Correspondence to contact European nations, he was appointed to the Middle Indian Department to contact all the Indian nations between the Cherokee on the south and the Six Nations on the north. Before a message was sent to C.W.F. Dumas at the Hague in December 1775 asking him to find out the disposition of European powers toward possible assistance or alliance with the United Colonies, messages were sent and meetings were held with a dozen Indian nations to determine their disposition and to seek their neutrality.[6]

Despite Franklin's recommendation, the United Colonies did not at first seek Indian alliances. Early in July 1775, the Second Continental

Congress considered the possibility of such alliances and decided to leave the initiative in that regard to the British. If the British entered into offensive alliances with any of the Indian nations, then "the colonies ought to avail themselves of an Alliance with such Indian Nations as will enter into the same, to oppose such British troops and their Indian Allies."[7] Otherwise, neutrality would be the goal of the colonists' negotiations with the Indians. In pursuit of this goal, the delegates to the Continental Congress wrote another of their long public appeals, this one addressed to the Six Nations of the Iroquois League. With modifications, it was to be presented to the other Indian nations as well.

The address to the Indians differed from the other public statements in which the delegates sought to justify the colonies' quarrel with Great Britain and give it universal significance. The colonial-British conflict was presented to the Indians as a family struggle. The metaphor has particular interest here because the imperial-colonial relationship was, in the mid-eighteenth century, frequently described in terms of parent and child. In 1775 the "child" was forcibly asserting maturity, and would not be likely to continue to use that particular metaphor, with its demeaning associations, unless there were some compelling reason. Persuading the Indians to neutrality was reason enough. The idea of a family struggle might well make the quarrel meaningful to societies where kinship was the primary basis of social organization. This conception also made it possible for the delegates to seek sympathy and understanding and at the same time to point out that, since the struggle was within their own family, the Indians did not need to be concerned in it at all.[8]

The family concept in the address to the Indians was worked out at length, and the colonies were compared to a younger son who had suffered for a long time under an increasing burden of taxation and injustice. The son's father, the king, did not know all that was happening. He was misled by his own servants while in private they mocked the son, stole what was rightfully his, and heaped new injustices upon him. When the son could not stand the burden any longer because "Such a weight would crush him down and kill him," he put it down and refused to carry it:

> Upon this, those servants are very wroth—and tell the father false stories respecting the child—they bring a great cudgel to the father, asking him to take it in his hand and strike the child.
>
> This may serve to illustrate the present condition of the king's American subjects or children.[9]

The colonists wanted to be sure that the Indians did not ally themselves with Great Britain, and they used the family metaphor to show that the neutrality that was being urged on them by the United Colonies was actually in the Indian's own interests. The outlook would be bleak indeed if Great Britain were to win: "For, if the king's troops take away our property, and destroy us who are of the same blood with themselves, what can you, who are Indians, expect from them afterwards?"[10]

This message was presented to the Six Nations at a meeting at Albany in August 1775, to some of the western nations at a meeting at Fort Pitt in September and October 1775, to the Cherokees at a meeting at Salisbury, North Carolina, in November 1775, and to the Creeks at a meeting in Augusta in May 1776.[11] There was no hint in the message that the colonists, as well as the king's troops, might constitute a threat to the Indians' property, but at Albany the Mohawks pointed out that past experience had taught them to be wary. They brought up a long-standing dispute between the Mohawks and the citizens of Albany to serve as a test of the colonists' intentions. As they saw the dispute, some citizens of Albany had taken two pieces of Indian land and had not made any payment. The Indians wanted the land returned. In the words of their speaker, Abraham: "If you refuse to do this, we shall look upon the prospect to be bad, for if you conquer you will take us by the arm and pull us all off [our land]."[12]

As for neutrality, the Mohawks had already made their position clear. They had met earlier that year with city officials of Schenectady and Albany. Speaking only ten days after the fighting at Lexington, Abraham had said that the Indians did not want to interfere "in the dispute Between old England and Boston and white People may settle their own quarrels between themselfs we shall never meddle in these Matters or be the agressor—if we are let alone."[13]

At Albany Abraham repeated this message to the continental commissioners who had brought the address from the United Colonies with its plea for Indian neutrality. "As for your Quarrels to the Eastward, along the Sea Coasts, do as you please." But Abraham also sounded a note of warning that if the quarrels spread into areas where the Indians felt their vital interests to be threatened, they would not hesitate to fight. The Indians had two purposes: to stay at peace and to protect their friends. This protection would be extended, even though war should ensue.[14]

One specific friend the Mohawks had in mind was Guy Johnson, who had been acting as British superintendent of Indian affairs in the Northern Department since the death in 1774 of his uncle and father-in-law, Sir William Johnson. The acting superintendent was then in Canada, as was Joseph Brant, the Mohawk leader whose sister Molly had long made a home with Sir William. More than two hundred Iroquois from New York were also there to help the British in case of an invasion of Canada by the United Colonies. In his talk to the continental commissioners at Albany, Abraham made it clear that the part of the Six Nations for which he spoke would consider any move toward those and other friends in Canada a hostile act. He emphasized that the Indians wanted to remain at peace but that the path of peace they were defending ran all the way to their friends in Canada. He warned the Americans not to defile the path with blood.[15]

Like the British before them, the continental commissioners at Albany used Iroquois terminology and concepts for their own purposes. They spoke of a "covenant chain," using the phrase not in its specific Iroquois application but in a general sense meaning a binding agreement between separate political groups. They referred to the Iroquois conception of peace as a vast tree in the shade of which all nations could sit down together, and tried to adapt that concept to the American policy of neutrality for the Iroquois:

> Brothers: we live upon the same ground with you. The same island is our common birthplace. We desire to sit down under the same tree of peace with you: let us water its roots and cherish its growth, till the large leaves and flourishing branches shall extend to the setting sun and reach the skies.[16]

Unlike the British, however, the Americans did not ask the Iroquois to send to the Ohio country and see that their allies and dependents there also remained neutral. The Anglo-Shawnee War had been fought only one year earlier, and the Shawnees, despite their defeat at Point Pleasant, were still seeking allies for a new stand against the incursion of whites into the upper Ohio Valley. Yet there were no American remonstrances at the Albany meeting with the Six Nations. They did not, as the British had done the previous summer, tell the Six Nations to keep their dependents in line or lose face. "If you do not," Guy Johnson had said to the assembled Iroquois, "your reputation as a powerful Confederacy will greatly suffer in the eyes of the English."[17]

The Americans did not make any such demand of the Iroquois because other steps were being taken, independent of the Iroquois Grand Council. A messenger was already in the Ohio country inviting the western Indians to talk to the Americans. Within two weeks of the meeting at Albany in the latter part of August, a meeting began at Fort Pitt, and a different group of continental commissioners conveyed the colonies' request for Indian neutrality to representatives of five western nations: Wyandot, Ottawa, Delaware, Shawnee, and Mingo (the Six Nations of the Ohio).[18]

If the Americans at Albany in August 1775 understood that the Iroquois tree of peace had often been watered by blood and that nations had sometimes been dragged by force under its spreading branches, they did not try to use that knowledge, as the British had done, to control the western nations through the Iroquois League. Yet there is no indication that the independent negotiations with the western nations were a deliberate attempt to undercut Iroquois prestige. Early in the war the Americans even upheld that prestige rather than side with the Delawares against it at a time when there were still hopes of keeping the bulk of the Six Nations neutral.

The independent American meeting with the western nations in September and October 1775 seems rather to have been an attempt to counter the efforts of the British among the western nations. Some of the Delawares and Mingoes who gathered at Fort Pitt in September to hear the Americans had met at Fort Pitt three months earlier and heard John Connolly state the British case. Similarly, some of the Wyandots who came from their villages on the upper Sandusky River to meet with the continental commissioners had already met with the British at Detroit. It is likely that most of the Indians in that fall meeting with the Americans had already spoken to a British agent or officer and had heard a different version of the colonial-British quarrel.[19] The colonists' universalist vision of a righteous struggle against tyranny was not nearly so useful in such a contest as the promises of ample supplies and of protection for Indian lands which the British could offer to the Indians with greater assurances that they would be believed.

The War Years

By September 1775 the contest for the loyalties and resources of groups, both Indian and white, was well underway. Differences within the groups, such as those between the western and eastern nations of the Iroquois League, or between the upper and lower divisions of the Creek Confederacy, were so many handholds for outsiders. While the British were drawing two hundred Iroquois to Montreal for the defense of Canada, the Massachusetts Provincial Congress was trying to persuade the Mohawks, Oneidas, and Onondagas to support the American cause. The American invasion of Canada, shortly after the August meeting in Albany, virtually assured Mohawk adherence to the British cause, which was, in general, supported also by Senecas, Cayugas, and Onondagas. The Oneidas and Tuscaroras tended to side with the Americans.[20]

These statements of general tendencies obscure the destructiveness of wartime divisions in Iroquois society. As provocations mounted, making neutrality impossible and forcing the Indians to choose sides, their society fragmented, and the scope of their consensual decision-making procedures grew ever smaller. There were many exceptions to the general tendencies noted above. Individuals and small groups split off and went their own way. Cayugas took arms against Cayugas, and Mohawks faced Mohawks as spokesmen for the view that each was maintaining at the cost of the League as a whole. "We have no reason to be ashamed of what we have done," said the Mohawk leader Aaron to the Mohawk leader Little Abraham when they met in 1780 at the British headquarters of Colonel Guy Johnson at Niagara. Little Abraham had brought a message from the Americans to the Mohawks at Niagara, a message that Aaron rejected on behalf of those Mohawks, who were fighting on the British side: "We have acted agreeable to our Treaties & Engagements with our Father the King, with whom our Ancestors have for many Ages been connected."[21]

This fragmentation made social expression on a League wide basis all but impossible, a fact noted by the Cayuga leader Kingageghta in 1780: "We have for some time past, substituted the smaller Kettle & the small Canoe (in which only a part join) to the large Kettle & great Canoe, which signified that the whole Confederacy were engaged in the Expedition." Worst of all, the ceremonial forms that had once expressed League unity and destiny were disappearing: "[A] Great Part of our ancient Customs & Ceremonies have, thro' the Loss of many of our principal men during the War, been neglected & forgotten, so that we cannot go through the whole with our ancient Propriety."[22]

But wartime did not bring decline to all Indian societies. What was tragedy for the Iroquois was opportunity for the western nations in their struggle against Iroquois dominance. In the South, the war between the whites meant opportunity of a different sort for some of the

Indians. Alexander McGillivray was able to use British supplies to help him in his rise to leadership of the Creek Confederacy, and militant groups in the Cherokee Nation took advantage of a shipment of British ammunition to launch their own separate war against the Americans. In 1776 Cherokees attacked the outlying settlements that had for so long been a grievance to them.

The Cherokee decision was a critical one, both for their own future and for the policies pursued by other southern Indian nations during the years of the American War for Independence. James H. O'Donnell, the leading historian of the part played by the southern Indians during those years, has concluded that the sufferings of the Cherokees, after they were defeated, made other Indians hesitant to act against the Americans, and that this severely hampered later British war efforts in the South.[23]

The British had tried to persuade the Cherokees to wait and coordinate their efforts against the Americans with those of Great Britain, but five thousands pounds of British powder and lead was a more forceful argument in favor of immediate war. Such leaders as Chincohacina (Dragging Canoe), who had long advocated war and who had opposed the land cessions of the early 1770s, took advantage of the opportunity the British had provided. The Cherokees set out to defend their long, exposed boundary.

The attempt ended in disaster. Invading forces from North and South Carolina destroyed the Cherokee Lower and Middle Towns, and Virginians were threatening the destruction of the Overhill Towns when the Cherokees sued for peace. This was not a case of a hunting people being driven further into the forest. When the Overhill Cherokees fled before the advancing Virginians, they abandoned horses, cattle, hogs, fowl, forty to fifty thousand bushels of corn, and ten to fifteen thousand bushels of potatoes, as well as the log cabins in which, by this period, most Cherokees lived. They were as dependent as the whites on peace and a settled existence to secure their means of subsistence, and they competed with whites for the same agricultural resources. They competed also, not very successfully, for allies who might give them aid. No other Indians came to their assistance, although the British tried to preserve Cherokee usefulness to their own cause by persuading the Creeks to do battle against the pursuing Americans. The Creeks refused.[24]

The Cherokees had little choice but to make peace on American terms, which included major cessions of Cherokee land, and a new

Cherokee-white boundary. The boundary was defined in three separate treaties. The Treaty of Dewitt's Corner, signed 20 May 1777, established the Cherokee boundary with Georgia and South Carolina, and two Treaties of Long Island (of the Holston), signed 20 July 1777, established the boundary with North Carolina and Virginia.[25]

The Creek Confederacy did not act as a whole during these years of fighting. The fate of the Cherokees made them cautious about committing themselves wholly to the British cause, despite the efforts of Alexander McGillivray, the Upper Creek leader who was also a British commissary and an advocate for the British insofar as British policy might coincide with the interests of the Creeks.[26] Those interests, in relation to the world outside the confederacy, can be summarized as protection of the Creek land-base and acquisition of a reliable source of supplies. The 1773 land cession to Georgia (made jointly with the Cherokees), in which proceeds from sales of the land went to pay debts incurred by the Creeks in the purchase of supplies, illustrates how these goals could be contradictory, and shows again the economic bind in which the southern Indians found themselves. The Creeks were in a better position than the Cherokees in that they were more protected from white competition for land and game. They were protected both by distance and by other Indian groups. Moreover, they were more favorably located for access to southern and Gulf ports. So long as there were European groups to the south contending with the Atlantic seaboard settlements, the Creeks had room to maneuver because they had access to alternative sources of supplies.

This did not mean, however, that Creek leaders agreed on how best to use the advantages they had. Throughout the war years there were disputes within the confederacy between those who agreed with McGillivray that, taken all in all, the British offered the best long-run means to achieve Creek goals, and those who were inclined to believe George Galphin's assertions that the Creeks would do better to look to the Americans, who could supply them better goods at cheaper prices. Galphin's influence was chiefly among the Lower Creeks, and McGillivray's among the Upper Creeks, a fact that reflects a persistent internal division in the confederacy's councils and actions.[27]

Despite divisions and disagreements, and a smoldering war with the Choctaws to the west, the Creeks made their presence felt during the years of fighting, particularly after Spain entered the war against Britain in 1779. By that time, also, some Cherokees were again engaged actively against the Americans, especially the breakaway group called the

Chickamaugas, led by Chincohacina. Choctaw councils were divided on the question of Spain versus Great Britain for their source of supplies, but substantial numbers of Choctaws, and of Chickasaws, too, became involved on the side of the British when Spanish forces from New Orleans moved east. At Mobile and Pensacola, and, later, at Augusta and Savannah, southern Indians took a significant part in battles that, in the long run, determined which whites they would be dealing with on the questions of land and supplies that were their chief concerns.[28]

By the war's end, the Creeks and Choctaws, and, to a lesser extent, the Chickasaws, were still strong, relatively untouched by the fighting, and in a position to exploit what opportunities might arise. They found their opportunities in a boundary dispute between Spain and the United States over the southern boundary of the new nation. It was a dispute that held little advantage for the Cherokees, situated as they were out of easy reach of Spanish possessions in East and West Florida and Louisiana. Moreover, the Cherokees had been greatly weakened during the war. Their settlements had been overrun again after Cherokee-American hostilities resumed in 1780. In the shadows of the past they rested for a time, defined as enemies in the minds of those who needed less excuse than that to appropriate their lands, temporarily in political disarray and the most vulnerable of all the southern Indians to the expansionary forces that were released by the closing of the British-American war.

North of the Ohio, diplomacy after 1783 was most deeply affected by the fact that the western nations had won most of their wartime encounters. Unlike the Cherokees or the Iroquois—who suffered a punishing American invasion in 1779—the western nations at the war's end still controlled their territory. Their policy for the next twelve years was based on this fact.

The struggle among the western nations for regional leadership also affected post-1783 diplomacy. The struggle was muted but ever present, even when the Indians were engaged in cooperative campaigns against the Americans. Set over against that struggle was a third factor that continued throughout the period of this study and beyond. There was among the western nations a feeling that shared problems required joint efforts for their solutions. Too feeble as yet to be called a sense of unity, the feeling might still be described as a sense of community. In this period it did not find a permanent institutional form, such as the Great Council of the Six Nations had been for the Iroquois, or a spokesman of the stature of Tecumseh. Yet it persisted. It can be seen in the

Indians' repeated efforts and repeated failures to subordinate small-group to regional interests, to move from the parochial to the shared outlook, to be, as one Indian leader said, "of one mind."[29] Faltering as the sense of community was among the western nations, it yet enabled them to combine their military efforts effectively enough to delay for twelve years American occupation of any significant portion of the lands north of the Ohio.

Most of the Indians north of the Ohio had fought with the British against the Americans. This was not from any loyalty to the British. Before the outbreak of British-American hostilities, the Indians of the Ohio country had been resisting Iroquois efforts to force a British alliance on them. They fought with the British because they perceived the Americans as the greater threat. Even those Delawares who had originally attempted to gain American friendship and use it for their own purposes eventually joined the rest of their nation in fighting the Americans. This was after it became apparent that the Americans did not have enough arms or troops even to protect their friends in the West, much less to supply them, and that the main American war effort was going to be directed to the eastern theater.[30]

By war's end the wartime alliance of western Indians included most of the Shawnees, Delawares, Mingoes (Six-Nations-of-Ohio), Wyandots, Miamis, Weas, Piankeshaws, Kickapoos, and Illinois, as well as large numbers of Potawatomis, Ottawas, and Chippewas (Ojibwas). Supplied by the British, often operating jointly with British rangers, they had by 1782 established effective control of the northwestern frontier. When news about the impending preliminary American-British peace treaty arrived at Fort Pitt in October 1782, the American commander there gladly abandoned plans for yet another expedition into the Indian country. He had neither the supplies nor the men to face combined Indian-British forces who were operating with the confidence of recent victories.[31]

In the struggle among the western nations for a position of regional leadership, there were several contenders. The Delawares made an early bid for a position of power. Their strategy was threefold. They sought independence from the Iroquois League, where they had for many years been subordinate to the Great Council at Onondaga. They sought a territorial base, and to this end asserted their claim to land in what is now eastern Ohio, western New York, and western Pennsylvania. Finally, they sought to be at the head of whatever Indian confederacy might form under the pressures generated by the British-American war, and, further, to gain United States sponsorship for their leadership. Because the efforts of the Delawares reflect some of the complexities of the diplomatic situation north of the Ohio during this period, they are worth examining.

The unchanging constraint on Delaware policy was economic need, a point that needs to be emphasized as they turned first to the British, then to the Americans, and then back to the British during the years of British and American fighting. No matter which way Delaware desires or inclinations might swing, they never swung free of the drag of daily necessities that could only be procured from the whites. Beyond that, however, the consistency of their own goals, separate from those of the whites, can be seen in their efforts in the early years of the war to get their land claim acknowledged by some group of whites capable of guaranteeing them possession. In the spring of 1775, when the quarrels between the colonists and Great Britain were just reaching the stage of open hostilities, the Delawares approached the British at Fort Pitt. By the fall of 1775 the colonists were in control there, and the Delawares adapted their strategy to the changed situation. They took advantage of the neutrality council called by the Americans, asserted their independence from the Six Nations of the Iroquois Confederacy, and tried to get the Americans to recognize their land claim.[32]

This Delaware effort was rebuffed by the Continental Congress the following spring in terms that reflected the desire of the United Colonies to keep the Six Nations neutral and avoid any action that might anger them and incline them toward the British:

> You tell us that your uncles, our brothers, the Wiandots, have given your nation a large tract of country, comprehended between the river Ohio on the south, the west branch of the river Muskingham and Sandusky on the west, Lake Erie on the north, and Presque Isle on the west [east]:
> Brothers, hearken to our advice. As we are informed that your uncles, our brothers, the Six Nations, claim most of those lands, we recommend it to you to obtain their approbation of this grant to you from the Wiandots in public council, and have it put on record. Such a step will prevent uneasiness and jealousy on their part, and continue the confidence and friendship which subsists between you and them. We wish to promote the lasting peace and happiness of all our brothers, the Indian nations, who live with us on this great island.[33]

The Delawares did not give up. A year later the Delaware leader Koquetakeghton (White Eyes) formally and contemptuously threw off the subordinate status that had been assigned to the Delawares by the Iroquois in their days of dominance.[34] Two years after that, in 1779, the Delawares again asserted a territorial claim and again attempted to get American acknowledgment of that claim. By then the situation with regard to the Iroquois had changed. Fighting had broken out between the Americans and part of the Six Nations, and the Americans no longer shaped their policy to secure Iroquois neutrality.

The situation with regard to the Delawares had changed also. In 1778 they had rendered useful service to the Americans in the protection of the frontier outpost of Fort Laurens on the Tuscarawas River in present Ohio. They had also become formal allies of the Americans and had guided an American expedition in a movement (later abandoned) against the British at Detroit.[35] The Delawares may have felt that they had a few loans outstanding with the Americans, and that the time had come to call them in. At any rate, when a group of Delaware leaders was in Philadelphia in 1779, they laid claim to a much larger territory than they had claimed in 1775, and tried to get American acknowledgment of their extended claim.[36] This time the Continental Congress made no mention of the Six Nations in its reply. It showed a strong desire to stay clear of the tangle of Indian politics, and simply pleaded lack of competence and jurisdiction—a feeling that did not survive the war:

> The great Council [Congress] have never interposed with respect to the claims and bounds of their Indian Friends. Their disputes ought to be settled by wise Men of your own Nations acquainted with your customs and your rights which we do not profess to be, nor have we time while the war continues to rage to examine into such matters altho at a future day we shall be glad to give you the best advices in our power after receiving the necessary information.[37]

Related to these Delaware moves for independence and a territorial base were their attempts to put themselves at the head of other Indian groups, in a position of leadership that would be sponsored and secured by the United States. The attempts can be seen in two never-implemented treaty articles, one in the 1778 Delaware-United States treaty of alliance, and the second in a Cherokee-United States treaty of alliance signed the following year. The articles make an explicit bid for Delaware leadership under the sponsorship of the United States:

> And it is further agreed on between the contracting parties [the Delawares and the United States in 1778, and the Cherokees and the United States in 1779], should it for the future be found conducive

for the mutual interest of both parties, to invite any other tribes who have been friends to the interest of the United States, to join the present confederation, and to form a state whereof the Delaware nation shall be the head, and have a representation in Congress: Provided nothing contained in this article [is] to be considered conclusive until it meets with the approbation of Congress.[38]

In the 1779 Cherokee-United States treaty, the Delawares were cosigners with the Cherokees and United States officials. Whatever the Cherokees' reasons for signing, it seems clear that the Delawares—or part of them, at any rate—were maneuvering to put themselves into a position of leadership.[39]

They were one among several contenders for the position, but the records offer only glimpses of the struggle for dominance that was taking place. These glimpses are chiefly through the eyes of baffled American or British administrators trying to find some center of power to deal with, some way of getting hold of the complex, shifting relationships in the Ohio country. At various times various white leaders thought they detected a new locus for the old power of the Iroquois. In 1777 George Morgan, American congressional agent at Fort Pitt, noted that the Mingoes of the Ohio, the small breakaway group from the New York Iroquois, were acting with the "air and authority of the Six Nations council." A little later, in 1778, George Rogers Clark was confident that the center of power in the Great Lakes-Ohio country lay farther west among the Piankeshaws near the old French post of Vincennes.[40] However accurate that assessment may have been, the various Wabash River groups, which included the Piankeshaws, do seem to have been rising in prominence and independence throughout this period. By 1783, when the British and Americans were ready to quit fighting and wanted to persuade the western Indian nations to do the same, the British found the Wabash River Indians the hardest to restrain.[41] From one of those groups, the Miami, came the leader Michikinikwa (Little Turtle) who was to lead united Indian forces to victory over American forces in 1790 and again in 1791.

But there were still other contenders. The Shawnees figure prominently in the rumors of impending Indian union that circulated throughout this period. In 1774 they had broken decisively with the Iroquois over the cession of their hunting grounds, so they were free to make what alliances they would and assert what leadership they could.[42] During this period they nurtured Tecumseh, the leader who, in the early

1800s, was to come the closest to making the rumors of Indian union come true.

Then there were the Wyandots, who had granted the Delawares the territory they were so anxious to secure. They were a mixed group of Hurons and Petuns, Indian nations that had been smashed and scattered by the Iroquois in the trade wars of the seventeenth century. Although many of the survivors had been adopted into the member nations of the Iroquois League, others had fled west and south for refuge among other Indian nations. Not until the eighteenth century did descendants of those refugees begin to drift back to the area around Detroit and along the southern shore of Lake Erie where, as Wyandots, they began their rise in influence among the western nations. They claimed most of what is now Ohio, and asserted preeminence over the other Indian nations there—an assertion symbolized by their right of lighting the council fire at inter Indian meetings. It was a Wyandot leader, Dunquad (Half King), who spoke out on behalf of the wartime alliance of western nations when the Delawares were seeking the backing of the Americans. "If you do not stop treating with the Americans I will kill you," he told the Delawares in 1779.[43]

His anger was more than personal. Indian leaders customarily used the first person singular when speaking on behalf of their group, and in this case his group was the whole alliance of western nations. "Consider yourself, Cousin," he went on, still addressing the Delawares and still using the personal form of address, "you alone are diverse from all other Nations. All the Nations are of one mind but you. I am quite astonished at you & your works."[44]

Dunquad's remonstrance to the Delawares, with its assertion of Indian unity and its dismay at actions that might destroy that unity, is a convenient summary of the situation of the western Indian nations at the close of the British-American war.

Peace and Boundaries
American and European Views

Like the Treaty of Paris of 1763, the treaties that marked the close of hostilities between Great Britain and the United States and its allies were partition treaties. As in 1763, the partitioning was done without consultation with the indigenous inhabitants, and in North America after 1783 this produced the same reaction it had in 1763. Possible

Indian opposition was not the first consideration of European policy-makers, however, as they juggled the familiar elements of European balance-of-power calculations to take into account the new and possibly disturbing element of an independent United States. So far as North America was concerned, the resulting bargains left Great Britain in possession of Canada and Newfoundland, returned East and West Florida to Spain, and gave the United States boundaries far beyond the area of actual American control, particularly in the West. The boundary there was the Mississippi River from the Lake of the Woods on the north north and west of Lake Superior), to the thirty-first parallel on the south (the southern boundary of the present state of Mississippi).

Long before the formal close of hostilities, the Continental Congress had turned its attention to the boundaries it hoped the war would establish for the new nation. The instructions to its peace commissioners, issued early in 1779 when the Congress still believed that Spain might formally ally itself to the United States and that the war would then be quickly over, were the first in a series of attempts to secure European acknowledgment of the widest possible boundaries for the United States. The success of these maneuvers in 1783 was, as Samuel Flagg Bemis has pointed out, as much a result of the European powers' mutual suspicions and determination to limit each other's imperial extent, as to any pressure that the United States was able to bring to bear.[45] A later student of the diplomacy of this period, J. Leitch Wright, Jr., has added to this the finding that none of the great European powers expected the boundaries of 1783 to be permanent ones. There were no definite plans to transgress the boundaries. It was just that paper agreements and lines on a map were only marginally relevant in an area that no one controlled, and where Britain, Spain, and—later—France were still actively contending with the United States for the influence that might lead to predominance.[46]

Within this European frame of reference, the Indians were not wholly forgotten. There are indications that American policymakers were willing to use the Indian presence as a bargaining counter in peace negotiations, should that become necessary. The Americans did not want to discuss the Indians with any European power. They preferred the establishment of a western boundary that would allow them to define the presence of the Indians as a domestic affair, not as a matter for international negotiation. But in 1781 when the Continental Congress was again formulating instructions to a peace commission, it had to decide what the commissioners should do if they could not get the western boundary that Congress had indicated was the most desirable. The following was considered:

> If that [western boundary] cannot be obtained, it is the wish of Congress that a peace be made without fixing the western limits but considering that territory as of right belonging to the Indian nations.[47]

The sparse records of debate in the Continental Congress do not provide information beyond the fact that this was one possible bargaining position discussed there. In the end, mention of the Indians was dropped from the instructions to the peace commission, as were other aspects of the boundary question. Congress left the matter of boundaries to the good judgment of the commissioners and of France, while referring them to previous congressional statements on the matter as a guide.[48]

The 1781 negotiations failed, but in 1782, after the American victory at Yorktown and the fall of the North ministry, peace talks were resumed with better prospects for success. America had to consider again what would happen if their peace negotiators could not get the preferred boundaries. Again the Indians were seen as something that could be brought up in case of need—if, for instance, Spain pressed its desire to limit the new nation, either by its own claims or by advocating boundaries that corresponded with actual possession at the close of hostilities. Early in 1782 Robert R. Livingston, American secretary for foreign affairs, wrote to Benjamin Franklin, a member of the American peace commission, and suggested that if the commissioners could not get the western boundary of the United States fixed at the Mississippi River, there might then be a four power guarantee of the independence of the Indians in the West, with free trade allowed throughout the area.[49]

The American peace commissioners never made this proposal at Paris because they did not have to retreat to such an extent from the boundaries they were demanding. United States policymakers, therefore, went into the postwar period with the assumption that, since they had won the war against Great Britain and secured a stunning victory in European bargaining, they were in a position to impose terms on the Indians who had fought against them in the war.

Indian opposition was to be expected. What American officials did not expect was the strength and extent of the opposition. Neither did they expect Great Britain to move from a position of apparent unconcern about the Indians who had been their wartime allies to a position of open diplomatic support. When the northern and western Indians asserted that the Fort Stanwix line was the only proper boundary between their land and that of white Americans, British officials backed the assertion. The officials assured the Indians that Americans had no claim whatsoever to land beyond the Ohio, since King George would not and could not have given to the Americans what he had no right to give.[50]

In his study of British postwar diplomacy, J. Leitch Wright has shown how the lack of central policy planning and pressure from Loyalist refugees, British merchants, fur traders, and Army officers combined to keep Great Britain deeply involved in North American affairs. Pressure was especially intense from officers in the field who were in direct contact with the northern and western Indians and heard the Indians' point of view. Many of the officers were not only sympathetic to that point of view, they were afraid of what might happen to British subjects in Canada if it were disregarded.[51]

While British policymakers moved gradually and rather absentmindedly toward a position of limiting the extent of territory under actual United States control, the Spanish consistently pursued the same end. Territorial limitation had been one of their goals at the Paris peace negotiations. Failing there, they set out to achieve limitation through other means. They supported the southern Indians as a check to American western expansion, and they asserted that the boundary between Spanish and American territory was not the thirty-first parallel, but a line much farther north, in one place going as high as the Ohio River near its junction with the Mississippi. As events would show, the Spanish advanced this extreme boundary argument chiefly to have something to give up in negotiations with Americans on the question of commercial transport on the Mississippi.[52] During the early 1780s, the Spanish position was useful to the southern Indians, however. The supplies and arms that the Indians needed to maintain their own boundary position came more readily from a Spain that wanted to keep pressure on the Americans in their separate boundary negotiations.

Peace and Boundaries: Indian Views

The predominant reaction of northern and western Indians to the European Peace of Paris of 1783 was bitterness. As Wright has shown, this mood was of great concern to British officials. Early in 1783, Sir Frederick Haldimand, governor of Canada, observed that it would require the utmost British exertion and attention to keep the Iroquois in good temper. They maintained with vehemence that they were allies of King George, not his subjects. They were a free people "subject to no power on earth," and the king had no right to grant to the United States any of their "rights or properties without a manifest breach of all Justice and Equity."[53] From the West the word was the same. The commanding officer at Detroit reported that a group of Wabash Indians had come to him demanding an explanation of the peace arrangements in a manner that was "very impertinent," and that they used "expressions not proper to be committed to paper."[54]

The British felt compelled to call a meeting of the Indians to reassure them that the boundary agreed on between the United States and Great Britain did not infringe upon the Indians' rights. Nor did the boundary as drawn in Europe in any way negate the Fort Stanwix line. Speaking at Sandusky in present-day Ohio in September 1783, Sir John Johnson, superintendent of Indian affairs for Canada, told the assembled Indians:

> You are not to believe, or even think that by the Line which has been described it was meant to deprive you of an extent of country of which the right of soil belongs to, and is in yourselves as Sole Proprietors as far as the boundary Line agreed upon and Established in the most Solemn and public manner in the presence and with the consent of the Governors and Commissioners deputed by the different Colonies for that purpose by your late worthy Friend Sir. Wm. Johnson in the year 1768 at Fort Stanwix.[55]

Johnson's statement of the British position was heard by representatives from the Six Nations of the Iroquois Confederacy, and from seven of the western Indian nations: Wyandot, Delaware, Shawnee, Mingo (Six Nations of the Ohio), Potawatomi, Ottawa, and Chippewa (Ojibwa). Present also were representatives from two southern Indian groups, the Creek Confederacy and the Cherokee Nation. The western and northern Indians might take comfort from Johnson's defense of the Fort Stanwix line, but it would have been small comfort for the southern Indians. It had nothing to offer them, even if the Americans accepted it, except the assurance that the main thrust of white expansion would continue to be diverted south of the Ohio River where they, not the Iroquois or the western nations, would have to deal with it.

The southern Indians were not in a strong position to do so. Much of the north-south boundary line they had worked out with British authorities was gone by 1783. The whole northern portion of the line had been destroyed by the very treaty that the Indians north of the Ohio were counting on as their best hope in negotiations with the Americans. The middle portion of the line, made up of the Cherokee boundary with the Carolinas and southwestern Virginia, had been drastically altered following the Cherokees' defeat in 1777. At the war's end only the southern portion of the line, the Creek-Cherokee-Georgia portion, was intact, and it came under immediate pressure by the state of Georgia. North Carolina was also actively expansionist. In May 1783 the North Carolina legislature unilaterally redrew the state's Indian-white boundary by expropriating all Indian land within its borders and reserving an area between the French Broad and the Tennessee rivers for the Cherokees.[56]

Thus the southern Indians who attended the British conference at Sandusky in September 1783 could not point to any one line and say to the Americans that it was the rightful boundary. The conference at Sandusky and the withdrawal of the British from southern posts, made it clear that, at their most helpful, the British could do little for the southern Indians. If they were to resist the expansionist pressures of the new United States, the southern Indians would have to find not only a common policy such as the one that the Indians north of the Ohio were working out. They would also have to find European patron to furnish them supplies, and a line that they could defend.

These were the very problems addressed by Alexander McGillivray, the Creek leader who rose to prominence in this period and remained the most prominent southern Indian leader until his death in 1793. Son of a noted Creek woman and a wealthy Scotch planter, McGillivray had the advantages of education and experience in both the European and Indian ways of life. While consolidating a position of leadership among the Creeks, McGillivray also managed to attain the title and pay of a British colonel. After the departure of the British, he turned to the Spanish. The terms of trade he secured from them in Pensacola in June 1784 and the Spanish commission as commissary in the Creek Confederacy helped him retain his leadership among the Creeks. By the following year, McGillivray was ready to claim a larger Indian constituency. In the name of the Creek, Cherokee, and the Chickasaw nations, he issued a document that was both a memorial to the Spanish king and a declaration of southern Indian aims.[57]

The occasion for the declaration was the beginning of negotiations between Spain and the United States over the disputed boundary between the United States and the Spanish possessions of East and West Florida. The document appeared in July 1785, which was the same month that Diego de Gardoqui, the Spanish negotiator, arrived in New York to begin talks with John Jay, U.S. secretary for foreign affairs. The document expressed the Indians' concern that the British-American peace treaty of 1783 would be made the basis of negotiations between Spain and the United States. They rejected any American claim to their land that was founded on this treaty and pointed out that, as the Indians had not been parties to the treaty, so they would not be bound by it. In words that echoed those of the northern Indians, they denied that the British king had the right to do anything with their lands:

> it being a Notorious fact known to the Americans, known to every person who is in any ways conversant in, or acquainted with American affairs, that his Brittanick Majesty was never possessed either by session, purchase, or by right of Conquest of our Territorys and which the Said treaty gives away. On the contrary it is well known that from the first Settlement of the English colonys of Carolina and Georgia up to the date of the said treaty no title has ever been or pretended to be made by his Britannic Majesty to our lands except what was obtained by free Gift or by purchase for good and valuable Considerations.[58]

Having set out the standard for a valid transfer of land, the Indians then used that standard to define the valid boundary between their land and that of the whites. Mention was made of the joint Creek-Cherokee land cession in 1773 and the payment that had been made for it:

> nor has any treaty been held by us Since that period for the purpose of granting any land to any people whatever nor did we the Nations of Creeks, Chickesaws, and Cherokees do any act to forfeit our Independance and natural Rights to the Said King of Great Britain that could invest him with the power of giving our property away unless fighting by the side of his soldiers in the day of battle and Spilling our best blood in the Service of his Nation can be deemed so.[59]

The Indians then noted that at a general Indian Congress in Pensacola in June 1784 the Spanish king had granted them his favor and had promised to protect them, their property, and their hunting grounds. They asked that in the current boundary negotiations Spain would "enter into no terms with the American States that may Strengthen their claims or that may tend to deprive us of our Just inheritance."[60]

A thorough evaluation of this document of July 1785 requires more information than is available. McGillivray said that it came out of a "general convention" of Indians at Little Tallassee in 1785, but did not indicate what Cherokees and Chickasaws were present.[61] Nor did he say why the Choctaws were not included in a general convention of southern Indians. Hostility between the Creeks and the Choctaws is a probable explanation, but the absence of the Choctaws reduces the credibility of McGillivray's claim to speak for the southern Indians. The Choctaws were at this time the most populous of the southern groups and were the object of solicitous Spanish concern. Moreover, the American boundary claim of the thirty-first parallel was certainly of interest to them, since it cut through their lands.

Beyond this, the Declaration of 1785 was misleading about what the southern Indians had been promised in the name of Charles III, the Spanish king. From June 1784 to early December, Spanish authorities had held meetings with southern Indians at various localities, and in some cases treaties had been signed, but only the treaty signed 1 June 1784 with the Creeks in Pensacola had any guarantee of protection. (On June 23 in Mobile the Alabamas acceded to the Pensacola Treaty. The Alabamas are usually considered to be part of the Creek Confederacy in this period.) The Spanish treaties with the Chickasaws and Choctaws were chiefly concerned with terms and conditions of trade, and the Cherokees in 1785 had no treaty with Spain. Even the guarantee to the Creeks was limited by the proviso that this not embroil the Spanish in conflict with the Americans.[62]

Then, too, the boundary that was set out in the southern Indian declaration of 1785 was not a comprehensive, defensible line like the line of Fort Stanwix. The Creek-Cherokee-Georgia boundary of 1773 that the document mentioned was only a small part of the line that had once extended from the Ohio River south to Georgia and west to the Mississippi. The fact that the Georgia segment was mentioned at all suggests that the document was issued as part of Creek resistance to Georgia's efforts to change the line.

That does not mean that the other southern Indians did not agree with the declaration's assertions of Indian sovereignty and with the principle of fair purchase that was invoked. It does indicate some of the difficulties that would have been involved in any joint endeavor they might have undertaken. They were hampered by the problems that are revealed in even an incomplete analysis of the document: lack of a defensible boundary and limited Spanish support, as well as limited experience in cooperative efforts. They were hampered, too, by a persistent fragmentation of authority that, for example, led some Creeks to sign treaties with Georgia when they were not authorized to do so.[63] This fragmentation was one of the chief causes of the political chaos of the period.

United States Policy

United States Indian policy in the period following the Revolution has been the subject of several studies. W. H. Mohr has given a detailed, annals-like listing of appointments, congressional committee reports, and the like through 1788. Francis Paul Prucha in his *American Indian Policy* has shown the consistency and continuity of federal policy aims from the first days of the Republic through the period of the removals in the 1830s and beyond. Reginald Horsman has convincingly placed Indian policy within the long-range framework of United States territorial expansion. Horsman has also distinguished two periods in Indian policy in the immediate postwar era: the conquest period to July 1787, and the succeeding purchase period.[64]

Within a diplomatic framework, there is more to be said about United States postwar Indian policy. "Conquest" and "purchase" do not adequately describe what was in fact a major policy retreat. From an assertion of full political sovereignty over the territory acquired from Great Britain, the United States was forced to an acknowledgment that it had only limited sovereignty and that the limitations were set by the rights of the Indians inhabiting the land. This retreat also involved a major change in the way that Indian affairs were defined by the United States government.

Indian affairs were at first seen as a domestic problem, equal to and linked with the problems of war debts, western land claims, orderly expansion, and so on. Diplomatic considerations entered in only as a possible hazard should unwise actions on the part of the United States drive the Indians into the camps of the British or the Spanish—but this was true also for the new western settlements and Vermont. It was only after the repeated failure of attempts to handle Indian affairs as a domestic problem that United States officials were forced to consider relations *with* the Indians, rather than a unilateral policy *for* the Indians. This shifted the whole basis of the relationship from the domestic to the diplomatic, a fact that was acknowledged in 1789 when Secretary of War Henry Knox suggested that under the new Constitution the

United States treat the Indian nations as if they were foreign nations. The principle of purchase, which Knox advocated at the same time, was grounded on this basic change in United States willingness to accept the Indians' own evaluation of their political standing. This was, in effect, a renunciation of the claim of absolute sovereignty over the Indians' land, a claim so sweeping that, under it, the Indians could occupy the land only at the pleasure of the United States. The changes proposed by Knox recognized that the Indians' possession of the land gave them the right of soil, that is to say, the right to occupy the land as long as they wished to do so.[65]

A second point that needs to be emphasized is the influence of the British-Indian prewar treaty system on the context within which United States Indian policy was formulated and carried out after the war. Existing studies either do not deal with this at all or touch lightly on the prewar years as the background to United States efforts. In fact, the boundary line that had been established through British and Indian endeavors from 1763 to 1768 was a critical factor in the postwar years. It became the policy ideal for Indians on both sides of the Ohio, and in the case of the western Indians the 1768 boundary was one for which they were willing to fight. More than that, however, the 1768–75 transformation of the prewar treaty system into a mechanism for land transfer set a pattern that continued into the postwar years. United States Indian policy contributed to this tendency, at the same time that it struggled against the fragmentation of authority that had accompanied the transformation of the treaty system and that also continued into the postwar years.

The goals of United States Indian policy in the period immediately following the war were peace, a boundary, regulation of trade, and congressional preeminence in Indian affairs. The latter was by definition a domestic problem. Regulation of trade was made part of the domestically oriented Ordinance of 1786. This administrative ordinance superseded the arrangements that had been made in 1775. It established two departments of Indian affairs, the northern and the southern, and made the two department superintendents responsible for the issuing of trading licenses and the regulation of trade.[66] The emphasis here was on trade as a domestic concern, amenable to administrative controls. The domestic focus of United States officials can be seen even more clearly in their pursuit of the remaining goals of United States policy, peace with the Indians and the establishment of an Indian-white boundary.

Peace was, of course, a primary concern. In April 1783, before the final peace treaty was signed with Great Britain, the Continental Congress considered the matter. In May it authorized the secretary of war to notify the Indians of the situation in regard to Great Britain and of the United States desire to make peace with the Indians as well. By October of that year the desire for peace had become indissolubly linked with the boundary question, and that, in turn, was linked with the new country's desire for expansion. In the thinking of its policy-makers, the diplomatic had become the domestic, and that in spite of the fact that Great Britain and Spain were deeply involved in Indian relations. British officials had interfered with the congressional peace envoys by determining what Indians they could see and what subjects could be discussed,[67] but the congressional emphasis remained domestic. The following spring, while Spanish officials were entertaining Alexander McGillivray and his contingent of Creeks in Pensacola, Congress was considering a committee report on the southern Indians that concerned itself chiefly with the need of the southern states for land and the desirability of prevailing upon the southern Indians "to make such cessions of uncultivated land to the States they inhabit respectively as may be convenient to those nations and commensurate to the present and approaching necessities of those States."[68]

Horsman has detailed the influence of such individuals as Philip Schuyler, George Washington, James Duane, and Thomas Jefferson on the various reports and resolutions in which the Continental Congress embodied its Indian policy in the immediate postwar years. The first congressional recommendation for a specific boundary between Indian and white land north of the Ohio was suggested by Washington, who chose it solely on the basis of domestic considerations. Among other matters, he was concerned with the best location for the new states that were to be formed from the land New York had ceded to the confederation government. At the time that Washington wrote, Virginia had still not given up its claims to the same land, but that controversy was then well on the way to being settled. It is another indication of the domestic outlook of United States officials that the congressional resolution of 12 August 1783, and the proclamation of 22 September 1783, forbidding settlement on Indian land and prohibiting private land purchases from the Indians, were aimed more at Virginia than at the Indians. Before Virginia would give up its claims in favor of the confederation government, it wanted assurances that the land would in fact go to the nation, with the exception of its own military grants in the area, for which it wanted congressional approval.[69]

There is little to be added to Horsman's meticulous recounting of the steps and influences in early United States Indian policy beyond noting that much of it was an exercise on paper. Congress—on paper—said that peace with the Indians would be contingent upon war reparations in the form of land cessions. These were set out in six separate treaties at meetings with various Indian groups at various locations from October 1784 to January 1786 (see Table 13).

Table 13   North American Treaty System, 1783–86

Date	Participants	Place	Land Cession	Level of Authority
31 May 1783	Cherokee Georgia	Augusta	x	State
9 July 1783	Cherokee Joseph Martin et al.	Long Island of the Holston	x	Private
1 November 1783	Creek Georgia	Augusta	x	State
6 November 1783	Chickasaw Virginia	French Lick	x	State
1 June 1784	Creek Spain	Pensacola	–	National
23 June 1784	Alabama Spain	Mobile	–	National
23 June 1784	Chickasaw Spain	Mobile	–	National
14 July 1784	Choctaw Spain	Mobile	–	National
22 October 1784	Six Nations United States	Fort Stanwix	x	National
October 1784	Six Nations Pennsylvania	Fort Stanwix	x	State
21 January 1785	Wyandot Delaware Chippewa Ottawa United States	Fort McIntosh	x	National
10 June 1785	Cherokee "state" of Franklin	Dumplin Creek	x	Private— "state"

Table 13 (continued)   North American Treaty System, 1783–86

Date	Participants	Place	Land Cession	Level of Authority
28 June 1785	Oneida Tuscarora New York	Fort Herkimer	x	State
12 November 1785	Creek Georgia	Galphinton, Georgia	x	State
28 November 1785	Cherokee United States	Hopewell	x	National
3 January 1786	Choctaw United States	Hopewell	x	National
10 January 1786	Chickasaw United States	Hopewell	x	National
31 January 1786	Shawnee United States	Fort Finney	x	National
15 May 1786	Ottawa Chippewa Great Britain		x	National
3 August 1786	Cherokee "state" of Franklin	Coyatee	x	Private– "state"
3 November 1786	Creek Georgia	Shoulderbone	x	State

SOURCE: See Appendix A.

Four of the six treaties had to be renegotiated after Congress was forced to discard the purely domestic focus that had dictated the terms of the treaties. The treaties failed to achieve either peace or a new Indian-white boundary. Instead of setting the conditions under which a magnanimous and victorious United States would grant peace to repentant Indians, as Congress intended, the treaties helped bring about a renewal of hostilities. Instead of securing war reparations grants that would—in the North—be co-terminus with the boundaries of the new states proposed in the Ordinance of 1784, or—in the South—be sufficiently "advantageous" to the adjoining states, the treaties angered the Indians without satisfying the whites.[70]

The Six Nations were pressured into a treaty on October 22, 1784, at Fort Stanwix, that denied their claims to any land west and south of the Ohio and reduced the amount of land remaining to them in New

York. It also ensured their continuing hostility, and drove the Mohawk leader, Joseph Brant, back to the British, although before the treaty negotiations began at Fort Stanwix he had said that he wanted to make friends with the Americans, since the British alliance had been so disastrous to his people. Friendship with the United States in the early postwar years would have been difficult for any Indian group, and much more for the Iroquois with their special sense of destiny and their claims to dominance in the entire area between the Great Lakes, the Mississippi, and the Ohio. When Captain Aaron Hill, a Mohawk leader, advanced these claims at the Stanwix negotiations, and then said that he spoke for the southern Indians as well, the U.S. commissioners promptly denied his right to do so. But in the treaty itself they seemed to recognize some kind of Iroquois suzerainty in the Ohio country, by forcing a renunciation of any Iroquois claim to land there. In these negotiations, the arrogance of the Iroquois was matched by the arrogance of the United States, and the resulting treaty helped to bring on ten more years of war.[71]

Since United States officials were not at all sure how far the League could make good on its sweeping claims, they also dealt with some of the western nations, and dealt on the basis of the conquest theory. These western treaties were not negotiated so much as simply imposed on those Indians who came to the treaty grounds. Reparations grants were exacted from the Wyandots, Delawares, Chippewas, and Ottawas at a council at Fort McIntosh in the Ohio country and peace was "granted" to them on 21 January 1785. The process was repeated with the Shawnees at Fort Finney in the Ohio country on 31 January 1786. None of the Wabash River Indians—the Miamis, Piankeshaws, or Weas— showed up for this meeting although the reparations grant exacted from the Shawnees extended to the Wabash River.[72] Since the United States could neither take possession of the land nor go to war if the Indians refused a grant of peace on such terms, the proceedings were simply a part of the paper policy that Congress was conducting at this period.

In the South, too, United States policy was one part actual and nine parts intentional. The paper prescription for peace in the South, as in the North, rested on the explicit assumption that the Indians could have no reasonable cause for complaint at the demand for reparations grants of land since:

They were themselves aggressors in the war, without even a pretence of provocation, and the barbarities which attend their mode of war fare are too shocking and of too great notoriety to be here recited. These circumstances are sufficient to manifest the obligation they are under to make atonement for their outrages, and a reasonable compensation for the expences and alarms to which they have exposed their unoffending neighbours, and they possess no other means to do this act of justice than by a compliance with the proposed terms.[73]

The peace prescription further assumed that the Indians ought to be grateful that the United States did not expel them from the land entirely. Instead they were only being asked to give up some of their "uncultivated land" for the needs of the southern states that, like the other states, were pledged for the payment of the public debt and were under obligations to their own military veterans. Room also had to be found for the population of the United States since it was growing rapidly both by natural increase and by emigration from abroad.[74]

These congressional proposals were seen by their authors as eminently reasonable, satisfying not only the claims of justice but of "Generosity, Clemency and Mercy," with the further merit of meeting the needs of a growing nation.[75] But the southern states were not satisfied. North Carolina and Virginia protested the "peace treaty" agreements with the Cherokees (28 November 1785), and with the Chickasaws (10 November 1786), and Georgia proceeded on an independent course with the Cherokees and the Creeks. Nor were the Indians grateful, or even resigned. The Cherokees at the 1785 negotiations informed the United States commissioners that they wanted "Kentucky" returned to them since they had never sold it to Colonel Henderson and his associates. They asked that the Indian-white boundary reflect that fact. When told that it was too late to do anything about the sale since the principals involved, both Indian and white, were no longer alive and the land was being settled, the Cherokees added that to their store of grievances. The Chickasaws and the Choctaws were also unhappy. Following their treaties with the Americans on 3 and 10 January 1786, they sent delegations to the Spanish to assure them that the American treaties meant nothing since the Indians who had signed them had no authority to cede land or make any other binding agreements. They had only gone to the meeting with the Americans to find out about trade. One Choctaw leader said frainkly that since he was down to his last shirt *(ya me á hallo á la última camisa)*, he had sent representatives to the meeting to see if the Americans would offer a larger trade on better terms than the Spanish had.[76]

As for the Creek Indians, the United States commissioners could not get enough of them to come to a meeting to justify a peace treaty on any terms. Instead, while the commissioners were in the South making treaty arrangements during the summer and fall of 1785, Alexander McGillivray was transmitting to the Spanish the messages that were sent to him by United States and Georgia officials. Throughout this period McGillivray functioned as a channel of information to the Spanish regarding the intentions of the United States. Since the Spanish opposed American expansion and wanted to exclude American trade from any territory claimed by Spain on the grounds that it was contraband, the situation lent itself to the manipulation in which McGillivray excelled.[77]

In early November 1785, about the time the United States commissioners were hoping McGillivray would appear with a large Creek contingent for a meeting with them in Georgia, McGillivray was writing to the Spanish about American ambitions. In a letter to Arturo O'Neill, Spanish governor at Pensacola, McGillivray noted the good effect that the British were having north of the Ohio. By retaining the posts at Niagara and elsewhere along the Great Lakes, by strengthening the garrisons and supplying the Indians, the British had made possible the continuation of the confederation of Indians that had fought against the Americans in the war. McGillivray pointed out that the same could be true in the South. If the Spanish would continue to supply the Indians, as they were doing, the Indians would be able to hold together their wartime confederation and would be a permanent check on American ambitions to possess all the land in the West.[78]

McGillivray's letter summarized the diplomatic factors that were involved in the situation that the United States was trying to handle as a domestic problem, and suggests as well some reasons for United States failure. With alternative patrons to turn to, both North and South, there was no reason for the Indians to acquiesce in the demand that they provide the means for the payment of United States war debts and for further territorial expansion that could only be at their expense. Still, some Indians, both North and South, did sign treaties which did just that, and thus lent justification to subsequent United States attempts to dispose of the land. In most cases the Indians were probably not authorized to sign the treaties. Other Indians said they were not. But treaties were negotiated anyway, as when a small group of Creeks met with Georgia officials in November 1785 after United States officials had given up hope of a Creek representation that would justify negotiations. The small group of Creeks and the Georgia officials signed a treaty that confirmed and extended an earlier cession of land to Georgia.[79]

The incident illustrates a decisive factor in the failure of United States policy and of Indian policy as well. The United States was only one treaty-making party in the field, and not the most active one. Of the twenty-one treaties listed in table 13 for the period 1783-86, the United States negotiated six, less than one-third. Georgia, by itself, negotiated four of the treaties, while three other states accounted for three more, making a total of seven state-level treaties. Private individuals, on their own or claiming the authority of a state, negotiated three treaties; Great Britain, one; and Spain, four. When it is considered that the Indian signers of many of the treaties probably represented only small factions in their nations, some idea can be gained of the political chaos of those years.

Nowhere along the seaboard or in the backcountry on either side of the Ohio River was there a clear-cut center of authority, white or red. There was no power great enough or with enough prestige to impose a system of stable relationships or to persuade groups into voluntary associations that could be counted on from one day to the next. The resulting flux frayed the diplomacy of sovereign groups to a thousand ragged ends. Councils were held, speeches made, terms offered, treaties signed, by individuals trying to stave off personal disaster, or by small groups trying to turn confusion to their own ends. For the scholar of the period this means that it is extraordinarily difficult to tell which people were pursuing the considered policies of a sovereign entity and which were simply striking out on their own. What the documents do clearly convey is a picture of the continued degradation of the treaty system between Indians and whites.

The degradation had begun before the war. What had been a set of formal relationships between separate peoples, embodying the arrangements by which they agreed to live near but not with each other, had by 1775 become almost exclusively a means of land transfer. Further, after 1770, there had been a rapid decline in the level of the authority of those entering into treaty agreements so that in some instances, as has been discussed, private individuals had procured or conveyed thousands of acres of land. The prewar treaty system, in its transformed and degraded state had, in effect, marked out the areas for postwar conflict: Kentucky, Tennessee, the backcountry of Georgia and North Carolina, the upper Ohio Valley. Moreover, the conflicts were not just between Indians and whites. They were also between whites (as in the struggles to form the separate state of Franklin) and between Indians (as in the struggles to be free of Iroquois domination). These conflicts fed into one another and became part of the large-scale, authority-less contention that created the treaty system of 1783–86.

By 1786 the tensions and contradictions within this system were too great to be contained in peace. War broke out again in the South where the Creeks were determined to defend the boundary that had been defined in the joint Creek-Cherokee-Georgia Treaty of 1773. As required under the terms of the Treaty of Pensacola of 1 June 1784, McGillivray notified Spanish officials of the outbreak of hostilities, and they in turn sent guns and supplies to the Creeks for their struggle.[80]

Hostilities were also increasing north of the Ohio. On the assumption that the treaties of Forts Stanwix, McIntosh, and Finney were valid, the Continental Congress had, in the Land Ordinance of 1785, authorized the survey of land north of the river. The Indians resisted the surveys and demanded a renegotiation of the treaties which, they said, were wholly invalid. In the words of the Confederated Council of the United Indian Nations, "we hold it indispensably necessary that any cession of our lands should be made in the most public manner, and by the united voice of the confederacy; holding all partial treaties as void and of no effect."[81]

It is not clear whether or to what extent the British were involved in the writing of this declaration. What is clear is that by 1786 the United States attempt to treat Indian affairs as a domestic problem and the Indians themselves as unwelcome guests on their own land was a total failure. That failure was compounded by the collapse of the treaty system through which Indian relations were customarily handled. The next ten years would see a change in United States attitude, and a restoration of the treaty system to the highest level of white authority. By then, however, warfare in North America and Europe had so sapped the Indians' strength and narrowed the choices open to them that they were reduced to colonial status in the land that had once been theirs.

Creation of a Colonial Treaty System 1787-96

The major events of the years 1787–96 are too well known to need detailed exposition here. The years in which a colonial treaty system was created in eastern North America were also years of renewed warfare in Europe and of the establishment of constitutional government in the United States. The complex of events leading to these results on either side of the Atlantic was in turn linked to the creation of the colonial treaty system in which North American Indians east of the Mississippi lost their freedom to maneuver and thus their ability to secure favorable terms as they bargained with the new United States. The Indians were, however, able to force an acknowledgment of their prior rights in the land that was sought so eagerly by white Americans, and to secure for themselves a toehold in the legal system of the United States that eventually gave them a wholly unique position in American society, both in relation to the federal government and to other members of the society. In this they were helped by advocates at the highest levels of United States government who—for whatever reasons—were unwilling to let the American experiment in nationhood rest on outright conquest and exploitation of those peoples who were the first-comers to the continent.

Warfare in Europe

North America, in the period from 1787 to 1796, sank to a position of unimportance in the thinking of European policymakers. No longer was the North American continent one of the centers for international and imperial struggles as it had been during the Seven Years War and the Wars of the Austrian and Spanish Successions. As events in France moved toward the Revolution (1789), the execution of Louis XVI (1793), and the French declaration of war on Great Britain (1793),

North America and its problems returned to the periphery of the world that most concerned leaders in London and Madrid. The rise of a militant revolutionary government in France, proclaiming its willingness to help any people anywhere throw off the chains of monarchy, effectively secured the attention of other governments in Europe and kept it to the virtual exclusion of other concerns.

After 1793, both Spain and Great Britain engaged in limited holding actions in North America. Local officials such as Britain's Lord Dorchester in Canada or Spain's Baron de Carondelet in Louisiana might give a stir to the stew of international intrigue that simmered in all the border areas where authority was not established and loyalties were unsure, but their initiatives were their own. They could not count on the backing of home governments that were far more concerned with the ramifications of events in France and with the difficult alliance of Great Britain, Spain, and Holland, than with the ramifications of events in the Maumee River Valley or the difficult alliance of Creeks, Choctaws, and other southern Indians. When Lord Dorchester overstepped the bounds of local initiative in an inflammatory speech to the northern Indians in early 1794, he got so little official support that he felt compelled to offer his resignation. As for Carondelet's efforts to secure Spanish territorial claims through an alliance of southern Indians under Spanish control, these were negated by Spanish home officials who, in 1795, conceded United States territorial claims as far as the thirty-first parallel. Carondelet, Dorchester, the American Indian nations, and the new United States were all bit players in the central drama of the 1790s that was, for Europeans, again preeminently a European affair.[1]

This being so, many events in North America during this period are like sketches for plays that were never produced. British and Spanish agents from field level to governor's palace busied themselves arranging a series of potentialities that could only be exploited if taken up by the authorities at home. Those authorities were the only possible producers for plays at the level of multilateral alliances, independent nation-states, and international wars. But Europe was busy with other matters, and the diplomatic potentialities of North American intrigue flattened out into squabbles for personal advantage. Thus it was that the Cumberland-Franklin-Kentucky intrigues of the late 1780s, and the renewed Kentucky intrigues of the early 1790s caused more excitement in New Orleans and Philadelphia than they did in Madrid. Since Madrid alone had the power to make General James Wilkinson president of an independent Kentucky allied to Spain, rather than an obscure adventurer scrambling for Spanish gold, this lack of enthusiasm was fatal.[2]

In a different locale, the same damper was put on the hopes of Canadian officials and of the Allen brothers, Levi and Ethan, for what might be made of Vermont while it was still separate from the United States. British officials were more concerned with European affairs. The focus of their concerns can be seen in their behavior in 1790 when it appeared that war between Spain and Great Britain would break out at any moment (the Nootka Sound controversy). As a hedge against the dangers in this eventuality, the British turned their attention briefly to some diplomatic outposts. They gave vague encouragement to the Vermont independence movement on the north flank of the United States and to William Bowles's "nation" of Muscogee on the south flank. They also, however, opened talks with Gouverneur Morris, George Washington's special diplomatic agent in London, with whom, until then, they had refused to talk. When the diplomatic crisis with Spain was over, the British withdrew support from Vermont and Muscogee and broke off talks with the United States. With the European situation in hand, the outposts could be left to local officials until European developments made them of possible importance again in the European frame of reference.[3]

William Bowles's attempt at nation-making is another reminder of the fragmentation of authority that had transformed the North American treaty system during the period of this study. As head of the "nation" of Muscogee, Bowles negotiated "treaty" agreements with nearby Creek Indians who were disgruntled with the leadership of Alexander McGillivray and were also on the lookout for an alternative source of European supplies. The firm of Panton, Leslie and Company, which had secured from the Spanish government the monopoly of the Creek Indian trade, was not universally loved among the Creeks. Moreover, if war did come between Great Britain and Spain and cut off Panton's source of supplies or cause the Spanish to revoke Panton's monopoly, it would be well to have another source. William Bowles promised such a source to the Creeks on the basis of his connections in the British West Indies and in England.[4]

Such bargain agreements were far removed from full-dress diplomatic negotiations in Paris or at Johnson Hall or in Augusta. They were as far removed from usual diplomacy as was William Bowles's little fleet of Muscogeean ships from the British Royal Navy. Even farther removed and at a still lower level of authority was Elijah Clarke's Trans-Oconee Republic, established in May 1794 on Creek land in what is now Greene County, Georgia, and disbanded four months later. Clarke held a commission from Citizen Edmond C. Genet, revolutionary

France's first minister to the United States, and not only claimed the protection of the French Republic but full sovereign rights for Trans-Oconee as well, including the right to negotiate treaties. With this declaration, the sovereign power through which alone treaties had any meaning was reduced to the ultimate absurdity of a handful of armed men in the North American backcountry.[5]

Absurd as it was, however, Trans-Oconee was simply an extreme instance of the tendencies that had created the chaos of the preceding years. A handful of armed men had "negotiated" the August 1786 land-cession treaty between the "state" of Franklin and the Cherokees, after first attacking the Cherokee town of Coyatee, killing two townsmen, and burning the council house.[6] Franklin, Trans-Oconee, Muscogee, an independent Vermont, the Kentucky intrigues, were all expressions of conditions in which the treaty system of independent sovereign entities had almost no meaning. If Great Britain or Spain had found it expedient to lend full support to any of these movements, or to concurrent Indian drives toward confederation and unified military action, the movements might have attained the diplomatic significance they sought. With the attention of Great Britain and Spain firmly fixed on Europe, all that the Spanish and British could spare for North America were some arms, some supplies, and a lot of advice.[7]

For the Indian nations of eastern North America this meant, of course, the reduction and eventual loss of the military and economic support they needed if they were to maintain their position vis-à-vis the United States. The fall of the Bastille led, in effect, to the fall of the Indian nations. Because of events in France, the major victories of the northern Indians over American troops led by Josiah Harmar (1790) and Arthur St. Clair (1791), did not secure them the support that military success might otherwise have done. The northern Indians implored British aid after their defeat at Fallen Timbers by troops under Anthony Wayne (1794), and were turned away from Fort Miamis by a British commander well aware of his precarious position on American soil and of the fact that he could not risk a war with the United States while Great Britain was engaged in a war with France.[8]

Similarly, in the South, lack of consistent Spanish support for the southern Indians was a result of Spanish reluctance to force the issue of their differences with the United States when more serious differences closer to home were coming to a head. Spanish support for the southern Indians was less consistent than British support for the northern Indians in the years after 1786. Consequently, the southern Indians were more inclined than the northern to hedge the future by negotiating with both the United States and Spain. The position of the southern Indians was put pointedly in 1787 by Choctaw leader Franchimistabe, who said that he was standing between Spain and the United States "stretching my arms to the south and the north to shake hands with both nations, waiting to see which one will be the first to tell the truth."[9]

So the situation seemed to the Indians, whose supplies might depend on policy decisions based on events in Europe that had no apparent connection with their affairs. When Alexander McGillivray realized that the Spanish would not back the Creeks to the extent necessary for an effective defense of the boundary line of 1773, he turned to the Americans to see what accommodation could be worked out with them. The resulting Treaty of New York (1790) undermined his reputation among the militant Creeks and robbed his leadership of much of its effectiveness. A subsequent rapprochement with Spanish authorities in New Orleans did little to restore McGillivray to his former position, and he died (February 1793) before Carondelet's general congress of southern Indians was held at Nogales, a congress that could have given McGillivray a chance to compete for the leadership of a confederation of southern Indians.[10]

Even had McGillivray lived, however, and succeeded in establishing the broad-based leadership that had been his dream, he would have seen the Southern Indian Confederation reduced to impotence by the Treaty of San Lorenzo (1795). Spain's withdrawal from active contention in eastern North America meant that the southern Indians had no place to turn for support or supplies except the United States. Britain had been eliminated as an effective alternative patron or ally by the provisions of Jay's Treaty (1794), and the defeat of the northern Indians at Fallen Timbers the same year had temporarily halted the attempts at united action by northern and southern Indians. For fifteen more years Spain and Great Britain were to be preoccupied by France, a circumstance that aided the new United States as much as it damaged the American Indian nations.[11]

The New United States

No period in American history has been more thoroughly studied than the late 1780s to the mid-1790s when the federal constitution was

adopted and a beginning was made toward an effective national government. There is scarcely an aspect of the proceedings that has not been
the subject of a scholarly monograph as subsequent generations have
sought to understand how the new American nation came into being
and why it developed the way that it did. So far as the new nation's
relations with American Indians are concerned, it remains only to emphasize what has been pointed out by others, that the whole
experiment in nation-making rested on the presumption that land could
be acquired for development and expansion and that most of that land
belonged to the American Indians.

A straightforward account of the various steps by which the United
States acquired title to the public domain can be found in many
sources.[12] Here it is only necessary to emphasize two aspects of the
process. The first is the fact that federal Indian policy was, from the
beginning, partly a product of local political struggles over land, as state
after state laid down the conditions under which it would give up to the
federal government its claims to the western (Indian) lands that became
the national domain. The second is the pot-of-gold reputation that land
had in this period. A straightforward recital of state cessions and federal ordinances does not adequately explain what happened, since it does
not take into account the emotional undercurrents of the process of
acquisition. In the thinking of early American policymakers, land had
an almost mystic significance that put it at the heart of the glorious
future that they foresaw for the new United States. Not the least of the
attractive qualities of such a resource was its versatility. It could be par-
celed out in sizes from a small freehold to state-size domains. It could
be sold for public revenues. It could be taxed. It could be granted to
discontented veterans of the war for independence. It could be made to
turn a profit simply by being held for a time and resold to later comers.
Finally, it could be farmed by the independent small-holders who were
the ideal citizens of early American policymakers—many of whom lived
on plantations or in the cities.[13]

United States policy from 1787 to 1796 can scarcely be understood
if the emotional significance of land to American policymakers is left
out of the account. Land as potential, land as the glorious future, was
the moving force behind legislative acts that bore little relation to
actual conditions. What the vast potential of the China market would
be to the imagination of future American policymakers and entrepreneurs, the vast potential of the North American interior was to the
policymakers and entrepreneurs of the early days of the Republic. In

each case, the imaginings were closer to desire than to reality. So the Confederation Congress passed the Northwest Ordinance of 1787 providing in detail for the government of a territory it could not govern. It could not even send its representatives into the territory without the permission of the British and of the Indians who occupied and controlled the ground.[14]

An indication of how far removed was the myth of land from the reality of land in the years under study can be seen in the amounts of land actually sold, and the revenue actually generated. In September and October 1787 occurred the first (and only) public sale of land in the Northwest Territory under the Ordinance of 1785. Fewer than one-third of the twenty-seven townships offered for sale were disposed of to buyers, and the average bid worked out to be less than $1.25 an acre. In July 1788 Congress authorized additional public sales in the seven ranges of townships that had been surveyed north of the Ohio (next to the western boundary of Pennsylvania), but there were no buyers. Large blocks of land were disposed of by Congress to the Ohio Company of Associates (July 1787), and to John Cleve Symmes (October 1788), but in 1792 both purchasers had to reduce the amount actually bought because sales were lagging badly. The Ohio Associates reduced their purchase from 1.5 to 1.1 million acres, and Symmes from 1 million to a little more than 100 thousand acres.[15]

As for the revenue generated by what was generally presumed to be the source of national treasure as well as national greatness, the figures naturally reflect the lagging sales. The gross receipts of the federal government from 4 March 1789 to 31 December 1792, broken down by categories such as customs duties, loans, etc., do not show *any* income from public lands. For the succeeding four years, ending 31 December 1796, the receipts from public lands were $4,836, a little more than one-third the income generated from postage for the same period. Customs receipts were the primary source of revenue for the federal government during this period. As a proportion of total receipts for 1792 to 1796, import duties accounted for 63 percent, and public lands for .01 percent. Not until after 1800 and the extension of credit for the purchase of public land did receipts for such land rise above a fraction of a percent of total government receipts (2 percent in the period from 1800 to 1804) and finally begin to assume any importance in the national economy.[16]

These myths regarding land were of great consequence to the American Indian nations. It was the dream of what land might be and not the reality of what it was that provided the driving force behind the various moves of the state and central governments to acquire land from the Indians immediately following the War for Independence. Their efforts continued into the period from 1787 to 1796, with this significant change, that the late-confederation and constitutional governments insisted ever more strongly that only the central government had the right to acquire Indian lands, or at least that any other acquisition must be with United States approval. During this period also, various acts and resolutions regarding Indian affairs were passed by Congress, and proclamations issued, all designed to strengthen the position of the federal government in relation to the states and to reassure the Indians of the government's good intentions. Like the various documents and acts regarding land, these acts should be seen not as descriptions of reality or what the federal government was able to do. Rather, they too were expressions of an American vision of the future, and of the way that things ought to be.

In September 1783 Congress issued a proclamation warning all intruders on Cherokee lands to leave immediately and in the future to abide by the federally negotiated Treaty of Hopewell (November 1785) which had established a boundary between white and Cherokee land. The proclamation was wholly ineffective except as a statement of good intent. Continuing in this line, the new Constitutional Congress in July 1790 passed the first of four Trade and Intercourse Acts of the decade of the nineties: 1790, 1793, 1796, and 1799. The purpose of the four bills was to put Indian relations firmly in the domain of the federal government. This was to be done through federal control of land acquisition, and federal regulation of trade, the liquor traffic, and the punishment of Indian-related crime. Beginning in 1793, the president was also authorized to disburse funds for education and technical aid for the Indians.[17]

Besides being statements of what federal policymakers thought ought to be done in Indian affairs, the Trade and Intercourse Acts were also acknowledgments in extensive detail of the Indians' right to peaceable possession of their land. The limits of this land would continue to be a matter for contention between the federal government and the states, and between the federal government and the Indians, but the principle of peaceable possession was here incorporated in statutes at the highest level possible in the new United States. This was far removed from the position held by United States officials from 1783 through 1786 that the Indians had forfeited any rights to their land through their conduct in the war, and that their possession was at the pleasure of the United States.

It was Indian resistance, of course, that had forced the reexamination and change of the earlier policy based on conquest. The effectiveness of Indian resistance was helped by the presence of Spain and Great Britain as alternative patrons. It was also helped by the fact that there were ideals within the American system of values that could be called upon by U.S. leaders to justify what might otherwise seem a humiliating policy turnabout. The ideals found expression after 1786 in the often-quoted section of the Northwest Ordinance of 1787 to the effect that the "utmost good faith" was to be shown to the Indians, and that their lands and property were never to be taken from them "without their consent."[18]

Continuing Indian resistance and the continued presence of Spain and Great Britain on soil claimed by the American nation created conditions in which ideals could justify the practical retreat of practical men, and at the same time open different possibilities for the future. In 1787, Henry Knox, Revolutionary War veteran and secretary of war under both the confederation and constitutional governments, called for an abandonment of the policy based on conquest in favor of purchasing land from the Indians. The practical men in the Confederation Congress of 1788 agreed with Knox to the extent of authorizing the renegotiation of the three treaties signed with Indians north of the Ohio in the 1784 to 1786 period, and payment for the land that had been "acquired" in those treaties under the right-of-conquest principle.[19]

After the new government was organized under the Constitution, Knox continued his campaign. He pointed out that authorization for the renegotiation of the treaties with the northern Indians was, in effect, congressional agreement with the view that had been expressed by the confederated Indians in their statement of 1786 "that they were the only rightful proprietors of the soil." Knox urged the new Congress:

> The principle of the Indian right to the lands they possess being thus conceded, the dignity and interest of the nation will be advanced by making it the basis of the future administration of justice toward the Indian tribes.[20]

The ideals that should guide United States policy were, in Knox's thinking, grounded in nature itself, and to go against them would be a "gross violation of the fundamental laws of nature, and of that distributive justice which is the glory of a nation."[21] Here Knox touched on one of the central concerns of the eighteenth century: how to relate the "laws of nature" to the practice of nations. Nature was conceived of not as an arena in which only the "fit" would survive but as the ultimate source of the ideals of justice and harmony. For the United States to achieve this just and harmonious balance in its relations with the Indians, several things were necessary. First, treaties of peace had to be signed and, on the part of the United States, observed "with the most rigid justice."[22] Second, boundary agreements had to be made, since disputes over boundaries were the primary causes of Indian wars. Further, the boundaries had to be worked out by the Indians and the federal government, not the state governments. In the final analysis, it was the federal government that had to see that the boundaries were observed. Finally:

> The independent nations and tribes of Indians ought to be considered as foreign nations, not as the subjects of any particular State. Each individual State, indeed, will retain the right of pre-emption of all land within its limits, which will not be abridged, but the general sovereignty must possess the right of making all treaties, on the execution or violation of which depend peace or war.[23]

In his study of the origins and effects of white views of American Indians, Robert F. Berkhofer, Jr., concludes that this statement of Knox's should be taken only as an assertion of federal supremacy in Indian relations, and that the contemporary domestic context of state versus federal governments is what gives the statement its meaning.[24] Certainly, Knox did have the domestic context in mind when he advocated that American Indian groups be "considered as foreign nations." He could, however, have made his case for federal supremacy without advocating that particular status for the Indians. It was because Knox also had in mind the diplomatic context of relations with the Indians that foreign nations came into the discussion.

In 1789, when Knox made his statement, the general impression conveyed by those European powers who paid any attention to the United States was that the new nation was of negligible importance in the affairs of the world and would probably not last very long. Great Britain still occupied the Northwest posts, and had not yet even sent a minister to represent its interests in the United States or to receive United States protests. Spain continued to refuse the navigation rights on the Mississippi that the United States had supposedly won in the war. Spain also had formal treaties of alliance and friendship with some of the southern Indian nations, and had made territorial guarantees of an extent not known by United States officials. Part of the context for Knox's statement of 1789 was this diplomatic situation. His advocacy of foreign-nation treatment for the Indians was immediately preceded by a discussion of the policy that Spain was following in the South. If the southern Indians, said Knox, perceived the United States as a threat, they would submerge their differences "and an union as firm as the six Northern nations may be formed by the Southern tribes."[25]

Knox pointed out that Spain would surely encourage such a union in order to prevent United States expansion. He then noted that Alexander McGillivray claimed a treaty guarantee of Creek lands on the part of Spain, and added that, however that might be, it was certain that Spain "actually claims a considerable part of the territory ceded by Great Britain to the United States."[26]

In 1789 it was impossible to separate the diplomatic aspects of United States relations with the Indians from the domestic aspects. Events or policies in one sphere affected events and policies in the other in complex ways that undid attempts to categorize them as this type or that and treat them accordingly. The United States attempt to treat Indian relations as a wholly domestic affair had ended in total failure. Knox was attempting to retreat from that position with honor and to establish different guidelines for the future. He had, of necessity, to consider federal relations with the states and the effect of these on Indian relations, but he had also to consider the relations of Indian nations with foreign nations and to concede the existence of the sphere in which those took place.

Knox had no choice, and neither did the new United States. In 1789 the American Indian nations were politically independent and were accustomed to handling their own relations with other groups, whether European, American, or Indian. So long as they had support or the hope of support from powers beyond the control of the United States, they continued to act in ways that forced the United States to deal with them in a diplomatic framework, "as foreign nations." The means of treating with them ran the full range from peaceful negotiations in which each party sought advantage, through the various combinations of persuasion and coercion, to the outright use of force—as with any nations. There were, however, differences from other nations, even small, militarily weak nations, and it was the presence of those differences and the difficulty even of defining them within a framework of

nascent nationalism that made Indian relations synonymous with per-
plexity.

A glimpse of some of the difficulties can be seen in Henry Knox's
attempts in 1789 to find a way back from the dead end of violence. In
the two short paragraphs that have been quoted here, Knox put together an extraordinary mix of jurisdictional prerogatives for the states, the
federal government, and the Indians. Since this became the formula
with which federal officials tried to solve the problems of relations with
the Indians, it is worth looking more closely at Knox's suggestions.
Central to this examination is the concept of sovereignty that is
implied.

Knox spoke as a representative of the United States, the "general
sovereignty" of his proposal. In the hierarchical array of powers that he
proposed, the United States stood at the top. As such, it had the final
decision on peace and war, hence on the treaties that might determine
which would be the outcome. But this was in relation to the states, not
to the Indians. They, being independent, could not be forced to treat
only with the United States and were, in fact, treating with both
Spanish and British officials, as Knox well knew. They were exercising
one of the prerogatives of sovereignty as it was understood in the
eighteenth century.

Like other top officials, Knox had to deal on practical grounds with
the fact of the Indians' behavior, while ignoring the sovereignty that
such behavior asserted. Thus, in Knox's words, the Indian nations were
"independent" (irrefutable fact), but the United States was to have the
sole right of treaty negotiation with them (unenforceable theory). The
Indians had a right to the land (they possessed it), but they were to give
it up on terms that would help solve the internal problems of the
United States (an ingenious but, in 1789, still unenforceable theory).
As a way out of the impasse, Knox proposed a kind of layering of
sovereign powers (which took account of the facts), with specified and
limited land rights (which fit the theories). First, the Indians were to be
recognized as independent, and treated as foreign nations. Second, on
the key issue of land, the Indians were to have possessory rights, the
states to have preemption rights, and the federal government was to
have the sole right of acquisition. It was on the face of it an impossible
mix, and, in fact, it proved to be quite as unsatisfactory as its appearance promised.

In this muddle of competing jurisdictions, however, Knox had
spoken to the central difference between American Indian nations and

other foreign nations. The Indians were *resident* "foreign" nations. They had no homeland across the ocean to which they might withdraw in case of need or defeat. The North American continent was their homeland. It was a problem for which the nationalism of a new country had no solution. With its exclusive claims to sovereignty and territorial control, nationalism did not even provide a vocabulary suitable for discussion of the problem. There was no conceptual category for resident "foreigners" who did not think of themselves as clients of the United States, much less as dependents, and who showed no signs of wanting to become a part of the new American nation.

How all of this worked out in practice can be seen by looking at what was actually done by the United States in the years from 1787 to 1796, rather than at what was said by American officials—interesting though such statements are as expressions of opinion and intent. The United States had, in effect, three separate Indian policies during those years, one for the South, one for the Northwest, and one for the Northeast. The fact is not as significant as it might be under other circumstances, since by 1796 the outcome was the same in all three areas of endeavor. This, however, was less the result of American efforts than of events in Europe.

What makes the separate policies of interest here is that they reflect the continuing influence of two factors emphasized in this study: British-Indian policies in the years 1763 to 1775, and the Indian setting. United States officials did not set out to treat different Indian groups differently. Their policy statements indicate a desire to establish a uniform policy at the federal level, and a belief that they were doing so. Perhaps this has helped to mislead scholars into accepting uniformity as the basic framework for studies of United States Indian policy. In fact, the adjustments that officials had to make to the forces of circumstance meant that until 1796 three different policies were pursued, and these different policies corresponded to the strength and cohesion of the Indians in the three sections of the country that have been mentioned. The three geographical sections corresponded, in turn, to the major political groupings of Indians during this period—groupings that were formed, for reasons that have been shown, during the period of British administration of the backcountry.

In the South, where Indian resistance was more fragmented than it was north of the Ohio, there was a gradual strengthening of federal authority. Some of the reasons for the fragmentation of southern Indian efforts have been explored in this study, and the inconsistency of

Spanish support has been pointed out. Added to these was the fact that, in this period, the Indians in the South were still at the tremendous disadvantage imposed on them by the breakdown and degradation of the treaty system of 1763-75. They could not point, as the northern Indians did, time and again, to one line—the Ohio—and say, thus far and no farther.[27] The hodgepodge of multilevel "treaties" before, during, and after the war had put organized western counties and incipient western states on the southern Indians' side of the Ohio. (Kentucky was admitted to the Union in 1792, Tennessee in 1796.) Further, the southern states' claims to western land were such as to keep those states deeply involved in Indian affairs.

Virginia made an early cession to the central government of the state's claims to western lands. The cession, which was accepted by Congress in 1784, did not include any land south of the Ohio. Specifically, it did not include the area that later became Kentucky. Georgia, in 1788, offered to cede part of its western land-claims, but the offer was refused by the Confederation Congress on the grounds of the distance of the land from the rest of the settled portions of the country. South Carolina had only a small claim to cede, and did so in 1787. North Carolina, after first making and then withdrawing an offer of cession in 1784, made a second offer five years later, which was accepted by Congress in 1790.

North Carolina's was thus the only substantial cession of state claims to western lands south of the Ohio from 1787 to 1796, and a closer look at that cession will show that even it was enmeshed in Indian affairs. In a report made in November 1791, Secretary of State Thomas Jefferson estimated the amount of North Carolina's cession at approximately 7.5 million acres, figuring only that part of the land lying outside the Cherokee and Chickasaw boundaries as defined in the United States-Indian treaties of Hopewell (November 1785, Cherokees; January 1786, Chickasaws), and Holston (July 1791, Cherokees). Of this 7.5 million, only 300 thousand acres of arable land had not already been granted by North Carolina for military bounties or under other legislative provisions, and those 300 thousand acres had been acquired from the Cherokees only four months earlier in the Treaty of Holston. Jefferson also estimated that the cession was actually considerably larger than the 7.5 million acres of non-Indian land, since North Carolina had also made some 2.2 million acres of military and other grants on land still belonging to the Indians.[28] Instead of getting from North Carolina a large disposable addition to the public domain, the federal government got instead all the problems that might be expected from the state's illegal grants of 2.2 million acres of Indian land.

What was most significant for the future was that, by the cession, these problems became *federal,* not state, problems; the fact that the grantees, the state, and the Indians would all be pressing the federal government for a solution strengthened the claim of federal primacy in Indian affairs and helped eventually to make it so. The method evolved by central authorities to handle the pressures generated by the situation south of the Ohio, where three states, one European nation, four major Indian groups, and the federal government were all competing for sovereignty and land rights, was to avoid outright confrontation with any one group in competition with the central government, and to play for time. Throughout this period the method worked well enough to keep hostilities on a small scale and to confirm the practice of looking to the federal government for a solution to the many problems that southern whites and southern Indians posed for each other.[29]

Contributing to the success of the federal government's cautious approach was the acquisition of two crucial tracts of Indian land. In the July 1791 Cherokee–United States Treaty of Holston mentioned by Jefferson, the United States acquired land in western North Carolina and eastern Tennessee that could easily have been one of the flashpoints for a general outbreak of hostilities. The cession included the junction of the Holston and French Broad rivers (present Knoxville), and embraced much of the central sections of those two rivers as well as such tributaries as the Nolichucky and a portion of the Clinch River. So far as recurrent tensions and hostilities were concerned, the area had for almost thirty years been the Rhineland of the American backcountry. Securing the cession from the Cherokees gave federal officials a respite from white pressure, and opened the possibility of thwarting—at least temporarily—the expansionary desires of whites in other areas.[30]

The other crucial tract of land was acquired by the United States from the Creek Indians in the August 1790 Treaty of New York. This acquisition, which lay in a vast inverted "L" around the settled portions of Georgia, defused the explosive situation that the state of Georgia had been creating since the war's end through unilateral acquisition of land from Creeks not authorized to negotiate. The circumstances that led Alexander McGillivray to negotiate with United States authorities have already been mentioned. For the new country, the 1790 Treaty of New York was a signal achievement, combining as it did both diplomatic and domestic success. Through the treaty, McGillivray was detached from his Spanish connection, which gave the United States a point against Spain. The detachment turned out to be only temporary, but it was long enough to undermine McGillivray's credibility among militant Creeks who had been following him in his defense of the 1773 British boundary line in Georgia—another diplomatic point for the United States, this one against the Creeks. Finally, expansionary pressure in Georgia could now be released safely into the hundreds of thousands of acres acquired in the treaty, acres that conveniently adjoined the settled areas. This was a domestic triumph of great importance for the government's Indian policy.[31]

It is not too much to say that the 1790 Creek-United States Treaty of New York and the 1795 Spanish-United States Treaty of San Lorenzo were the most important factors in making the central government of the United States—not Spain, not the Creek Confederacy, not an independent Kentucky allied with Spain, and not a recalcitrant Georgia—the dominant power south of the Ohio.

As for the Indians of the various southern groups securing dominance by acting under a unified command, as did the Indians north of the Ohio, there is little evidence that this was ever a possibility. The claim made by Alexander McGillivray in the Declaration of 1785, that he was authorized to speak for the Cherokees and Chickasaws as well as for the Creeks, is at least open to question for reasons already given. When the Spanish governor of New Orleans, baron de Carondelet, attempted to put together an effective Indian alliance under Spanish patronage in the early 1790s, he did not find the Indians looking naturally to the Creeks for leadership. The location chosen for the grand-alliance congress of southern Indians in October 1793 indicates that in this period the Spanish did not look to the Creeks either. The congress met at Nogales on the Mississippi River (the Walnut Hills of American records). This post in the Chickasaw country was an odd location to choose if Creek leadership were to be emphasized. Further, Manuel Gayoso de Lemos, Spanish governor at Natchez, who conducted the proceedings at Nogales, informed Carondelet that he had been told by a Choctaw leader that all the major southern Indian groups—the Choctaws, Cherokees, Creeks, and Chickasaws—had formed a defensive alliance under the leadership of the Chickasaws ("for their chief they had chosen the king of the Chickasaws," were Gayoso's words).[32]

At this stage of research, about all that can be said with certainty is that the southern Indian alliance, whatever its form or leadership, did not make its presence felt in the period from 1787 to 1796 as did the alliance of the northern Indians.

In the Old Northwest, American officials faced conditions that, in the end, made them more willing and better able to make concessions to the views of the Indians than in the South. Two factors dominated in the Old Northwest. One was the effectiveness of the northern Indian alliance, due in part to support given to the Indians by local British leadership. The other was the relative lack of domestic competition with the states for dominance in the area. By 1787, the states had ceded their claims to most of the territory (New York in 1781; Virginia, 1783; Massachusetts, 1785; Connecticut, 1786). In the Old Northwest, the federal government was free to carry out the centralized policy that was supposed to reduce friction with the Indians.

The prolonged warfare that was the result of unhampered federal jurisdiction should stand as a warning of the limitations of unilateral policymaking in a diplomatic situation. Within the domestic framework, it was significant that in this one geographic area the federal government did not directly compete with the states. The fact made little difference to the Indians of the Old Northwest. They were still not consulted in matters that concerned them more deeply than anyone else.

For federal officials, the lesson of the limitations of unilateral action was a hard one to learn. They made a reluctant start on the lesson when they accepted the principle of the purchase of Indian lands rather than acquisition by right of conquest. In the long run, the principle of purchase made a great deal of difference to the Indians; in the short run, its effect was diluted by the practices of negotiation. Thus, Congress, when authorizing the renegotiation of the postwar conquest-treaties with the Northern Indians, did not authorize a renegotiation of the conquest-cessions—unless the cessions could be enlarged. Payment was indeed authorized, so the principle of purchase was satisfied. The Indians were not satisfied, however, because as usual they were not consulted. They were summoned to the renegotiation councils, and the few who came were told what the United States had decided. Treaties were signed (the two Treaties of Fort Harmar, 9 January 1789), but they did not stop the widespread fighting.[33]

What the new federal government found itself engaged in during this period was an undeclared war against the resident foreigners north of the Ohio. This war against the western Indian nations was one of three undeclared wars in which the United States was involved in the 1790s, the others being against the Barbary pirates (ca. 1793–96) and France (1798–1800). American ideology could accommodate war if it were a just war, as Knox had noted in one of his reports in 1789,[34] but this one against the Indians created unease among U.S. officials from the first, and they made repeated attempts to negotiate an end to hostilities. They also continued the behavior that fired hostilities, as when Congress tried to raise money from the Ohio Company and John Cleve Symmes by selling them some of the land "purchased" in the renegotiated treaties of 1789. It took four more years of fighting to convince American officials that this purchase did not seem valid to the Indians. The Indians were not convinced by government assertions of fair purchase, or by an ingenuous letter from Symmes himself, explaining why white settlement in the disputed area should be allowed: "We come to live here on these lands, for we have bought these lands from the nations of red people and paid the red people for them, and you gave us a deed and signed your names to the deeds you gave Congress."[35]

United States policy north of the Ohio was to acquire land for the public domain and to preserve peace with the Indians. By 1793, federal officials had realized that the two goals were incompatible, and they were ready to settle, at least temporarily, for peace. A peace commission was dispatched with an offer to return to the Indians all the postwar acquisitions of Indian land north of the Ohio, with the exception of the tracts already sold to Symmes and the Ohio Company. When the negotiations failed, the officials again resorted to force. Their method throughout the period had been a combination of force and negotiation—those staples of eighteenth-century diplomacy. So, in August 1794, Anthony Wayne moved American forces down the Maumee River valley toward the battle at Fallen Timbers that gave victory to the United States and convinced the Indians that Great Britain had, indeed, withdrawn effective support.

The subsequent Treaty of Greenville (1795) was a landmark treaty in the diplomacy of the new American nation. In it the United States specifically relinquished its claims to absolute sovereignty over unceded Indian land north of the Ohio, east of the Mississippi, and south of the Great Lakes, reserving only the right of purchase when the Indians wanted to sell. That there might be no mistake about the Indians' rights in the land, these were spelled out in Article V of the treaty:

> To prevent any misunderstanding about the Indian lands relinquished by the United States in the fourth article, it is now explicitly declared, that the meaning of that relinquishment is this: The Indian tribes who have a right to those lands, are quietly to enjoy them, hunting, planting, and dwelling thereon so long as they please, without any molestation from the United States: . . .[36]

The Treaty of Greenville also drew a boundary between white and Indian land in the Old Northwest. The line gave the whites less than they had claimed on the basis of the postwar treaties of 1784-86 and the renegotiated treaties of 1789. It gave the Indians less than they could have had in the U.S. proposal of 1793 and, of course, less than the 1768 Stanwix line along the Ohio River. With the Greenville line, the United States completed a comprehensive Indian-white boundary from Lake Erie on the north to a point on the thirty-first parallel in southeastern Georgia, the border of Spanish territory.[37]

The boundary was incorporated in the Trade and Intercourse Act of 1796 which was, so far as the boundary was concerned, an enabling act authorizing the president to ascertain and mark the line that had already been largely established by treaty. The legislation had only to add one portion along the Ohio River and around Clark's Grant to connect the Greenville Treaty line of 1795 with the Holston Treaty line of 1791. This, in turn, connected with the New York Treaty line of 1790, and the boundary was complete along the entire western front of Indian-U.S. contact, just as it had been in 1768 under British administration. The southern portion of the 1796 line, with its sweeping curve below Kentucky and deep into the Cumberland region, showed the effects of the British period when the Stanwix treaty broke the southern backcountry open to white speculation and settlement, and individuals bargained for areas the size of European nations. The northern portion, describing a rough right angle from the mouth of the Kentucky River on the Ohio, to its Lake Erie terminus at the mouth of the Cuyahoga River, reflected the sustained resistance of the northern Indians to the American assumption that European peace terms were sufficient for the disposition of American land.[38]

It remains only to look at the Northeast, where the United States pursued yet a different policy toward the Indians. The major concern in that area was, of course, the Iroquois League. Government policy toward the Iroquois has not, in other studies, been sufficiently distinguished from the policy pursued in the South and the Northwest, but it was, in fact, different in goals and method. The difference is yet another instance of the way that the Indian setting helped determine policy, irrespective of the wishes of those Europeans or Americans who proposed and implemented it. In the Northeast, federal officials did not pursue the goal of land acquisition, as in the Northwest, or exert themselves to placate and control expansionist states, as in the South. Their chief goal throughout the period of the undeclared war with the western nations was to keep the Six Nations of the Iroquois neutral or, failing in that, to see that the militant among them fought on the side of the United States and not for the western nations. The officials hoped also to use the good offices of the Iroquois to persuade the western Indians to accept peace on government terms.[39]

It was Iroquois "good offices" that federal authorities hoped for, not Iroquois ability to command their dependents to stop fighting. The difference in the two is a measure of the realization that came gradually to officials such as Secretary of War Henry Knox, that the League no longer had enough influence to command anything. In the early 1790s, the Iroquois were at one of the lowest points in their fortunes, in the trough of disorganization and despair that preceded the Handsome Lake revitalization movement among the Senecas, a movement that has been studied and described by Anthony F. C. Wallace. They saw the bulk of British aid going to the militant western Indians, some of whom openly derided the Iroquois and repudiated their leadership. They saw their own leaders' pride turn to a passion for rum. "Brant will get drunk," wrote Timothy Pickering in 1791, while on a special mission to the Six Nations, "The Farmer's Brother will get drunk. Red Jacket will get drunk. . . . At times, most of them will make any sacrifice to Rum."[40]

The demoralization of the Iroquois was reflected in complex ways in United States policy and method in the Northeast. This is of particular interest here because, of the three areas of federal concern, the Northeast, after early 1791 and the admission of Vermont as a state, was the one least involved in international diplomacy. It is true that worry about possible Iroquois participation in the western Indians' war for the Ohio boundary, plus continuing suspicion of British contacts with the Iroquois, kept the diplomatic elements in the minds of American officials. Still, after 1791, they did not have the same fears that parts of the Northeast might be snatched away by foreigners, whether resident or overseas, that they had about the Old Northwest and the South. Because of this, and the weakness of the Iroquois, the Northeast was the area where, if anywhere, the United States was free to define and handle Indian relations as a domestic affair.

What happened was not at all simple, and not at all part of the stated policy of the government toward the Indians. It can be taken as an illustration of how difficult it was for policymakers to handle the situation of resident foreigners—that intractable contradiction in their nationalist frame of reference. Except for a very brief period at the close of the

Revolution, there was no serious consideration of moving the Iroquois out of New York, which meant that the problems inherent in Henry Knox's proposed layering of sovereign powers and land rights had to be dealt with immediately. They could not be postponed, as they were elsewhere, by the withdrawal or removal of the Indians.

In the Northeast, the United States had an ambiguous attitude toward state acquisition of Indian lands. This was in marked contrast to policy in the South, where every effort was made to prevent state acquisition and to reserve the right of land acquisition to the federal government. The difference in the Northeast was a result of the special context created there by a set of particular conditions. The most important was Iroquois weakness. State acquisition of Indian lands did not provoke open Indian hostilities as it did in the South, hence the federal government was not forced to intervene.[41] The weakness of the Iroquois was felt in another way. Because the Six Nations were still politically independent, they retained the right to dispose of their lands—within the guidelines laid down by the victorious Americans. They were, however, now too weak to control the actions of their individual members, and it was with the active participation of individual Iroquois that most of their land passed to the states of New York and Pennsylvania. Finally, the relative lack of British activity in the Northeast meant that white American officials, while still working with the forms of diplomacy, were free of the restraints that, in normal diplomatic discourse, would have been imposed by stronger antagonists, whether whites or Indians.

An illustration of the difference that strong antagonists could make is found in the dramatic change in the official attitude toward retrocession of Indian lands. The change took place between 1791 and 1793. After the formation of the new government under the Constitution, the Seneca nation began to press for the return of land taken from the Six Nations under terms of the conquest-treaty of October 1784 at Fort Stanwix. As Farmer's Brother, a Seneca leader, noted in November 1790, "The 6 Nations are in a bad situation since all their land was taken from them....We should be very happy, now the United States have taken up the matter, if we could have our land back again."[42] In December that same year, a delegation of Senecas went to Philadelphia to press the Iroquois request for retrocession.

The matter was considered at the highest executive level, and the request was denied. Grounds for the denial were expressed by President George Washington in a letter to Secretary of War Knox early in 1791.

Washington said that he did not want to give the Indians assurances that might involve the federal government in a dispute with any individual state, and that, at any rate, he doubted his authority to give such assurances without Senate consultation. There was a further objection to be considered: to undo or revise treaties that were already made "would be to open a door to certain inconvenience, and probable difficulty."[43] To the Senecas, Washington said that he could not annul treaties made before his administration, nor could he alter boundaries that the Indians had agreed on twice. "The lines fixed at Fort Stanwix and Fort Harmar must therefore remain established."[44]

In 1793, when the United States was preparing terms for the peace mission to the western Indian nations, the subject of the retrocession of Indian lands came up again for executive consideration. Washington asked his department heads whether he should consult with the Senate "as to the propriety of instructing the Commissioners to recede from the present boundary, provided peace cannot be established with the Indians upon other terms."[45] At a cabinet meeting at Washington's house on February 25, the question was debated under two heads. First, did the executive, or the executive together with the Senate, have the authority to relinquish to the Indians "the right of soil" in any of the lands north of the Ohio that had been validly obtained by treaties? Second, would it be expedient to do so, if that were necessary to obtain peace?

On both parts of the question, the cabinet divided three to one, with Knox (War), Alexander Hamilton (Treasury), and Edmund Randolph (attorney general) of the opinion that the president and the Senate did have the authority to retrocede and should do so, provided that the rights of individuals or states were not infringed and that the retrocession did not include any special reserves. Opposed on both counts was Jefferson (State), who thought that the Senate and the executive had only the authority necessary to negotiate favorable conditions for peace, such as promising not to settle any of the lands outside the special reserves.[46]

In this discussion, the fact that the retrocession offer was rejected by the Indians is not so important as the fact that it was made at all. This represented a complete reversal of the government's position in 1791 when the Senecas asked for the return of Iroquois land. One complicating factor in that case was, of course, the fact that the Iroquois were within the bounds of organized states, and a retrocession by the federal government would have embroiled it in disputes with Pennsylvania and

New York. This, however, only emphasizes the role played by strength in the diplomacy of the day—and hence, in United States policy. There being no state entanglements in the Northwest Territory, the government had been, in theory, free to retrocede land north of the Ohio at any time. It did not offer to do so until after the two severe defeats of American troops in the early 1790s, followed by accounts of a great massing of Indians during the summer of 1792.[47]

The effectiveness of force in diplomacy was not often so nakedly revealed as in this instance when the United States, under pressure on many fronts besides the Ohio backcountry, offered to retrocede land to the western Indian nations. It would, however, be an oversimplification to conclude that federal policy was shaped solely by those opponents who had the biggest sticks. The principle of retrocession, once accepted, then worked to the benefit of the Iroquois. In 1794 at the Treaty of Canandaigua, the United States made a retrocession of some 1,600 square miles of Iroquois land in western New York, between the mouth of Buffalo Creek and the western boundary of the state. The tract had been part of the Iroquois conquest-cession of 1784 at Fort Stanwix, and had, ever since, been one of the Senecas' chief grievances. Timothy Pickering, who conducted negotiations for the United States, told the Indians, "All this tract you, by former treaties ceded to the United States: but I am now willing to relinquish *all their claim to it.*" Pickering reported that the Indians were greatly satisfied. " 'This settlement (said one of the Chiefs to me) appears like a great light to us.'— And to me it seems like a new era."[48]

In a letter to Secretary of War Knox, Pickering offered a detailed explanation of this return of Iroquois land. His rationale was apparently accepted by the Senate, which approved the treaty on January 9, 1795.[49] Why this did not mean a new era in United States–Indian relations can only be seen by looking at the special circumstances of the Northeast where the layering of sovereign powers and land rights that was envisioned by Knox as a solution to the problems of Indian affairs was in actual operation and was creating a situation that became a prelude to social tragedy. To understand what happened, it is necessary to go back briefly to 1783.

The Pattern of the Future

At the war's end, there were many active contenders for sovereignty, or land rights, or both in the Iroquois area of the Northeast. These included five of the Six Nations of the Iroquois (during the war the Mohawk Nation had withdrawn to Canada): Seneca, Cayuga, Onondaga, Oneida, and Tuscarora; the states of New York, Pennsylvania, and Massachusetts; the central government of the United States under both the Confederation and the Constitution; and a number of influential entrepreneurs such as John Livingston, Robert Morris, Oliver Phelps, and Nathaniel Gorham. The involved contest got under way immediately upon the close of hostilities. By July 1790, when the new central government under the Constitution passed the first Indian Trade and Intercourse Act, stipulating that only the United States had authority to acquire land from the Indians, the entire Iroquois area was already covered by various forms of land-disposition agreements, many of them conflicting, and most of them contested by one or another contender. The major exception to this statement is Pennsylvania's land acquisition during this period.

Pennsylvania authorities had early secured from the Indians the preemption title to the northwestern third of their state through agreements with the Iroquois (23 October 1784), and with some of the western nations (19 January 1785). These agreements were made at the United States–sponsored negotiations at Fort Stanwix and Fort McIntosh, and with the knowledge and approval of United States officials. The land transactions did not become a cause for friction since the Iroquois never denied the validity of the sale, and the western nations were no longer contending in that area. In 1789, when the United States renegotiated its early treaties with the northern Indians, Pennsylvania negotiated a new agreement also (9 January 1789), again with the Iroquois, and again with United States approval.[50]

New York officials also got an early start on an active program of land acquisition, but until 1796 their program was independent of federal authority. At the Fort Stanwix negotiations of 1784, New York tried unsuccessfully to acquire land from the whole Iroquois Confederacy. After that failure, state authorities negotiated separately with the different nations of the League. Their intense activity is reflected in table 14, where seventeen Iroquois land-disposition agreements are listed for the period from 1783 to 1796. Twelve of the seventeen, or 70 percent, were with the state of New York.[51]

The three agreements that were the key to the future, from the point of view of New York expansionists, were the two of September 1788 and the one of February 1789. By those three, *all* the land belonging to the Onondaga, Oneida, Tuscarora, and Cayuga nations were

Table 14   Land-Disposition Agreements of the Six Nations of the Iroquois, 1783–96

Date	Indians	Others	Disposition
22 October 1784	Six Nations	United States	Conquest-Cession
23 October 1784	Six Nations	Pennsylvania	Sale
28 June 1785	Oneida Tuscarora	New York	Sale
5 March 1787	Seneca Cayuga	Private individuals	Lease
8 July 1788	Six Nations	O. Phelps N. Gorham	Sale
12 September 1788	Onondaga	New York	Sale[1]
22 September 1788	Oneida Tuscarora	New York	Sale[1]
9 January 1789	Six Nations	Pennsylvania	Sale
25 February 1789	Cayuga	New York	Sale[1]
16 June 1790	Onondaga	New York	Affirming sale of 1788
22 June 1790	Cayuga	New York	Affirming sale of 1789
11 March 1793	Onondaga	New York	Sale
27 July 1795	Cayuga	New York	Sale
28 July 1795	Onondaga	New York	Sale
15 September 1795	Oneida	New York	Sale
30 May 1796	St. Regis[2]	New York	Sale[1]
31 May 1796	Seven Nations of Canada[3]	New York	Quit-Claim

SOURCE: See Appendix A.
1. Sale of entire holdings, from which certain tracts were reserved for Indian residence.
2. A Catholic Iroquois group at Akwesasne on the south bank of the St. Lawrence River.
3. Groups of mixed background, probably including some Iroquois.

transferred to the state, which then, by terms of the same agreements, reserved certain portions for the Indians. This fundamental change in basic ownership once made, expansionists in the future could direct their efforts toward whittling away at the reserves—and did so. A point that needs to be emphasized in this discussion is that the pressures on the Iroquois nations for cession of their lands were internal as well as external. Witnesses who signed the treaty of 12 September 1788, for example, by which the Onondaga gave up title to all of their land in New York, included Senecas, Oneidas, and Cayugas, as well as New Yorkers, and there were twenty-three Onondagas who signed on behalf of their nation.[52]

The intense state negotiations with the Indians during these years took place in a context of equally intense negotiations on the part of private individuals. One unexpected result of the settlement of the contest between New York and Massachusetts for the western section of the state of New York was that it provided an entry for individual entrepreneurs into Indian negotiations at the highest level. That was not the intent of the New York–Massachusetts Treaty of Hartford (1786), but it was the result. The intent of the Hartford agreement was to resolve the dispute between the two states by giving Massachusetts the preemption rights for the land, and letting New York retain the right of sovereignty, or political jurisdiction.

Preemption rights were thus distinguished from the Indians' possessory rights, which no one was disputing. Neither was anyone disputing the Indians' political independence. In fact, the settlement depended on it. What Massachusetts had been given was the monopoly of acquiring the land of western New York from the Indians who possessed it and who retained enough vestiges of sovereignty to negotiate regarding its disposition. It was a right that Massachusetts could not well exercise on its own behalf, however, since New York retained political sovereignty vis-à-vis the other states. Under these conditions, the preemption rights awarded to Massachusetts became an economic resource that Massachusetts could exploit only by selling to someone else. In April 1788, the Massachusetts legislature sold the rights to Oliver Phelps and Nathaniel Gorham, thus giving official state sanction to the entry of private individuals into Indian negotiations.[53]

It is not necessary here to follow the course of events through which John Livingston and Robert Morris became involved in the Phelps and Gorham purchase and in the attempts to gain land rights from the Indians—attempts that were largely successful by 1797.[54] What is important here is the context that was created by Iroquois weakness and by the layering of sovereign powers and land rights in the Iroquois area. In such a context, the political independence of the Indians, vis-à-vis the other and stronger political entities in the area, became the freedom to negotiate away the Iroquois land base. Further, the restrictions placed upon that freedom by the federal government were restrictions that favored New York, not the Indians.

An illustration of the way that federal restrictions favored New York can be found in 1791, a year when federal officials were expressing concern about the active policy of land acquisition being pursued by state officials and private citizens in New York. The concern was consistent with the policy of requiring all negotiations with the Indians to be either by the United States or under its sponsorship (a policy that found expression in the Trade and Intercourse Acts of 1790, 1793, and 1796). Thus, George Washington, in April 1791, wrote to Secretary of the Treasury Alexander Hamilton to express his exasperation that the New York legislature was negotiating with the Indians after the Indians have been told that in the future only the federal government would treat with them: "To sum the whole up in a few words: the interference of States, and the speculation of Individuals will be the bane of all our public measures." In his reply, Hamilton, as might be expected from his views of the needs of the central government, lamented that the "public peace of the Union" was left "at the mercy of each State government."[55]

Later that same year, however, New York's independence of action was given indirect support by the federal government when both Washington and Secretary of War Knox explicitly disavowed land-disposition agreements that had been concluded at a U.S.-sponsored conference with the Six Nations. The agreements conflicted with New York's program of land acquisition and, further, had not met standards that had been imposed by Massachusetts in its disposition of preemption rights. Given these circumstances, the central government might have chosen to assert its authority by saying that the agreements were valid so long as they were made in conformity with the requirements of the Trade and Intercourse Act of 1790, which was then in force, and if the Senate approved. Instead of that, before the conference proceedings were submitted to the Senate, Knox wrote to New York Governor George Clinton to disavow the agreements, and Washington assured Clinton that Knox had written "by my orders." When Washington submitted the proceedings to the Senate, he again backed away from a confrontation with New York by a further disavowal, saying that the federal commissioner, "with good intentions, but incautiously, made certain ratifications of lands, unauthorized by his instructions and unsupported by the constitution."[56] So far as land-disposition agreements were concerned, the Iroquois were already securely within the legal net of imposed government restrictions.

Again, in 1794, the federal government deferred to state and private interests in the Northeast. The American-sponsored Treaty of Canandaigua, which has already been mentioned, acknowledged certain Oneida,

Onondaga, and Cayuga reservations, thus validating the New York treaties that had determined them. The treaty also described the Seneca lands by using some of the boundary lines of the Phelps-Gorham purchase, thus validating that state-private arrangement. It was at Canandaigua, too, that Timothy Pickering made the retrocession of land that the Senate sustained; Pickering's reason was that the United States had but a "shadow claim," the various state and private arrangements with the Indians taking precedence over it.[57]

It is not clear why the federal government was so adamant in the South about its powers in Indian relations, and so accommodating to the desires of the states in the Northeast. One can speculate that in the South, government officials feared the Spanish and the militant southern Indians more than they did the states, and in the Northeast they feared the very powerful state of New York more than they did the Indians, who were by then not militant, and the British, whose attention was chiefly elsewhere. But this is speculation.

The same 1791 agreements that provoked the disavowals from Knox and Washington provoked some Iroquois to argue their right to dispose of their land as they saw fit. The agreements had been approved by U.S. Commissioner Timothy Pickering at a meeting with the Six Nations at Newtown, New York, in June and July 1791. Some Senecas asked Pickering to give approval to a grant of land that they wanted to make to Ebenezer Allan's two Indian daughters. After discussion, and a clarification of the size of the grant, Pickering agreed. He agreed also to a Cayuga request for approval of a lease of their reserved land to John Richardson for twenty years. Later, Pickering defended his actions by saying that he interpreted the Trade and Intercourse Act of 1790 to mean that the Indians had a right to dispose of their land as they wished, so long as it was done at a public treaty held under the authority of the United States.[58]

Federal disavowal of the Seneca grant and the Cayuga lease meant that New York arrangements prevailed, and this angered some of the Indians. Fish Carrier, a prominent Cayuga leader, refused to go to Philadelphia in 1792 with other Iroquois leaders because, he said, he had thought that the lease of the Cayuga lands would stand firm. Now he saw that the United States were all liars, and he would fight them again.[59] As late as 1794, some Cayuga and Onondaga leaders at the Canandaigua negotiations were still trying to get U.S. approval of their right to lease their lands under their own arrangements, saying that as the state of New York had gotten almost all their land for practically nothing they did not see why they could not rent out the two small pieces remaining to them for income to feed their women and children.[60]

At issue, of course, was the degree of Indian sovereignty and what, in fact, this meant in the mid-1790s in the Northeastern United States. The Oneida leader, Good Peter, put his finger exactly on the central issue in the statement that was quoted at the beginning of this study: "It seems to us we are not really free men, nor have we had the real disposal of our property." Good Peter spoke for many. The Northeast Indians were, in this period, bereft by circumstance of the flexibility of maneuver that was essential for the maintenance of a bargaining position in diplomatic negotiations. They were also faced by vigorous, acquisitive states and individuals whose actions were tacitly approved by the federal government. The pattern of state-federal-Indian relations that was set then in the Northeast was to prevail for many years.

Elsewhere, too, the patterns of relationships that emerged during the twelve or thirteen years following the end of the American Revolution were the patterns that continued on into the next century. These patterns, in turn, were strongly influenced by what had happened during the period of British administration, and by the actions and relationships of the Indian nations. In the South, the federal government continued to assert its primacy in Indian affairs, and to try to placate both the states and the Indian nations by a program of land acquisition that was gradual and under United States authority. In the Northwest, until after the Black Hawk War in 1832, federal officials kept a wary eye on the British in Canada, and on the various combinations of Indian groups that formed when the Indians recovered from their 1794 defeat and looked to a future that included organized states and territories in the area they had lost.

Conclusion

By 1796 a single treaty system encompassing whites and Indians had been reestablished in the United States. On the surface it looked much the same as the Anglo-Indian treaty system of the early 1760s. The same diplomatic forms were observed as in the past. Invitations to treaty councils were still issued to the Indians. Supplies were still provided. Special commissioners were appointed, and the resulting treaties—like any treaties entered into by the United States—were submitted to the Senate for its advice and consent. The profound difference between the treaty system that was established by 1796 and the system of the early 1760s lay in the disparity of power between the participants. For all the reasons that have been discussed in these pages, the Indians had lost their freedom of maneuver and thus their negotiating leverage. The great disparity of power between them and the United States could not help but skew the treaty relationship into one so unequal that it can only be called colonial. The system no longer expressed mutual compromise and accommodation, but rather the domination of the Indians by the United States.

The treaty system of 1796 was the unplanned outcome of the decisions and events that have been analyzed in this study. It took thirty-three years of such activity in eastern North America and in Europe to create the colonial treaty system of 1796. The system was to stay in place for the next seventy-five years—expanding, adding secondary functions, but never changing its primary function of transferring land from Indian ownership to ownership by the United States.

In some respects, a treaty system can be seen as a kind of planned social order, in which the participants agree on common rules of behavior to reduce the friction of their differences and competition. The system also, however, infallibly expresses the power relationships of the participants. So the treaty system that was created, destroyed, and re-created in eastern North America after 1763, changed drastically without the conscious intention of anyone involved, from an accommodation system to a colonial system in which the Indian nations had little say in their own destiny. The course was set for the social disaster that followed, and that still troubles Americans today. What is not well understood today is that behind the disaster's well-publicized clash of cultures, lay the old question of political power. By birth and by inclination, the Indians were for many years outside the domestic political system in America, and, until recently, they did not have the power to make the diplomatically based treaty system very much more than what it became for the United States: a license for empire.

Appendix A

Sources for Figure 4
and Tables 6, 8, 10, 12, 13, 14

Table 15.   North American Indian Treaties, 1763–96

Date	Place	Indians	Source
		For the Period 1763–74[a]	
10 November 1763[b]	Augusta, Ga.	Cherokees Lower Creeks Choctaws Chickasaws Catawbas	*Journal of the Congress of the Four Southern Governors . . . with the Five Nations of Indians, at Augusta, 1763* (Charleston, S.C.: Peter Timothy, [1764]); *The State Records of North Carolina*, 17 vols. (1895–1905) 11: 199–203.
3 April 1764	Johnson Hall, N.Y.	Senecas	Clive Parry, ed., *The Consolidated Treaty Series, 1648–1918* (hereafter cited as *CTS*), 175 vols. (Dobbs Ferry, N.Y.: Oceana Publishing, 1969) 42: 499–502; *Documents Relative to the Colonial History of the State of New York*, hereafter cited as *NYCD*), 15 vols. (1853–87) 7: 621–23.
18 July 1764	Niagara	Hurons of Detroit	*NYCD* 7:650–51.
12 August 1764	Presque Isle	Delawares Shawnees Hurons of Sandusky	"Terms of Peace," in "State Papers," *Annual Register* (1764), p. 181.
7 September 1764	Detroit	Ottawas Chippewas Potawatomis Hurons	"Transactions of a Congress held with the Chiefs of the Ottawa and Chippewa Nations," Col. John Bradstreet to Maj. Gen. Thomas Gage, 12 September 1764, General Thomas Gage Papers, William L. Clements Library, University of Michigan, Ann Arbor.

Date	Location	Tribes	Source
10 September 1764[b]	Pensacola, W. Fla.	Creeks	"Proceedings of the Congress at Pensacola, Sept. 5-10, 1764," Gage Papers, Clements Library, Ann Arbor, Mich.
26 March 1765[b]	Mobile, W. Fla.	Choctaws Chickasaws	Dunbar Rowland, ed., *Mississippi Provincial Archives, 1763-1766, English Dominion*, (Nashville, Tenn.: Mississippi Department of Archives & History, 1911), pp. 249-55; *NYCD* 8:31-32 (extract).
8 May 1765	Johnson Hall, N.Y.	Delawares	*NYCD* 7:738-41.
11 May 1765	Fort Pitt	Shawnees Delawares Mingoes	*Pennsylvania Colonial Records* 9:249-64.
28 May 1765[b]	Pensacola, W. Fla.	Upper Creeks Lower Creeks	Rowland, ed., *English Dominion*, pp. 211-15.
8 July 1765	Ouiatenon on the Wabash	Kickapoos Miamis Weas Piankeshaws Mascoutens	*Illinois Historical Collections* 11:41.
18 July 1765	Ouiatenon on the Wabash	Ottawas Illinois Confederacy	Ibid., p. 42.
13 August 1765[b]	Natchez, W. Fla.	Arkansas (Quapaw) Small Tribes of the Lower Mississippi	Lt. Thomas Ford to John Stuart, 21 June, 16 July 1765; Maj. Robert Farmer to Gen. Thomas Gage, 25 April, 16 December 1765, Gage Papers, Clements Library, Ann Arbor, Mich.

Date	Place	Indians	Source
28 August 1765	Detroit	Wyandots (Hurons) Ottawas Chippewas Potawatomis Saginaws Miamis Weas Piankeshaws Kickapoos Mascoutens	*Illinois Historical Collections* 11:43–46, 56–57.
19 October 1765[b]	Fort Prince George, S.C.	Cherokees	"Cession of Lands by the Cherokee Indians at Fort P: George," 19 October 1765, Gage Papers, Clements Library, Ann Arbor, Mich.;*NYCD* 8:33 (extract).
18 November 1765[b]	Fort Picolata, E. Fla.	Lower Creeks	"Proceedings of the Congress of Picolata, Nov. 12–18, 1765," Gage Papers, Clements Library, Ann Arbor, Mich.; *NYCD* 8:32 (extract).
31 July 1766	Fort Ontario	Ottawas Potawatomis Wyandots (Hurons) Chippewas Six Nations	"Proceedings of Sir William Johnson with Pondiac and other Indians," *NYCD* 8:854–67.
1 June 1767[b]	Tiger River (in present S.C.)	Cherokees	*Colonial Records of North Carolina* 7:462–66, 502–5.

Date	Place	Nations	Source
14 October 1768[b]	Hard Labor, S.C.	Cherokees	"Proceedings of the Congress of Hard Labor, October 13–17, 1768," Gage Papers, Clements Library, Ann Arbor, Mich.
5 November 1768	Fort Stanwix, N.Y.	Six Nations	"Proceedings at Fort Stanwix," *NYCD* 8:111–34.
12 November 1768[b]	Augusta, Ga.	Lower Creeks	Copy of treaty abstract from Papeles procedentes de Cuba, AGI, Seville, in the Edward E. Ayer Collection, Newberry Library, Chicago.
22 July 1770	German Flats, N.Y.	Six Nations	"Proceedings of the Congress at German Flats," *NYCD* 8:227–44.
18 October 1770[b]	Lochaber, S.C.	Cherokees	"Proceedings of the Congress of Lochaber, Oct. 18–22, 1770," in *Documents of the American Revolution, 1770–1783*, Colonial Office Series, 2:210–15.
22 February 1771[b]	(?)	Cherokees	Colonial Office Records, America and West Indies, vol. 661: 192–94, British Public Record Office, London.
2 November 1771[b]	Pensacola, W. Fla.	Upper Creeks	*Documents of the American Revolution* 3:229–31.
6 January 1772[b]	Mobile, W. Fla.	Choctaws Chickasaws	"Proceedings of the Congress of Mobile, Dec. 31, 1771–Jan. 6, 1772," Gage Papers, Clements Library, Ann Arbor, Mich.
? May 1772[b]	Virginia-Cherokee border area	J. Donelson Attakullakulla	*Calendar of Virginia State Papers* 1:291; for discussion: DeVorsey, Jr., *Indian Boundary*, pp. 78–92.
1 June 1773[b]	Augusta, Ga.	Cherokees Creeks	Colonial Office Records, America and West Indies, vol. 662: fols. 51–58d, Public Record Office, London.

Date	Place	Indians	Source
20 October 1774[b]	Savannah, Ga.	Creeks	Ibid., vol. 664:fols. 11–13d; Treaty of Savannah, October 20, 1774, Gage Papers, Clements Library, Ann Arbor, Mich.
? October 1774	Camp Charlotte (in present Ohio)	Shawnees	Thwaites and Kellogg, ed., *Documentary History of Dunmore's War, 1774*, p. 386; *American Archives*, 4 ser., 1:1014.

For the Period 1783–86[c]

Date	Place	Indians	Source
31 May 1783			*American State Papers, Indian Affairs*, 2 vols. (Washington, D.C.: Gales & Seaton, 1832–34) 1:23–24. See also Chapman J. Milling, *Red Carolinians* (Chapel Hill, N.C.: University of North Carolina Press, 1940), pp. 322–23, and R.S. Cotterill, *The Southern Indians* (Norman: University of Oklahoma Press, 1954), p. 58.
9 July 1783			Cotterill, *The Southern Indians*, pp. 58–59; Samuel C. Williams, *History of the Lost State of Franklin* (Johnson City, Tenn.: The Watauga Press, 1924), pp. 14–15.
1 November 1783			Sources are the same as for the treaty of 31 May 1783.
6 November 1783			R.S. Cotterill, "The Virginia-Chickasaw Treaty of 1783," *Journal of Southern History* 8 (1942):483–96.
1 June 1784			*Papeles Procedentes de Cuba* (Cuban Papers), legajo 2360, Archivo General de Indias (AGI), Seville, "Cuban Papers Transcripts," Edward E. Ayer Collection Newberry Library, Chicago. For a description of the proceedings, see Martin Navarro to José de Galvez, 27 July 1784, ibid., legajo 2351, no. 239, pp. 1–3, in the transcripts. For printed copies of the treaty in English translation, see *American State Papers, Foreign Relations*, 6 vols. (Washington, D.C.: Gales & Seaton, 1832–59) 1:278–79, and John W. Caughey, *McGillivray of the Creeks* (Norman: University of Oklahoma Press, 1938; 2d printing, 1958), pp. 75–76.

23 June 1784a — Cuban Papers, legajo 2360, AGI, no. 209, pp. 22–23, transcripts, Ayer Collection, Newberry Library, Chicago.

23 June 1784b — Ibid., pp. 16–21.

14 July 1784 — Cuban Papers, legajo 15, AGI, no. "B," pp. 1–15, transcripts, Ayer Collection, Newberry Library, Chicago. For a printed copy, see Manuel Serraño y Sanz, *España y los Indios Cherokis y Chactas* (Sevilla: Tip. de la "Guía, Official," 1916), pp. 32–85. Also in *CTS* 49:109–12.

22 October 1784 — Charles J. Kappler, comp. and ed., *Indian Affairs, Laws, and Treaties*, 2 vols. 2d ed. (Washington, D.C.: Government Printing Office, 1904) 2:5–6. Also in Parry, ed., *CTS* 49:169.

23 October 1784 — *Minutes of the Second Session of the Ninth General Assembly* [of Pennsylvania], Appendix, "Proceedings of the Treaties held at Fort Stanwix and Fort McIntosh," pp. 318–20, cited by Donald H. Kent before the Indian Claims Commission, docket 344, p. 55, printed as Kent, *Iroquois Indians I: History of Pennsylvania Purchases from the Indians* (New York: Garland Publishing, 1974), p. 98 [Garland pagination].

19 January 1785 — Kent, *Iroquois Indians* p. 125 [Garland].

21 January 1785 — Kappler, ed., *Indian Affairs* 2:6–8; *CTS* 49:217–18.

10 June 1785 — *State Records of North Carolina*, 22:649–50; Williams, *Franklin*, pp. 77–78.

28 June 1785 — *Indian Treaties and Laws and Regulations Relating to Indian Affairs* (Washington, D.C.: Way & Gideon, 1826) (hereafter cited as *Indian Treaties*), pp. 17–18. For preliminaries and proceedings: New York Indian Commissioners, *Proceedings of the Commissioners of Indian Affairs* (hereafter cited as New York, *Proceedings*), comp. and ed. Franklin B. Hough, 2 vols. in one (Albany, N.Y.: Joel Munsell, 1861) 1:72–109.

12 November 1785 — *American State Papers Indian Affairs* 1:20, 23.

Date	Place	Indians	Source
28 November 1785	Kappler, ed., *Indian Affairs* 2:8–11. Also in *CTS* 49:443–46. Minutes are in *American State Papers, Indian Affairs* 1:40–43; and the attempts of some Cherokees to get redress from Spain, in *American State Papers, Foreign Relations* 1:280–81.		
3 January 1786	Kappler, ed., *Indian Affairs* 2:11–14. Also in *CTS* 49:453–56. Proceedings are in the Frontier Wars MSS (U), 14U58–92, Draper Manuscript Collection, State Historical Society of Wisconsin, Madison; and the repudiation by some Choctaws in Serraño y Sanz, *España y los Indios Cherokis*, pp. 36–40.		
10 January 1786	Kappler, ed., *Indian Affairs* 2:14–16. Also in *CTS* 49:459–61. Proceedings are in the Draper Manuscript Collection, 14U93–107; and the denial by some Chickasaws in Serraño y Sanz, *España y los Indios Cherokis*, pp. 36–41.		
31 January 1786	Kappler, ed., *Indian Affairs* 2:16–18. Also in *CTS* 49:477–78. Treaty minutes are in the Draper Manuscript Collection, 3U186–202.		
15 May 1786	[Canadian government], *Indian Treaties and Surrenders, 1680-1890*, 2 vols. in one (Ottawa: Brown Chamberlin, 1891) 1:272.		
3 August 1786	J.G.M. Ramsey, *The Annals of Tennessee to the End of the Eighteenth Century* (Philadelphia: J.B. Lippincott & Co., 1860), pp. 344–46; Williams, *Franklin*, pp. 102–3.		
3 November 1786	*American State Papers, Indian Affairs* 1:23–24.		

For the Iroquois, 1783–96

Date	Reference
23 October 1784	*Minutes of the Second Session of the Ninth General Assembly* [of Pennsylvania], Appendix, "Proceedings of the Treaties held at Fort Stanwix and Fort McIntosh," pp. 318–20; cited by Donald H. Kent before the Indian Claims Commission, docket 344, p. 55, printed as Kent, *Iroquois Indians I: History of Pennsylvania Purchases from the Indians* (New York: Garland Publishing, 1974), p. 98 [Garland pagination].
28 June 1785	*Indian Treaties*, pp. 17–18. For the preliminaries and proceedings, see New York, *Proceedings* 1:72–109.
5 March 1787	MS copy, no. 422 in Ruth Lapham Butler, *A Check List of Manuscripts in the Edward E. Ayer Collection* (Chicago: Newberry Library, 1937), Edward E. Ayer Collection, Newberry Library, Chicago.
8 July 1788	A summary of the terms of cession is in New York, *Proceedings* 1:160n.
12 September 1788	Ibid., pp. 198–203.
22 September 1788	MS copy, no. 428 in Butler, *Check List*, Ayer Collection, Newberry Library. Printed in New York, *Proceedings* 1:241–47, and *Indian Treaties*, pp. 19–22.
9 January 1789	Kappler, *Indian Affairs* 3:698–701.
25 February 1789	*Indian Treaties*, pp. 22–24; New York, *Proceedings* 2:306–12.
16 June 1790	New York, *Proceedings*, pp. 400–402; *Indian Treaties*, p. 25.
22 June 1790	*Indian Treaties*, pp. 24–25.

Date	Place	Indians	Source
11 March 1793			Noted in New York State Legislature, *Report of the Special Committee to Investigate the Indian Problem of the State of New York* (hereafter cited as New York, *Report*) (Albany, N.Y.: Troy Press, 1889), p. 9.
27 July 1795			Ibid.
28 July 1795			Ibid.
15 September 1795			MS copy, no. 429 in Butler, *Check List*, Ayer Collection, Newberry Library, Chicago.
30 May 1796			New York, *Report*, p. 11.
31 May 1796			Kappler, *Treaties* 2:45–46; *Indian Treaties*, pp. 27–29.

[a]Some of these sources refer not to the treaty itself but to the negotiations from which the provisions of the treaty can be inferred. Where a treaty is available in print that has been the preferred source even when the printed version is only an extract. Edmund B. O'Callaghan, ed., *Documents Relative to the Colonial History of the State of New York*, 15 vols. (Albany, N.Y.: Weed, Parsons & Co., 1853–87) (cited as *NYCD*), is a particularly rich source, as is the Colonial Office Series edited by K.G. Davies, *Documents of the American Revolution, 1770–1783*, 19 vols. cont. (Shannon, Ireland: Irish University Press, 1972–). Even when a treaty is not printed in this series, but is mentioned in a letter from America, the location of the treaty in the British Public Record Office is given.

Three secondary works, based on close study of the Thomas Gage Papers in the William L. Clements Library, University of Michigan, Ann Arbor, and papers in the Public Record Office, London, indicate the location of other treaties or discussions of treaties: John R. Alden, *John Stuart and the Southern Colonial Frontier*, University of Michigan Publications in History and Political Science, vol. 15 (Ann Arbor: University of Michigan Press, 1944); Louis DeVorsey, Jr., *The Indian Boundary in the Southern Colonies, 1763–1775* (Chapel Hill: University of North Carolina Press, 1966); and Howard H. Peckham, *Pontiac and the Indian Uprising* (Princeton, N.J.: Princeton

University Press, 1947). Specific locations taken directly from these works are: 7 September 1764, Peckham, *Pontiac*, p. 261, n. 9; 10 September 1764, Alden, *John Stuart*, p. 194, n. 14; 13 August 1765, ibid., pp. 203–4, n. 54, 55; 19 October 1765, ibid., p. 219, n. 21; 18 November 1765, ibid., p. 231, n. 87; 14 October 1768, ibid., p. 272, n. 41; 22 February 1771, DeVorsey, Jr., *Indian Boundary*, pp. 162–63, n. 60, 61; 6 January 1772, Alden, *John Stuart*, p. 323, n. 48; 20 October 1774, ibid., p. 311, n. 80.

^{b}Listed in table 12.

^{c}To facilitate research in this neglected area of relations between American Indians and whites, several references are given for each treaty. Where a primary source is known or a copy of the treaty is available, that reference is listed first. Charles J. Kappler's compilation has been used here for United States–Indian treaties, but copies can also be found in volume 7 of the *United States Statutes at Large* (Boston: Little, Brown & Co., 1853).

Appendix B
Duties under the Spanish Commission Held by Alexander McGillivray 20 July 1784

Instructions for Mr. Alexander McGillivray, Spanish Commissary in the Creek Nation.

1. Your first and chief duty will be to keep the different towns of your nation dependent on and subordinate to our Sovereign, using whatever means your well-known activity and talent may dictate to keep the Indians on our side.

2. You are to give all your attention to seeing that the traders who go to your Nation behave decently, both politics and friendship requiring that the Indians have not the least cause for complaint.

3. You are to give preference to those particular traders whose prices conform exactly to those in the tariff schedule agreed on at the general Congress of Pensacola May 31 and June 1 of this year, neither raising nor lowering the established prices.

4. You are also to see to the observance of the general instructions for traders that were established in the said Congress, not allowing any contravention of them no matter how urgent the reason.

5. It will be your duty to be vigilant in maintaining peace and harmony in the Nation, not only between the different Creek tribes but with the rest of the Nations as well, especially the Choctaws and Chickasaws, and in encouraging agriculture and commerce.

6. One of the points demanding your utmost attention is to see that no trader enters the Nation without a passport, on which you are to note the conduct of the trader while in the Nation, as well as the day of entrance and of departure.

    You will arrest those traders who come into the Nation without posting the required bond with the Governor of Pensacola, requiring

---

Source: Legajo 2360, "Papeles Procedentes de Cuba," Archivo General de Indias, Seville; transcripts in Edward E. Ayer Collection, Newberry Library, Chicago.

those traders who are already in the Nation to help you without the least delay. If they do not, they will be severely punished.

7. You are always to exert yourself to unite the Nation in whatever course of action will promote its best interests and its glory, keeping the Governor of Pensacola informed of what you do.

8. You are to see that no trader gives credit to any Indian for more than thirty pounds of dried skins or the same value in unfinished skins, and all Indian debts that exceed that amount are to be considered as irrevocable.

9. You are not to permit any trader to sell more than five pounds of powder or twelve balls at any one time.

10. On our order, you are to prohibit traders taking part in the Indian hunts, unless the Indians voluntarily permit it.

11. Of equal importance, you are to see that traders do not conduct business in towns other than those for which they have been given permission by the Governor.

Finally, we hope that your well-known zeal, activity, and talent will keep the Creek Nation and its allies in the most perfect harmony and union, always promoting, whenever the occasion should occur, the honor, glory, and interest of the Spanish Nation and the tranquility of the Creek tribes.

Given in the Governor's House, signed by our hand, sealed with the seal of our Arms, and referred for copying to the Governor's Secretary, in New Orleans on July 20, 1784. Estevan Miro. (Signed.)

Notes

Chapter One

1. Red Jacket's reply to Timothy Pickering, 23 November 1790, council at Tioga Point, New York, Letters and Papers of Pickering's Mission to Indians, 1786-1809, vols. 59-62 of Pickering Papers (hereafter cited as Pickering Papers), Massachusetts Historical Society microfilm edition, 61:94.

2. Good Peter, with the Iroquois delegation in Philadelphia, April 1792, ibid., vol. 60:122.

3. Francis Jennings, "The Constitutional Evolution of the Covenant Chain," *Proceedings of the American Philosophical Society* 115 (1971): 88-96; Gunther Michelson, "The Covenant Chain in Colonial History," *Man in the Northeast* 21 (Spring, 1981): 115-26.

4. Good Peter's portrait, which is owned by the Yale University Art Gallery, New Haven, is reproduced in William C. Sturtevant, ed., *Handbook of North American Indians,* 20 vols. (projected), (Washington, D.C.: Smithsonian Institution, 1978-), vol. 15: *Northeast,* ed. Bruce G. Trigger, p. 312.

5. "La Situation coloniale: approche théorique," *Social Change: The Colonial Situation,* ed. Immanuel Wallerstein (New York: John Wiley & Sons, 1966), p. 55.

6. Introduction to the first edition. In reprint ed., 2 vols. (Paris: Guillaumin et Cie, 1864) 1: 45-56, 57. See also Martens's preface to the second edition (1801), reprinted in ibid., p. 23. Martens's work went through many editions including the one in English listed in the following note.

7. Translated by William Cobbett. Published as *Summary of the Law of Nations* (Philadelphia: Thomas Bradford, 1795), p. 24.

8. Ibid., pp. 343-72; *Recueil des principaux traités d'alliance, de paix, de trêve... conclus par les puissances de l'Europe,* 7 vols. (Goettingue: J. C. Dieterich, 1791-1802).

9. Etienne Grisel, "The Beginnings of International Law and General Public Law Doctrine: Francisco de Vitoria's *De Indiis prior,"* in *First Images,* ed. Fredi Chiapelli, 2 vols. (Berkeley: University of California Press, 1976) 1:305-25; Lewis Hanke, *The Spanish Struggle for Justice*

in the Conquest of America (Philadelphia: University of Pennsylvania Press, 1949); James B. Scott, *The Spanish Origin of International Law, Part One: Francisco de Vitoria and His Law of Nations* (Oxford: Clarendon Press, 1934). For a perceptive discussion of the beliefs and debates of the Spanish jurists and their place in the intellectual baggage of Europeans in the New World, see Wilcomb Washburn, *Red Man's Land/ White Man's Law* (New York: Charles Scribner's Sons, 1971), pp. 3–23.

10. *De Jure Belli ac Pacis* (1625; reprint ed., The Classics of International Law, 2 vols., Oxford: Clarendon Press, 1925).

11. 1758; reprint ed., Classics of International Law, 3 vols., Washington, D.C.: Carnegie Institution, 1916.

12. *Summary,* pp. 3–4, 4–5.

13. Max Savelle makes 1748 the date of the shift from Europe to the world: "The American Balance of Power and European Diplomacy, 1713–78," in *The Era of the American Revolution,* ed. Richard B. Morris, 1939; reprint ed., New York: Harper & Row Torchbook, 1965), p. 158. Since, however, the peace treaty of 1748 restored most of the places captured during the war, the Partition of 1763 has been chosen here. Jack M. Sosin notes that this struggle with the French and the Peace Treaty of 1763 marked a turning point in the thinking of British ministers from a European to a colonial outlook. "Britain and the Ohio Valley, 1760–1775: The Search for Alternatives in a Revolutionary Era," in *Contest for Empire, 1500–1775,* ed. John B. Elliott (Indianapolis: Indiana Historial Society, 1975), p. 60.

14. Clive Parry ed., *The Consolidated Treaty Series,* 175 vols. (Dobbs Ferry, N.Y.: Oceana Publications, 1969), (hereafter cited as *CTS*), vols. 42–45, is the basis for this and subsequent tables and figures up to the point in the text where Anglo-Amerindian treaties for the period 1763–74 are brought into the discussion. In the case of languages in the European treaty system, a word of explanation is necessary. Of the sixty-nine treaties counted here as having French for one of the official languages, Parry prints a French version in sixty-six cases. In three cases he docs not: 12 November 1764, France and Spain, Spanish version (*CTS* 43: 119–20); 29 September 1765, France and Spain, Spanish version (ibid., pp. 213–15); 12 May 1766, France and Zweibruchen, German version, (ibid., p. 341). These three treaties have been included in the French-language total on the basis of an assumption that it seemed reasonable to make, which is that since France was a signatory to all three treaties there must at one time have existed a version in French as well as in the language of the other signatories.

15. The Russian-Turkish treaties have been included in the European treaty figures since by territory and by history Turkey was at that time part of the European treaty system.

16. Great Britain's presence in India, where the bulk of the British treaties were signed, was in the form of the Honorable United Company of Merchants of England trading to the East Indies (the English East India Company). Until the 1750s, this presence was relatively insignificant, but from then until the company's formal dissolution in 1858 its

history "is the history of the growth of the British empire in India and the east," in the words of D. K. Fieldhouse, *The Colonial Empires* (London: Weidenfeld & Nicolson, 1966), p. 152. After 1764, the company was the ruler of Bengal and "one of the great powers of India" (ibid., p. 167), a change of status that deeply involved the British government on the Indian subcontinent (ibid., pp. 149–52, 161–73). Vincent T. Harlow discusses in detail the process by which the British government gradually assumed control of the East India Company: *Founding of the Second British Empire, 1763–1793*, 2 vols. (London: Longmans, 1952–64) 2: 7–224.

17. *CTS* 42: 499–502.

18. George Croghan's Journal, "February 28, 1763–October 8, 1765," in *Illinois Historical Collections* 11 (1916) :1–64, records a meeting at Fort Pitt with the Shawnees in May 1765, and two July meetings at Ouitenon (a Wea village) on the Wabash. The first of the July meetings was with Indians who lived on or near the Wabash River, and the second was with a group of Ottawas under Pontiac, as well as with some members of the Illinois Confederacy. While Croghan was trying to smooth the way for British troops from the east, efforts were also being made by the British to get to the Illinois country from the south, and in this connection a meeting was held in August 1765 at the mouth of the Margot River (near Natchez) with some Arkansas Indians and some members of the groups known to European officials as the Small Tribes of the Lower Mississippi. The meeting is discussed by John R. Alden, *John Stuart and the Southern Colonial Frontier*, University of Michigan Publications in History and Political Science, vol. 15 (Ann Arbor: University of Michigan Press, 1944), pp. 201–4.

19. Nicholas B. Wainwright, *George Croghan, Wilderness Diplomat* (Chapel Hill: University of North Carolina Press for the Institute of Early American History and Culture, 1959), pp. 219–23.

20. These figures for the extended European treaty system will have to be revised again as work being done now on Africa and Asia turns up other treaties that did not get into the standard sources.

21. A talk from the Creek leaders Yakatastanage (the Mortar) and the Gun Merchant, 8 May 1763, in *The Colonial Records of the State of Georgia*, compiled by Allen D. Candler, 25 vols. (Atlanta, Ga.: State Printer, 1904–15) 9: 73.

22. Francis Jennings's painstaking work in uncovering and disentangling the realities of Iroquois diplomatic relations is embodied in his *Ambiguous Empire: The Iroquois League and Its Covenant Chain* (New York: W. W. Norton, forthcoming), the second volume in his continuing study of the formation of American society. See also Richard L. Haan, "The Covenant Chain: Iroquois Diplomacy on the Niagara Frontier, 1697–1730" (Ph.D. diss., University of California, Santa Barbara, 1976).

23. Jennings, "Covenant Chain," pp. 93–94; Jennings, "The Delaware Interregnum," *Pennsylvania Magazine of History and Biography* 89 (1965): 185, 186–92.

24. *Le droit des gens* 3: 3 (Introduction, no. 1).

25. Ibid., p. 5 (ibid., no. 10).

26. In the words of the Spanish minister, Julio Alberni, the European powers "cut and pared states like Dutch cheeses." Quoted by Samuel Flagg Bemis, *The Diplomacy of the American Revolution* (1935; reprint ed., Bloomington: Indiana University Press, Midland Books, 1957), p. 14.

Chapter Two

1. The relationship of the League to France and to Great Britain was the subject of much negotiation between the two European powers before the signing of the Treaty of Utrecht (1713): Frances G. Davenport, ed., *European Treaties Bearing on the History of the United States and Its Dependencies*, 4 vols. (Washington, D.C.: Carnegie Institution, 1917–37) 3: 198–213. It was France's Louis XIV who pointed out the essential futility of such negotiations. His objection was that if the Indians were dependent on either Crown, because of territory, it was useless to stipulate for them since they would in that case be subjects of the respective Crowns. If, on the other hand, they were independent, no proposals could realistically be made for them (ibid., p. 200). In the end, the French agreed that in the future they would not interfere with the Five Nations or districts of Indians who were subject to Great Britain *(ne molesteront point à l'avenir les Cinq Nations ou cantons des Indiens soumis à la Grande Bretagne)* (ibid., p. 213). It was a fine point, since the Five Nations did not acknowledge themselves as subject to anybody, and were not involved in the negotiations. Moreover, France continued to "interfere" as late as the 1750s. However, the haggling as well as the "interference" shows the importance that was attached to the Iroquois.

2. George T. Hunt, *The Wars of the Iroquois* (Madison: University of Wisconsin Press, 1940); George Snyderman, "Behind the Tree of Peace," *Pennsylvania Archaeologist* 18 (1948): 2–93.

3. Lewis H. Morgan, *League of the Ho-dé-no-sau-nee or Iroquois* (Rochester, N.Y.: Sage & Bros., 1851), pp. 12–13; Jennings, "Covenant Chain," pp. 91–94; Jennings, *Ambiguous Empire.*

4. J. N. B. Hewitt, Iroquois article in *Handbook of American Indians North of Mexico*, Bureau of American Ethnology Bulletin no. 30, ed. Frederick W. Hodge, 2 vols. (1907–10; reprint ed., New York: Pageant Books, 1960) 1: 619. Elizabeth Tooker, "The League of the Iroquois . . . ," Sturtevant, ed., *Handbook*, vol. 15: *Northeast*, p. 420, has a number of estimates, all lower.

5. The term is Angel Rosenblat's. Quoted by Woodrow Borah, "The Historical Demography of Aboriginal and Colonial America: An Attempt at Perspective," *The Native Population of the Americas in 1492*, ed. William N. Denevan (Madison: University of Wisconsin Press, 1976), p. 32.

6. Henry F. Dobyns, *Native American Historical Demography: A Critical Bibliography* (Bloomington: Indiana University Press for the

Newberry Library, 1976), pp. 10–13; Douglas H. Ubelaker, "The Sources and Methodology for Mooney's Estimates of North American Indian Population," ed. Denevan, *Native Population*, pp. 236–37. For a general account of disease as a factor in population loss, see Alfred W. Crosby, Jr., *The Columbian Exchange* (Westport, Conn.: Greenwood Publishing Co., 1972).

7. For the invasion concept, and a full discussion of the significance of population estimates, see Francis Jennings, *The Invasion of America* (Chapel Hill: University of North Carolina Press, 1975; New York: Norton Library, 1976), esp. pp. 15–31.

8. W. M. Beauchamp, *Civil, Religious, and Mourning Councils and Ceremonies of Adoption of the New York Indians,* New York State Museum Bulletin 113 (Albany: 1907), p. 407.

9. Sir William Johnson, "Enumeration of Indians within the Northern Department," 18 November 1763, *Documents Relative to the Colonial History of the State of New York* (hereafter cited as *NYCD*), ed. Edmund B. O'Callaghan, 15 vols. (Albany: Weed Parsons & Co., 1853–87) 7: 582. Tooker, in her table of population estimates, *Handbook* 15: 420, omits figures for the Tuscaroras, Nanticokes, and others included by Johnson in his 1763 estimates.

10. Anthony F. C. Wallace, *The Death and Rebirth of the Seneca* (New York: Alfred A. Knopf, 1970), pp. 41–42.

11. William N. Fenton, Introduction to *The Iroquois Book of Rites,* ed. Horatio Hale (1883; reprint ed., Toronto: University of Toronto Press, 1963), pp. xx–xxi.

12. Anthony F. C. Wallace speculates that the founding tradition of the League is an orally transmitted version of an ancient revitalization movement, and that the movement not only saved the Five Nations from destruction but transformed them from an ethnic to a political confederacy. "The Dekanawidah Myth Analyzed as the Record of a Revitalization Movement," *Ethnohistory* 5 (1958):118–24. See also James A. Brown, "The Impact of the European Presence on Indian Culture," *Contest for Empire,* ed. John B. Elliott (Indianapolis: Indiana Historical Society, 1975), p. 15.

13. This is a much simplified description of the political structure of the League, a structure that also varied at different periods in the League's history. Mary E. Fleming Mathur has pointed out some of the differences between a demoralized League in the mid-nineteenth century, when L. H. Morgan did his work on the Iroquois government, and the functioning of the League in the early part of the eighteenth century when Lafitau was investigating their government. "The Iroquois in Ethnography," *The Indian Historian* 2 (1969): 12–18.

14. Paul A. W. Wallace, *The White Roots of Peace* (Philadelphia: University of Pennsylvania Press, 1946), p. 30. Paul Wallace's account, a synthesis of several different texts of the founding myth, is the best introduction to the subject if the reader keeps in mind that Wallace accepted as fact the Iroquois' own idealized version of themselves. Other more detailed accounts are Arthur C. Parker, "The Constitution of the

Five Nations," *Parker on the Iroquois,* ed. William N. Fenton (Syracuse, N.Y.: Syracuse University Press, 1968), and Horatio Hale, ed., *The Iroquois Book of Rites* (1883; reprint ed., Toronto: University of Toronto Press, 1963). The Mohawk Nation has also published an account, *The Great Law of Peace of the Longhouse People* (Akwesasne via Rooseveltown, N.Y.: White Roots of Peace, Mohawk Nation at Akwesasne, 1971). For a discussion of the different texts see Fenton, ed., *Parker on the Iroquois,* pp. 39–40, and A. F. C. Wallace, "Dekanawidah," *Ethnohistory* 5 (1958): 125–29.

15. Hale, *Book of Rites,* pp. 28–30.

16. Richard R. Johnson, "The Search for a Usable Indian: An Aspect of the Defense of Colonial New England," *Journal of American History* 64 (1977): 632–44; Jennings, "Covenant Chain," p. 91.

17. A. F. C. Wallace, *Seneca,* pp. 94–98.

18. Mohawk Nation, *Great Law of Peace* (no pagination), sec. 2 and 72–92.

19. Robert C. Newbold, *The Albany Congress and the Plan of Union of 1754* (New York: Vantage Press, 1955), is a general account that, as its title indicates, emphasizes the national aspects of the congress.

20. Claude de Contrecoeur, "Summons to the British Troops at the Monongahela," 16 April 1754, *NYCD* 6: 842.

21. Lawrence H. Gipson, *The British Empire before the American Revolution,* 14 vols. (rev. ed., New York: Alfred A. Knopf, 1958–69), vols. 4–8. Gipson closes the war with the Paris treaty of 1763, although fighting continued in North America until 1765 and, so far as the Indians were concerned, was part of the same war.

22. The concern of colonial officials is reflected in Governor George Clinton's letter to the Board of Trade, "Notes on the Governor of Canada's Letter of 10 August 1751," *NYCD* 6: 734–36; Cadwallader Colden, "The Present State of Indian Affairs," 8 August 1751, ibid., pp. 738–47; Albany Commissioners, "Representation to the Board of Trade," 9 July 1754, ibid., pp. 885–88.

23. Speech of Hendrick, 16 June 1753, ibid., p. 788.

24. Board of Trade to Sir Danvers Osborne, 18 September 1753, ibid., pp. 800–801. The Board was at the peak of its power during this period, so its opinion counted. See Charles M. Andrews, *The Colonial Period of American History,* 4 vols. (1934–38; reprint ed., New Haven, Conn.: Yale University Press, Yale Paperbound, 1964) 4: 422.

25. Board of Trade to James DeLancey, 5 July 1754, *NYCD* 6: 845–46.

26. Ibid., p. 887.

27. A. F. C. Wallace, *Seneca,* pp. 39–44, has a good discussion of the working of the various leadership councils at different political levels to assure consensual decision-making.

28. For example, the British agreed to provide thirty wagons and provisions for the home-bound Iroquois following the Albany Congress (*NYCD* 6: 884).

29. Ibid., p. 862.

30. William H. Fenton, *American Indian and White Relations to 1830: Needs and Opportunities for Study* (Chapel Hill: University of North Carolina Press for the Institute of Early American History and Culture, 1957), pp. 21–22, speaks of the Iroquois insistence on the ceremony.

31. Jennings, "Covenant Chain," pp. 88–96, but see especially 89 and 94.

32. *NYCD* 6: 862–63.

33. Ibid., pp. 869–70. The Iroquois maintained this position throughout the period of this study, although other Indians disputed the claim. Even in 1754, the Iroquois could not have enforced their claim without the help of the British.

34. In 1710 Hendrick accompanied a party of Mohawks to England where, among other activities, he was presented at Court, and had his portrait painted by John Verelst (*Dictionary of American Biography* 8: 532).

35. *NYCD* 6: 872–73.

36. Paul A. W. Wallace, *Conrad Weiser, 1696–1760, Friend of Colonist and Mohawk* (Philadelphia: University of Pennsylvania Press, 1945); Milton W. Hamilton, *Sir William Johnson: Colonial American, 1715–1763* (Port Washington, N.Y.: Kennikat Press, 1976).

37. *NYCD* 6: 876.

38. See chapters 4 and 5 for details.

39. "Search for a Usable Indian," *Journal of American History* 64 (1977): 623–51. Credit for the *machina* phrase goes to Johnson, p. 643.

40. Again, this is dealt with more fully in later chapters.

41. Donald H. Kent, report presented in Docket 344 before the Indian Claims Commission, published as *History of Pennsylvania Purchases from the Indians*, vol. 1 of *Iroquois Indians* (New York: Garland Publishing, 1974), p. 88 (Garland pagination).

42. Ibid., p. 95 (Garland).

43. Knox to Pickering, 9 April 1791, Pickering Papers 61. 172 73.

44. Dunbar Rowland, ed., *Mississippi Provincial Archives: English Dominion, 1763–1766* (Nashville, Tenn.: Mississippi Department of Archives and History, 1911), p. 198.

45. Jennings, "Covenant Chain," pp. 89, 94.

Chapter Three

1. Andrews, *Colonial Period* 4: 299–302; Richard Pares, *King George III and the Politicians* (Oxford: Oxford University Press, 1953), esp. pp. 3–4.

2. Lawrence H. Gipson, *The Coming of the Revolution, 1763–1775* (1954; reprint ed., New York: Harper & Row, Harper Torchbook, 1962), pp. 55–56.

3. John P. Moore, "Anglo-Spanish Rivalry on the Louisiana Frontier,

1763–68," *The Spanish in the Mississippi Valley, 1762–1804,* ed. John F. McDermott (Urbana: University of Illinois Press, 1974), pp. 85–86.

4. The warning came at least as early as the summer of 1762, before the war officially ended. See the reference in Johnson's letter of 1 July 1763 to the Board of Trade, *NYCD* 7: 525.

5. Lord Egremont, secretary of state for the Southern Department, to North Carolina Governor Arthur Dobbs, 16 March 1763, in *Colonial Records of North Carolina,* ed. William L. Saunders, 10 vols. (Raleigh, N.C.: State Printer, 1886–90) 6: 974.

6. Andrews, *Colonial Period* 4: 419–22, 424.

7. This is brought out vividly by Alden in his *John Stuart and the Southern Colonial Frontier.*

8. Egremont to Dobbs, *Colonial Records of North Carolina* 6: 974.

9. John R. Swanton, *The Indians of the Southeastern United States,* Bureau of American Ethnology Bulletin 137 (Washington, D.C.: Government Printing Office for the Smithsonian Institution, 1946), p. 110. For a comprehensive list of Lower, Middle, and Overhill settlements. see Swanton, *The Indian Tribes of North America,* Bureau of American Ethnology Bulletin 145 (Washington, D.C.: Government Printing Office for the Smithsonian Institution, 1952), pp. 216–18. Sometimes the valley towns were also considered a separate contingent. See the map of southern Indian villages by Helen H. Tanner in *Atlas of Early American History,* ed. Lester J. Cappon (Princeton, N.J.: Princeton University Press for the Newberry Library and the Institute of Early American History and Culture, 1976), p. 19. For a discussion of the general characteristics of the southeastern culture area, see Raymond D. Fogelson's article, "Southeast American Indians," in the fifteenth edition of the *Encyclopaedia Britannica* (1974). Two general accounts are of particular interest: Charles Hudson, *The Southeastern Indians* (Knoxville: University of Tennessee Press, 1976), and James Leitch Wright, Jr., *The Only Land They Knew* (New York: The Free Press, 1981).

10. David H. Corkran, *The Cherokee Frontier: Conflict and Survival, 1740–1762* (Norman: University of Oklahoma Press, 1962), pp. 191–272, has a detailed account of the Anglo-Cherokee War of 1760–61 and of the peace negotiations (see esp. pp. 255–72).

11. John R. Swanton, *Early History of the Creek Indians and Their Neighbors,* Bureau of American Ethnology Bulletin 73 (Washington, D.C.: Government Printing Office for the Smithsonian Institution, 1922), pp. 215–16.

12. *The Appalachian Indian Frontier: The Edmond Atkin Report and Plan of 1755,* ed. and with an introduction by Wilbur R. Jacobs (1954; Lincoln: University of Nebraska Press, Bison Book, 1967), p. 62.

13. Ibid.

14. Letter to North Carolina Governor William Tryon, 28 May 1766, *Colonial Records of North Carolina* 7: 213–15; Stuart to Board of Trade, 10 July 1766, ibid., pp. 232–40; Stuart and George Johnstone, Governor of West Florida, to Lord Halifax, 12 June 1765, *Mississippi Provincial Archives: English Dominion,* pp. 184–88.

15. Swanton, *Indians of the Southeastern United States,* p. 73–78, 116–18, 121–22.

16. John Stuart to the Board of Trade, 2 December 1766, in *Colonial Records of North Carolina* 7: 281; Swanton, *Indian Tribes,* pp. 139–43; Swanton, *Early History of the Creek Indians,* pp. 399–400; Charles L. Mowat, *East Florida as a British Province, 1763–1784* (Berkeley: University of California Press, 1943); talk of Colonel Ayres, Catawba leader at Congress of Augusta, November 1763, in *State Records of North Carolina,* ed. and comp. Walter Clark, 17 vols. (Winston, N.C.: M. I. & J. C. Stewart, 1895–1905) 11: 189, 201–2.

17. *State Records of North Carolina* 11: 204.

18. *Colonial Records of North Carolina* 6: 975; Treaty of Augusta, 10 November 1763, *State Records of North Carolina* 11: 199–203. For the Creek War of 1774: *Documents of the American Revolution, 1770–1783,* Colonial Office Series, ed. K. G. Davies, 19 vols. to date (Shannon, Ireland: Irish University Press, 1972–75) 7: 193, and *American Archives,* 4 ser., comp. Peter Force, 6 vols. (Washington, D.C.: M. St. Clair Clarke and Peter Force) 1: 1137–38.

19. *Colonial Records of North Carolina* 6: 976.

20. Ibid., p. 975.

21. Talk of James Wright, governor of Georgia, to the Gun-Merchant and other Indian chiefs, 4 January 1763, *The Colonial Records of the State of Georgia,* comp. Allen D. Candler, 25 vols. (Atlanta: State Printer, 1904–15) 9: 14.

22. Wilbur R. Jacobs, *Diplomacy and Indian Gifts* (Stanford, Calif.: Stanford University Press, 1950), pp. 5, 11–17, 28. The 1763–65 war with the Indians north of the Ohio is attributed by Jacobs directly to Britain's failure to supply gifts to the Indians (see pp. 182–85).

23. Stuart to the Board of Trade, 2 December 1766, *Colonial Records of North Carolina* 7: 281.

24. John F. McDermott, Introduction to *Spanish in the Mississippi Valley,* p. vii.

25. "Journal of Proceedings," *State Records of North Carolina* 11: 156–99.

26. Egremont to Dobbs, 16 March 1763, *Colonial Records of North Carolina* 6: 974–76; Governor Arthur Dobbs, "Report to the North Carolina Council and Assembly," 3 February 1764, ibid., p. 1090.

27. Adam Shortt and Arthur G. Doughty, ed., *Documents Relating to the Constitutional History of Canada, 1759–1791* (Ottawa: S. E. Dawson, 1970), pp. 119–23, for a copy of the Proclamation of 1763.

28. Jack M. Sosin, *Whitehall and the Wilderness* (Lincoln: University of Nebraska Press, 1961), pp. 27–51.

29. Francis Paul Prucha, *American Indian Policy in the Formative Years* (Cambridge, Mass.: Harvard University Press, 1962), p. 13. It should be noted that the designation "Indian Country" was still within the European frame of reference in which Great Britain claimed ultimate sovereignty over the whole area. Francis Jennings has pointed out that maps prepared to show the Proclamation Line labeled Indian terri-

tory as "Crown land." Memo to the author, spring, 1979.

30. The Earl of Halifax to Sir Jeffrey Amherst, 19 October 1763, *NYCD* 7: 571–72.

31. The older mercantilistic view and the emerging imperial view can be seen in two reports made to the Board of Trade in the spring of 1763: "Hints Relative to the Division and Government of the Conquered and Newly Acquired Countries in America" (generally attributed to Egremont), and "Sketch of a Report Concerning the Cessions in Africa and America at the Peace of 1763," by John Pownall. Both reports recommended a boundary back of the English settlements, but the author of the "Hints" was concerned only with the protection of English manufactures from possible competition should North American settlements extend far into the interior. For discussion and references, see Prucha, *American Indian Policy,* pp. 15–17.

32. In 1770 John Stuart was forced to renegotiate the Virginia-Cherokee boundary he and the Cherokees had worked out in 1768. See the proceedings of the Treaty of Lochaber, *Documents of the American Revolution* 2: 210–15.

33. *State Records of North Carolina* 11: 183–89, 204–5.

34. For Dragging Canoe, see the article in *Handbook of American Indians* 1: 399–400.

35. *State Records of North Carolina* 11: 199.

36. Talk of John Stuart, 5 November 1763, ibid., pp. 179–82.

37. "A Talk from the Mortar and Gun Merchant at the Okchoys," 8 May 1763, *Colonial Records of Georgia* 9: 73.

38. *State Records of North Carolina* 11: 181–82; Egremont to Dobbs, 16 March 1763, *Colonial Records of North Carolina* 6: 975.

39. *Colonial Records of North Carolina* 6: 974.

40. *State Records of North Carolina* 11: 199, 200.

41. *Colonial Records of Georgia* 9: 72–73; *State Records of North Carolina* 11: 201–2, 204–5.

42. "Report," 6 February 1764, *Colonial Records of North Carolina* 6: 1090.

43. "Jud's Friend's Talk to Governor William Tryon," 2 June 1767, ibid., 7: 464.

44. "Report of Congress with the Cherokees," 18 October 1770, *Documents of the American Revolution* 2: 212, 213.

45. The Creek–East Florida segment was defined in the Treaty of Fort Picolata, 18 November 1765. An extract of the treaty is in *NYCD* 8: 32.

46. The location of every segment of the southern boundary has been worked out by Louis DeVorsey, Jr., and published in his geographical study, *The Indian Boundary in the Southern Colonies, 1763–1775* (Chapel Hill: University of North Carolina Press, 1961).

47. 21 May 1763, *Colonial Records of Georgia* 9: 78.

48. *State Records of North Carolina* 11: 187–88, 190–91, 198.

49. For the Cherokees as trading partners, see W. Stitt Robinson, "Virginia and the Cherokees," *The Old Dominion,* ed. Darrett B. Rut-

man (Charlottesville: University Press of Virginia, 1964), pp. 21–40; W. Neil Franklin, "Virginia and the Cherokee Indian Trade, 1753–1775," *East Tennessee Historical Society Publications* 5 (January 1933): 22–38.

50. *State Records of North Carolina* 11: 183–84, 186, 189.

51. Report of 10 November 1763, ibid., p. 205.

52. "Plan for the Management of Indian Affairs," 7 March 1768, *NYCD* 8: 24. The expense of the Board of Trade's plan for imperial control was a major factor in its defeat but, as Peter Marshall has pointed out, not the only one. See his "Colonial Protest and Imperial Retrenchment: Indian Policy, 1764–1768," *Journal of American Studies* 5 (1971): 1–17.

53. "Plan for the Future Management of Indian Affairs," 10 July 1764, *NYCD* 7: 641.

54. Alden, *John Stuart*, pp. 192–239, 262–81, for an account of Stuart's travels. A map of the southern Indian–white boundary is in DeVorsey, Jr., *Southern Indian Boundary*, p. 232.

55. "Plan," Board of Trade to the King, 7 March 1768, *NYCD* 8:22.

56. "A Talk from the Mortar and Gun Merchant at the Okchoys," 8 May 1763, *Colonial Records of Georgia* 9: 73. Quoted in David Corkran, *The Creek Frontier, 1540–1783* (Norman: University of Oklahoma Press, 1967), p. 234.

57. Ibid.

58. Treaty of Pensacola, 28 May 1765, *Mississippi Provincial Archives: English Dominion*, pp. 211–15. Signatories are on p. 214.

59. John Stuart to Board of Trade, 10 July 1766, *Colonial Records of North Carolina* 7: 238; "Talk of Mortar at the Pensacola Congress," 29 May 1765, *Mississippi Provincial Archives: English Dominion*, pp. 204–5: "Talk from the Creeks to Governor George Johnstone of West Florida," 16 May 1766, ibid., pp. 526–31.

60. "Talk of Alibamo Mingo at the Mobile Congress," 1 April 1765, *Mississippi Provincial Archives: English Dominion*, pp. 240–41; for the treaty, pp. 249–55, the goods are listed on p. 254.

61. Stuart to John Pownall, Secretary to the Board of Trade, 24 August 1765, *Colonial Records of North Carolina* 7: 109.

62. DeVorsey, Jr., *Indian Boundary*, p. 123; Alden, *John Stuart*, pp. 218–20; John Stuart to Governor William Tryon of North Carolina, 5 February 1766, *Colonial Records of North Carolina* 7: 165; Stuart to Board of Trade, 10 July 1766, ibid., p. 233.

63. Cameron to Stuart, 10 May 1766, *Colonial Records of North Carolina* 7: 207.

64. "A Talk from the Cherokee Chiefs ... to their Father in Charles Town," 22 September 1766, ibid., p. 257.

65. "Jud's Friend's [Osteneco's] Talk to Governor William Tryon," 2 June 1767, ibid., pp. 465, 466.

66. 7 March 1768, *NYCD* 8: 22.

67. Quoted in Max Farrand, "The Indian Boundary Line," *American Historical Review* 10 (1905): 789, an early study that emphasizes the place of the boundary in British policy.

Chapter Four

1. Howard H. Peckham, *Pontiac and the Indian Uprising* (Princeton, N.J.: Princeton University Press, 1947). For reasons that are explained later in the text, Peckham's account supersedes the better-known work by Francis Parkman, *The Conspiracy of Pontiac*, 2 vols. (rev. ed., 1870; reprint ed., New York: Charles Scribner's Sons, 1915).

2. Johnson to the Board of Trade, 30 August 1764, *NYCD* 7: 648–50.

3. Peckham, *Pontiac and the Indian Uprising,* p. 255; "Proceedings of Sir William Johnson with Pontiac and other Indians," *NYCD* 7: 854–67.

4. Proceedings of Sir William Johnson, *NYCD* 7:864.

5. Johnson to the Board of Trade, 13 November 1763, ibid., pp. 572–73.

6. Ibid., p. 573. As subsequent events made clear, the Ohio and Michigan Indians did not agree with this theory of the Iroquois right of conquest. The point here is the effect of the theory on British policy.

7. Comment of Good Peter, an Oneida leader, at the Council at Newtown Point, July 1791, Pickering Papers, vol. 60: 104.

8. Jennings, "Covenant Chain," pp. 91–94, discusses these ambiguous relationships. For an instance of the Shawnee deference-defiance attitude, see *Minutes of the Provincial Council of Pennsylvania, 1693–1776, Colonial Records of Pennsylvania, 1683–1790* (hereafter cited as *Pennsylvania Colonial Records*), 16 vols. (Philadelphia: Theo Fenn & Co., 1852–53) 9: 527–30, 538–39. The instance is discussed in more detail later in this chapter.

9. Randolph C. Downes, *Council Fires on the Upper Ohio* (Pittsburgh: University of Pittsburgh Press, 1940), pp. 133–78.

10. C. A. Weslager, *The Delaware Indians* (New Brunswick, N.J.: Rutgers University Press, 1972), p. 242; Glenn Tucker, *Tecumseh* (Indianapolis: Bobbs-Merrill, 1956).

11. Weslager, *Delaware,* pp. 227–37.

12. Johnson, "Enumeration of Indians," *NYCD* 7: 584.

13. Ibid., 584, 648; for the 1764 council, see also Peckham, *Pontiac and the Indian Uprising,* p. 253.

14. Harold Blau, et al., "Onondaga," *Handbook of North American Indians,* vol. 15, *Northeast:* 494–95.

15. Information about each Indian group mentioned is scattered throughout the Northeast volume of the *Handbook of North American Indians* (vol. 15), but for brief historical accounts, particularly for the smaller groups, see the older two-volume publication edited by Hodge, *Handbook of American Indians.* A map of northern Indian villages, prepared by Helen H. Tanner, is in the *Atlas of Early American History,* p. 20. The complex movements and relationships of all these Indian groups are worked out in detail in a forthcoming work by Tanner et al., *Atlas of Great Lakes Indians* (Norman: University of Oklahoma Press). For the Delawares and their relations with the Six Nations see Jennings, "Covenant Chain," pp. 91, 94.

16. Johnson to the Board of Trade, 26 December 1764, in Parkman, *Pontiac* 2 (appendix F): 409–11.

17. 13 November 1763, *NYCD* 7: 574.

18. Toward the close of the winter of 1763–64, Johnson sent messages throughout the whole Ohio-Great Lakes area to invite the Indians to a meeting at Niagara in July and August. The Menominees, among many others, sent a delegation (Parkman, *Pontiac* 2: 176, 180).

19. As example, George Croghan's journey in the early summer of 1765 (*Illinois Historical Collections* 11: 1–64). Parkman's *Pontiac* and Downes's *Council Fires* contain other instances of the functioning of the Indians' communication system.

20. John Stuart, southern superintendent of Indian affairs and George Johnstone, governor of West Florida, to Lord Halifax, 12 June 1765, *Mississippi Provincial Archives, English Dominion*, p. 185; "Proceedings of the Congress at German Flats," July 1770, *NYCD* 8: 227–44; Lieutenant-General Thomas Gage to John Stuart, 16 October 1770, *Documents of the American Revolution* 2: 203–4.

21. "Enumeration," *NYCD* 7: 583.

22. "Proceedings of Sir William Johnson with Pontiac and other Indians," *NYCD* 8: 854–67; A. F. C. Wallace, *Seneca*, pp. 114–15; and, in general, Peckham, *Pontiac and the Indian Uprising*.

23. Fort Pitt, April and May 1768, *Pennsylvania Colonial Records* 9: 530.

24. Peckham, *Pontiac and the Indian Uprising*, pp. 71–73; Downes, *Council Fires*, pp. 93–122.

25. Alexander Henry, *Travels and Adventures in Canada and the Indian Territories between the Years 1760 and 1776* (New York: I. Riley, 1809), p. 44.

26. Speech of Shingas to the British at Fort Pitt, 26 June 1763, The Military Papers of Colonel Henry Bouquet, 1754–1765 (hereafter cited as the Bouquet Papers), British Library, Additional MSS 21655, fol. 218.

27. 13 November 1763, *NYCD* 7: 575.

28. Ibid.

29. Onondaga speaker at meeting at Johnson Hall, 6 May 1765, United States Congress, *Papers of the Continental Congress, 1774–89* (hereafter cited as *PCC*), Record Group 360, National Archives Microfilm Publication M247, reel 69: 45–46.

30. George Croghan to Sir Jeffrey Amherst, 30 April 1763, Bouquet Papers, British Library, Additional MSS 21634, fol. 235; "Description and History, Louisiana, 1680–1755, Moreau St. Mery," Series F.3, vol. 24, in *Report Concerning Canadian Archives for the Year 1905*, 3 vols. (Ottawa: S. E. Dawson, 1906) 1: 472; "A Copy of the Minutes of a Council held at the place of M. de St. Ange...," 4 April 1765," ibid., p. 473.

31. Croghan, "Journals," *Illinois Historical Collections* 11: 47–48.

32. To the Board of Trade, 8 October 1764, *NYCD* 7: 665.

33. Amherst to Croghan, 10 May 1763, Bouquet Papers, Additional MSS 21634, fol. 245.

34. See, for example, Jack M. Sosin, *Whitehall and the Wilderness* (1961), and "Britain and the Ohio Valley, 1760–1775," in *Contest for Empire*, ed. John B. Elliott (1975), pp. 60–76. In these detailed and excellent studies of British policy, the Indians appear as little more than stage props in a drama that was written, directed, and acted by the British.

35. Thomas P. Abernethy, *Western Lands and the American Revolution*, University of Virginia Institute for Research in the Social Sciences, Monograph no. 25 (New York: D. Appleton-Century, for the Institute, 1937); Shaw Livermore, *Early American Land Companies* (New York: The Commonwealth Fund, 1939); *The Papers of Benjamin Franklin*, ed. Leonard W. Labaree et al., 19 vols. to date (New Haven, Conn.: Yale University Press, 1959–) 12: 395–400, 403–6; 15: 264–65, 275–79.

36. An early study is Clarence W. Alvord, *The Mississippi Valley in British Politics*, 2 vols. (Cleveland, Ohio: Arthur H. Clark Co., 1917), 2: 61–89.

37. *NYCD* 7: 637–41. Possibly the Board of Trade did not intend the two superintendents of Indian affairs to act on the boundary without further authorization. They did, however, proceed with negotiations on the basis of the proposed plan, a fact that the board acknowledged and approved in March 1768.

38. Lord Egremont to the Board of Trade, 5 May 1763, *NYCD* 7: 521.

39. 13 November 1763, ibid., p. 578.

40. See, for example, Stuart's objection to Virginia's plan for a publicly funded trading company, a plan that would undercut imperial trade control through Stuart. John Stuart to the Board of Trade, 10 July 1766, *Colonial Records of North Carolina* 7: 232–40. The Board of Trade's 1764 plan for the management of Indian affairs greatly strengthened imperial direction (*NYCD* 7: 637–41).

41. To the Board of Trade, 30 October 1764, *NYCD* 7: 674.

42. Wainwright, *George Croghan*, pp. 203–7. Croghan himself claimed title to 200,000 acres of land near the forks of the Ohio, on the basis of a grant from the League Council at Onondaga in 1749, confirmed by the Iroquois of the Ohio the same year. While in London in early 1764, on the business of the Philadelphia merchants, Croghan did not seek direct financial advantage from his own grant. Instead, he petitioned the Board of Trade for permission to exchange the Ohio land for a tract of equal size in the Mohawk country, near his friend, William Johnson. The board refused permission. See ibid., pp. 26, 28, 207.

43. 20 January 1764, *NYCD* 7: 603.

44. Ibid.

45. George E. Lewis, *The Indiana Company, 1763–1798*, Old Northwest Historical Series no. 4 (Glendale, Calif.: The Arthur H. Clark Co., 1941). A clear account of the subsequent history is in Peter Marshall, "Lord Hillsborough, Samuel Wharton, and the Ohio Grant, 1769–1775," *English Historical Review* 80 (1965): 717–39.

46. Sosin, *Whitehall and the Wilderness*, pp. 181–210, summarizes these developments.
47. Board of Trade to Lord Shelburne, 23 December 1767, *Colonial Records of North Carolina* 7: 538.
48. Treaty at Johnson Hall, 8 May 1765, *NYCD* 7: 740.
49. *PCC*, Record Group 360, Microfilm M247, reel 69: 32–33, 34.
50. Ibid., p. 38.
51. Ibid., pp. 66–67.
52. Ibid., p. 72.
53. Ibid., pp. 70–71.
54. 12 December 1765, *Papers of Benjamin Franklin* 12: 398.
55. *NYCD* 7: 754.
56. The standard bibliography is Imre Sutton, *Indian Land Tenure* (New York: Clearwater Publishing Co., 1975). See also George S. Snyderman, "Concepts of Land Ownership Among the Iroquois and Their Neighbors," in *Bureau of American Ethnology Bulletin 149* (Washington, D.C.: Government Printing Office, 1951), pp. 13–14, and Anthony F. C. Wallace, "Political Organization and Land Tenure Among the Northeastern Indians, 1600–1830," *Southwestern Journal of Anthropology* 13 (1957): 309–21.
57. Snyderman, "Concepts of Land Ownership," p. 15.
58. Elizabeth Tooker, "History of Research," *Handbook of North American Indians*, vol. 15, Northeast: 12: T. J. Brasser, "Early Indian-American Contacts," ibid., p. 84; Brasser, "Mahican," ibid., p. 200; Conrad E. Heidenrich, "Huron," ibid., p. 380.
59. Wallace, "Political Organization and Land Tenure," p. 312, n. 7.
60. This account of the territorial concepts of the Indians of the Northeast is based largely on Wallace, "Political Organization and Land Tenure," especially pp. 311–18. Wallace's account is based on material gathered over fifteen years as part of his work for several legal firms representing Indians before the Indian Claims Commission. Wallace points out that his conclusions are based not on inference from arch aeological remains or on sentimental reminiscences, but on "historical accounts of observed Indian behavior" (p. 302). He also emphasizes the importance of placing generalizations within a specified time period. For example, the pan-Indian concept of land tenure, in which no one group could convey land without the permission of all the rest, only began to be articulated in the early 1800s when the theme was sounded by Tecumseh and other leaders (p. 312, n. 7). In fact, there are signs of the concept as early as the 1780s, but this was twenty years after the treaties of 1765 and was probably a response to them as well as to other events of the intervening years. To make the pan-Indian land-tenure concept part of an analysis of the 1760s would be anachronistic.
61. Francis Jennings has pointed out another possible element in the subsequent resistance of the Shawnees and Delawares to the 1765 treaties: the many different Indian land rights that might exist at any one time for one piece of land. The Delawares, for example, were still con-

ceded to have certain rights in their ancestral lands in the Delaware Valley, although those lands had long since been sold. (Memo to the author, spring, 1979.) In some cases of dislocation-tenure, several different rights can be distinguished: settlement, free passage, hunting, fishing. The Shawnees and Delawares could lose settlement rights by the actions of the Iroquois—to which, in need, they might agree—and still feel that they retained hunting and fishing rights. In later years, the retention of these particular rights was frequently written into treaties, but it was not included in the treaties of 1765.

62. Wallace, "Political Organization and Land Tenure," pp. 318–19.

63. *PCC,* Record Group 360, Microfilm M247, reel 69: 56, 58; *NYCD* 7: 754. There is, of course, the possibility that what was read aloud was not what was actually in the treaties, but I have not found a statement from the dissident groups claiming that they were deceived.

64. *NYCD* 7: 757.

65. Ibid., p. 754.

66. Sosin, *Whitehall and the Wilderness,* pp. 128–64, sets Shelburne's plan within the context of British politics.

67. Lord Shelburne to William Johnson, 5 January 1768, *NYCD* 8: 2: Lord Hillsborough to William Johnson, 12 March 1768, ibid., pp. 35–36. Shelburne's instructions were an indication of the defeat of his plan. By the end of the same month, responsibility for the American colonies had been taken from him.

68. Ibid., p. 36.

69. Lord Hillsborough to North Carolina Governor William Tryon (and to the other colonial governors), 15 April 1768, *Colonial Records of North Carolina* 7: 708. The boundary location was specified in the Board of Trade report to Lord Shelburne, 23 December 1767, ibid., p. 538, and in the board's revised "Plan for the Management of Indian Affairs," 7 March 1768, *NYCD* 8: 22. For a copy of one of the maps sent to Johnson, see ibid. between pp. 30 and 31.

70. "Deed Determining the Boundary Line between the Whites and Indians," 5 November 1768, *NYCD* 8: 136.

71. Sosin, *Whitehall and the Wilderness,* p. 177; Ray Allen Billington, "The Fort Stanwix Treaty of 1768," *New York History* 25 (1944): 189–94. Johnson himself said that he knew that Virginia was determined to settle the land, and that this was a factor in his decision to accept the Iroquois cession. Johnson to Hillsborough, 26 June 1769, quoted in Peter Marshall, "Sir William Johnson and the Treaty of Fort Stanwix, 1768," *Journal of American Studies* 1 (1967): 178.

72. *NYCD* 8: 135.

73. "At a Treaty with the Six Nations, Shawanese . . . ," 29 October 1768, in "Minutes" of Sir William Johnson, Public Archives of Canada, Ottawa, Indian Records 8: 115–16, photostats, Manuscript Division, Library of Congress.

74. *Pennsylvania Colonial Records* 9: 481, 483.

75. At a council at Fort Pitt, April and May 1765, ibid., p. 528.

76. Ibid., pp. 529–30.

77. Ibid., pp. 538–39.
78. Ibid., pp. 531–32, 539, 541–43.

Chapter Five

1. *Pennsylvania Colonial Records* 9: 528.
2. Teyawarunte to William Johnson, 7 April 1773, at a congress at Johnson Hall, *Documents of the American Revolution* 6: 123.
3. For a discussion of the diplomatic and record-keeping uses of wampum belts, see Tooker, "Iroquois," *Handbook of North American Indians,* vol. 15, *Northeast:* 422–24, and Jennings, *Invasion of America,* pp. 120–21.
4. *Mississippi Provincial Archives, English Dominion,* p. 204.
5. Ibid., p. 205.
6. Croghan journal of meetings at Fort Pitt, May 1765, *Pennsylvania Colonial Records* 9: 249–64.
7. Stuart to Board of Trade, 10 July 1766, *Colonial Records of North Carolina* 7: 234, 236.
8. Ibid., p. 236; talk from the Creeks to Governor George Johnstone of West Florida, 16 May 1766, *Mississippi Provincial Archives, English Dominion,* p. 530.
9. Stuart to Board of Trade, 10 July 1766, *Colonial Records of North Carolina* 7: 235, 236.
10. Ibid., p. 235; W. Neil Franklin, "Virginia and the Cherokee Indian Trade," *East Tennessee Historical Society Publications* 5 (1933): 29–31.
11. "Plan for the Management of Indian Affairs," Board of Trade to the king, 7 March 1768, *NYCD* 8: 24; Lord Hillsborough to North Carolina governor, William Tryon, 15 April 1768, *Colonial Records of North Carolina* 7: 707.
12. DeVorsey, Jr., *Indian Boundary,* map on p. 232. As an example of the continuation of work on the lower portion of the southern boundary, even while the upper portion was collapsing, the Choctaws and the British sent out a surveying party early in 1772 to mark their mutual boundary north of Mobile. They had agreed on a line in 1765 and confirmed it at a conference in Mobile in late 1771 and early 1772 (see ibid., p. 222).
13. Johnson to Hillsborough, 18 February 1771, *Documents of the American Revolution* 3: 41–42; "Map of the Frontiers of the Northern Colonies with the Boundary Line Established between them and the Indians at the Treaty held by S. Will Johnson at Fort Stanwix in Novr. 1768," *NYCD* 1: between 586 and 587.
14. All quotations from Hillsborough to Johnson, 4 January 1769, British Public Record Office, Colonial Office Series 5: America and the West Indies (CO 5), vol. 70: 1–3, microfilm edition, Library of Congress.
15. "Proceedings of the Congress at German Flats," July 1770, *NYCD* 8:239.
16. See Thomas Gage quotation in the next paragraph of the text.

17. Gage to Stuart, 16 October 1770, *Documents of the American Revolution* 2: 204.

18. Ibid.

19. Johnson to Hillsborough, 18 February 1771, ibid., 3: 40.

20. Ibid., p. 41.

21. Ibid.

21. Ibid.

22. *NYCD* 8: 163.

23. William Johnson to the Earl of Hillsborough, 4 April 1772, *Documents of the American Revolution* 5: 60.

24. Ibid., p. 59.

25. Ibid., pp. 59–60.

26. Johnson to the Earl of Dartmouth, 4 November 1772, ibid., p. 212.

27. *Documents of the American Revolution* 6: 122.

28. For the reference to Augastarax's support for the Shawnee position, as well as for Johnson's defense of his own actions, see Johnson to Hillsborough, 4 April 1772, *Documents of the American Revolution* 5: 60. Dunmore's actions in asserting Virginia's claims as against those of Pennsylvania precipitated the fighting.

29. Historians have usually not distinguished between the two portions of the Iroquois cession, that above and that below the mouth of the Kanawha River, nor have they placed Shawnee actions within the overall setting of Iroquois attempts to retain suzerainty. For examples, see Samuel Eliot Morison *The Oxford History of the American People* (New York: Oxford University Press, 1965), pp. 210–11, and Richard B. Morris, *Encyclopedia of American History* (rev. ed., New York: Harper & Row, 1965), p. 438. The exception to these general statements regarding the Indian setting of Shawnee actions is Randolph C. Downes's pro-Shawnee account in *Council Fires on the Upper Ohio*, pp. 152–78.

30. Johnson to Hillsborough, 4 April 1772, *Documents of the American Revolution* 5: 60; Johnson to the Lords of Trade, 13 November 1763, *NYCD* 7: 573.

31. Johnson to Hillsborough, 4 April 1772, *Documents of the American Revolution* 5: 59.

32. "At a Treaty with the Six Nations, Shawanese...," 29 October 1768, in "Minutes" of Sir William Johnson, Public Archives of Canada, Ottawa, Indian records, vol. 8: 134, photostats, Manuscript Division, Library of Congress.

33. The Board of Trade Reported to the Privy Council in 1771 that the colonies had always given preference to actual settlement and improvement, whether legal or not, when it came to granting land titles. Noted in Amelia C. Ford, *Colonial Precedents of Our National Land System as It Existed in 1800,* University of Wisconsin Bulletin 352 (Madison: University of Wisconsin, 1910), pp. 124–25.

34. Ramsey, *Annals of Tennessee,* p. 93.

35. *Calendar of Virginia State Papers, 1652–1869,* 11 vols. (Richmond, Va.: Superintendent of Public Printing, 1875–93) 1: 260–63.

36. At the time of the Cherokee visit in March 1768, a treaty of peace, friendship, and alliance between the Cherokees, the Six Nations of the Iroquois, and the Seven Nations of Canada was negotiated and signed. For a copy of the treaty see *NYCD* 8: 50; for the proceedings of the congress, ibid., pp. 38-53.

37. Oconostotah to Stuart, 18 October 1770, *Documents of the American Revolution* 2: 213. See also Franklin, "Virginia and the Cherokee Indian Trade," *East Tennessee Historical Society Publications* 5 (1933): 35-38.

38. DeVorsey, Jr., *Indian Boundary*, pp. 162-63; Stuart to Hillsborough, 27 April 1771, *Colonial Records of North Carolina* 8: 553-54; Hillsborough to Stuart, 3 July 1771, ibid., 9: 8.

39. *Colonial Records of North Carolina* 9: 8. For the "New Purchase" treaty of 1 June 1773: CO5, vol. 662: 51-58d, as noted in *Documents of the American Revolution* 4: 333. For the treaty of peace, 20 October 1774: CO5, vol. 664: 11-13d, noted in ibid., 7: 193. See also *American Archives*, 4 ser., vol. 1: 1137-38, for Georgia Governor Wright's proclamation that trade with the Creeks might resume.

40. A copy of the Treaty of Lochaber, 18 October 1770, is in CO5, vol. 72: 29-31, in the microfilm edition, Library of Congress. For the journal of proceedings: ibid., pp. 22-28, and in *Documents of the American Revolution* 2: 210-15. For a discussion of the controversy with Virginia, see Alden, *John Stuart*, pp. 275-80.

41. Devorsey, Jr., *Indian Boundary*, pp. 78-92, discusses the Donelson-Attacullaculla Agreement of 1772. The agreement is included in the Cherokee land cessions mapped by Charles C. Royce, *The Cherokee Nation of Indians*, Bureau of Ethnology Fifth Annual Report, 1883-1884 (Washington, D.C.: Government Printing Office, 1887), plate 8, but it is there listed as an agreement between the Cherokees and the governor of Virginia, a labeling that obscures the degradation of authority that was involved as private interests captured the treaty system. For the 1775 "Treaty" of Sycamore Shoals, the standard source is Archibald Henderson, *The Conquest of the Old Southwest* (New York: Century Co., 1920), an extended defense of Richard Henderson's purchase from the Cherokees.

42. For the 1770 proceedings, see *Documents of the American Revolution* 2: 210-15. DeVorsey's discussion of the private agreement, *Indian Boundary*, pp. 78-92, is the fullest available. The bounds of Henderson's 1775 purchase can be found in extracts from the "Treaty" of Sycamore Shoals, Kentucky MSS (CC), 1CC17, Draper Manuscript Collection, State Historical Society of Wisconsin, Madison, and some discussion of the proceedings is in the Thomas Jefferson Papers, vol. 2: 229-56, microfilm edition, Manuscripts Division, Library of Congress.

43. Introduction by Clarence W. Alvord, ed., *Illinois-Oubache Land Company Manuscripts* (Chicago: C. H. McCormick, 1915). The question of William Murray's direct purchases from the Indians was not finally settled within the American legal system until 1823, in the U.S. Supreme Court decision in *Johnson and Graham's Lessee v. William*

M'Intosh, US 21 (Wheaton 8): 543.

44. Haldimand to Johnson, 15 September 1773, Sir Frederick Haldimand: Unpublished Papers and Correspondence, 1758–84 (hereafter cited as Haldimand Papers), British Library, Additional MSS 21670, fols. 78–79. Haldimand was commanding temporarily in the absence of Thomas Gage.

45. Johnson to Haldimand, 30 September 1773, Haldimand Papers, ibid., fols. 82–83.

46. Sosin, *Whitehall and the Wilderness,* pp. 259–67. Sosin's account supersedes the hitherto standard accounts in Thomas P. Abernethy, *Western Lands and the American Revolution* (New York: D. Appleton-Century, 1937), and Clarence W. Alvord, *The Mississippi Valley in British Politics,* 2 vols. (Cleveland: Arthur H. Clark Co., 1917).

47. Percival Spear, *A History of India,* vol. 2 (Hammondsworth, England: Penguin Books, 1968), pp. 61–92.

48. Sosin, *Whitehall and the Wilderness,* p. 205.

49. For Johnson's response, see Johnson to Dartmouth, 4 November 1772, *Documents of the American Revolution* 5: 213.

Chapter Six

1. *Journals of the Continental Congress* (hereafter cited as *JCC*), ed. Worthington C. Ford, 34 vols. (Washington, D.C.: Government Printing Office for the Library of Congress, 1904–37) 1: 88–89, 103; 2: 206, 217–18.

2. Ibid., vol. 1: 105–13.

3. Ibid., vol. 2: 70.

4. Ibid., vol. 2: 195, 199. For a discussion of Franklin's concern about the international anarchy of the eighteenth century, see Gerald Stourzh, *Benjamin Franklin and American Foreign Policy* (Chicago: University of Chicago Press, 1954), pp. 59–60.

5. *JCC* 2: 198.

6. Walter H. Mohr, *Federal Indian Relations, 1774–1788* (Philadelphia: University of Pennsylvania Press, 1933), pp. 34–35; Franklin to Dumas, 19 December 1775, in *The Revolutionary Diplomatic Correspondence,* ed. Francis Wharton, 6 vols. (Washington, D.C.: Government Printing Office, 1889) 2: 65.

7. *JCC* 2: 123.

8. In only one other of their public addresses in 1775 did the delegates portray the colonies' relationship with Great Britain in family terms. There is a brief reference in the address to the people of Ireland in which certain British actions are characterized as "refinements in parental cruelty." *JCC* 2: 216. This may have been a lapse into customary terminology. At any rate, the comparison is only in passing. In the address to the Indians, the metaphor is structural.

9. Ibid., p. 181.

10. Ibid., p. 182.

11. For an account of the meeting at Albany, and a preliminary meeting a few days earlier at German Flats, New York, see U.S. Congress, *Papers of the Continental Congress, 1774-1789* (hereafter cited as *PCC*) (Washington, D.C.: National Archives Microfilm Publication M247, n.d.), roll 144, item 134, and "Proceedings of Commissioners Appointed to Treat with the Six Nations of Indians," *American Archives*, 4 ser., 3: 473-90. The speech, as delivered to the Iroquois, can be found on 481-84. For the meetings with the western nations, see Reuben G. Thwaites and Louise P. Kellogg, ed., *The Revolution on the Upper Ohio, 1775-1777*, Draper Series, vol. 2 (Madison: Wisconsin Historical Society, 1908), pp. 25-127, and with the southern Indians, *North Carolina Records* 10: 329-30, and Mohr, *Federal Indian Relations*, p. 34.

12. *American Archives*, 4 ser., 3: 487; *PCC* (M247), roll 144, p. 37.

13. Abraham, Chief of the Mohawks, to the Magistrates and Committee of the town of Schenectady, and Major Corporation and Committee of the City of Albany, 20 May 1775, N.A. 6, Edward E. Ayer Collection, Newberry Library, Chicago.

14. *American Archives*, 4 ser., 3: 486; *PCC* (M247), roll 144, p. 35.

15. *PCC* (M247), roll 144, p. 35. The continental commissioners warned by Abraham were Volkert P. Douw, Turbot Francis, General Philip Schuyler, and Oliver Wolcott. Ralph T. Pastore has studied the work of this group in "The Board of Commissioners for Indian Affairs in the Northern Department and the Iroquois Indians, 1775-1778," (Ph.D. dissertation, University of Notre Dame, 1972).

16. *JCC* 2: 182; *American Archives*, 4 ser., 3: 483.

17. "Proceedings at a Congress with . . . the Six Nations in June and July, 1774," *NYCD* 8: 483.

18. This meeting fell within the jurisdiction of the Middle Department, but Franklin did not attend. Only James Wilson of the three men originally appointed to the Middle Department was present. The other continental representative was Lewis Morris. For a brief account of the meeting, see Mohr, *Federal Indian Relations*, p. 34.

19. John Connolly, "A Narrative of the Transactions, Imprisonment, and Sufferings of John Connolly, an American Loyalist and Lieut. Col. in His Majesty's Service," *Pennsylvania Magazine of History and Biography* 12 (1888): 310-24, 407-20; 13 (1889): 61-70, 153-58, 281-91; Thwaites and Kellogg, eds., *Revolution on the Upper Ohio*, pp. 43-44.

20. Massachusetts Provincial Congress, "Address to the Mohawks," 4 April 1775, *American Archives*, 4 ser., 1: 1349-50. For a detailed account of the wartime alliances and activities of the Iroquois, see Barbara Graymont, *The Iroquois in the American Revolution* (Syracuse, N.Y.: Syracuse University Press, 1972), and John C. Guzzardo, "The Superintendent and the Ministers: The Battle for Oneida Allegiances, 1761-75," *New York History* 57 (1976): 255-83, for the Oneidas in particular. See also Francis Jennings, "The Indians' Revolution," in *The American Revolution: Explorations in the History of American Radicalism*, ed. Alfred E. Young (DeKalb, Ill.: Northern Illinois Univeristy Press, 1976), for a general discussion within an analytical framework

that compares the struggles of the Indians with the wars of Irish peasants in defense of their lands and independence.

21. Aaron to Little Abraham, 17 February 1780, Niagara, "Minutes" of Colonel Guy Johnson, Public Archives of Canada, Ottawa, vol. 12, pt. 2: 170, photostat, Manuscript Division, Library of Congress.

22. Kingageghta to Colonel Johnson, 25 January 1780, ibid., pt. 1: 126–27.

23. *Southern Indians in the American Revolution* (Knoxville: University of Tennessee Press, 1973), pp. 52–53.

24. Ibid., pp. 43–49.

25. For the Treaty of Dewitt's Corner, 20 May 1777, see *American State Papers, Public Lands,* 8 vols. (Washington, D.C.: Duff Green, 1834–1861)1: 59–60. The two Treaties of Long Island, 20 July 1777, can be found in *North Carolina Historical Review* 8 (1931): 103–5 (Cherokee-Virginia), and 107–8 (Cherokee-North Carolina). For a detailed, pro-Cherokee account of these and subsequent events, see Randolph C. Downes, "Cherokee-American Relations in the Upper Tennessee Valley, 1776–1791," *East Tennessee Historical Society Publications* 8 (1936): 35–53.

26. For a biographical account of McGillivray, see the introductory chapter to a collection of his correspondence, with related papers from Spanish archives, John W. Caughey, *McGillivray of the Creeks* (Norman: University of Oklahoma Press, 1938; 2d printing, 1958), pp. 3–57.

27. R. S. Cotterill, *The Southern Indians: The Story of the Civilized Tribes before Removal* (Norman: University of Oklahoma Press, 1954), pp. 40–41.

28. This summarizes O'Donnell's detailed account in *Southern Indians in the American Revolution.*

29. Half King to the Delawares at Coshocton, 9 February 1779, printed in Louise P. Kellogg, ed., *Frontier Advance on the Upper Ohio, 1778–1779,* Draper Series, vol. 4, *Wisconsin Historical Collections* 23 (1916): 223. Rumors of the union of Western Indians were as vague as they were persistent throughout this period. For example, late in 1778 the Chickasaws sent a message to the Delawares saying that it was their understanding "that all the nations in your locality had united to form but one." The message was mentioned by a Wyandot in a talk at Detroit, 2 January 1779, printed, ibid., p. 191.

30. C. A. Weslager, *The Delaware Indians* (New Brunswick, NJ: Rutgers University Press, 1972), pp. 312–17.

31. Downes, *Council Fires,* pp. 248–76.

32. The Delaware attempt to get British confirmation of their land claim was noted by Arthur St. Clair in a letter to Joseph Shippen, 12 July 1775, in *Pennsylvania Archives,* 1st ser., ed. Samuel Hazard, 12 vols. (Philadelphia: J. Severns & Co., 1852–56) 4: 637. For the 1775 attempt at American confirmation, see Thwaites and Kellogg, eds., *Revolution on the Upper Ohio,* pp. 86–87.

33. Congressional answer to Captain White Eyes, 10 April 1776, *JCC* 4: 269–70.

34. John Heckewelder, *A Narrative of the Mission of the United Brethren among the Delaware and Mohegan Indians* (Philadelphia: M'Carty & Davis, 1820), pp. 140–41.

35. Weslager, *Delaware Indians,* pp. 306–7; "The Deputies of the Delaware Nations to the United States Congress in answer to the Address of their Committee to the Said Deputies," 29 May 1779, "Brodhead Papers," (H), 1H91–92, Draper Manuscript Collection, State Historical Society of Wisconsin, Madison. It should be noted that the formal United States–Delaware alliance (1778) mentioned in the text, was denied by these Delaware deputies in 1779. They said that the Delawares had been deceived, and that they wanted to remain neutral (ibid., p. 76). Weslager discusses the unlikelihood of this claim of deception being true, at least for a man as knowledgeable and perceptive as the Delaware leader White Eyes, one of the signers of the formal treaty of alliance (see *Delaware Indians,* pp. 304–5).

36. Delaware statement of purposes, 10 May 1779, Draper MSS, 1H76.

37. Ibid., p. 87.

38. Delaware–United States treaty of 1778. Kappler, *Treaties,* vol. 2: 4, and *CTS* 47: 89. A copy is in the Draper MSS, 1H10–13, State Historical Society of Wisconsin, with minor differences from the version printed in Kappler and Parry. For the Cherokee-United States treaty of 1779, see ibid., 1H111–14, printed in Kellogg, ed., *Frontier Advance,* pp. 397–400.

39. Raymond D. Fogelson, professor of anthropology, University of Chicago, notes that "There seems to have been a longstanding tradition of Cherokee deference to the Delawares," and that this might account for their signing the treaty of 22 July 1779. Fogelson, 17 June 1977, to the author.

40. Quoted and noted in Downes, *Council Fires,* pp. 197, 236.

41. Captain Arent De Peyster to Lord Frederick Haldimand, 3 May 1783, in *Michigan Pioneer and Historical Collections,* 40 vols. (Lansing: Michigan Historical Commission, 1877–1919) 11: 363.

42. Even before the Six Nations' cession of Shawnee land, there were tensions between the Great Council and their supposed tributaries. The tensions and the Shawnee attempts to act independently can be seen in the Fort Pitt council, April–May 1768, that has been discussed in the text. For further details, see *Pennsylvania Colonial Records* 9: 527–30. In early 1775, despite their defeat by Lord Dunmore's forces, the Shawnees were still taking independent action and the Six Nations were still asserting their authority. When the Shawnees invited the Six Nations to a meeting to be held with representatives from Virginia in the spring of 1775, the Six Nations refused to go on the grounds that it was no business of the Shawnees to set a place for negotiations. Rather, the Six Nations would summon the Shawnees to a meeting at one of the traditional locations: Onondaga, or the residence of the superintendent of Indian affairs. See "At a Meeting with the Six Nations Chiefs at Guy Park," 24 January 1775, "Minutes" of Guy Johnson, Public Archives

of Canada, Ottawa, Indian Records, vol. 11: 49, photostat, Manuscript Division, Library of Congress.

43. For Wyandot history, see Swanton, *Indian Tribes*, pp. 233–36, and Elizabeth Tooker, "Wyandot," *Handbook of North American Indians*, vol. 15, *Northeast:* 398–404. For the view that disease and not trade wars decimated and scattered the Hurons, see Karl H. Schlesier, "Epidemics and Indian Middlemen: Rethinking the Wars of the Iroquois, 1609–1653," *Ethnohistory* 23 (1976) :129–45. Dunquad's statement to the Delawares, 9 February 1779, is in Kellogg, ed., *Frontier Advance*, p. 223.

44. Kellogg, ed., *Frontier Advance*, p. 223.

45. *The Diplomacy of the American Revolution* (1935; rev. ed., Bloomington: Indiana University Press, 1957), p. 255.

46. *Britain and the American Frontier*, p. 46.

47. *JCC* 20: 609.

48. Ibid., p. 617.

49. Wharton, ed., *Revolutionary Diplomatic Correspondence* 5: 89–90.

50. Discussed in detail later in this chapter.

51. *Britain and the American Frontier*, pp. 15–35.

52. Samuel Flagg Bemis, *Pinckney's Treaty* (1926; rev. ed., New Haven, Conn.: Yale University Press, 1960), pp. 62–66.

53. Brigadier General Allan Maclean to General Haldimand, 18 May 1783, in *Michigan Historical Collections,* 20: 119.

54. Speaker for the Ouiats (Weas), 3 May 1783, in *Michigan Historical Collections* 11: 370.

55. "Transactions with the Indians at Sandusky from 26 August to 8th September 1783," *Michigan Historical Collections* 20: 177.

56. *State Records of North Carolina* 24: 479. For a discussion of North Carolina's aims, see Cotterill, *Southern Indians*, p. 55.

57. McGillivray for the chiefs of the Creek, Chickasaw, and Cherokee nations, 10 July 1785, in Caughey, ed., *McGillivray*, pp. 91–93.

58. Ibid., p. 91.

59. Ibid.

60. Ibid., p. 92.

61. Ibid., p. 93.

62. For the preliminaries to the Spanish guarantee, see McGillivray to Arturo O'Neill, governor of Pensacola, 1 January 1784, in Caughey, ed., *McGillivray*, pp. 64–66; José de Galvez, Minister of the Indies, to José de Ezpeleta, acting captain-general at Havana, 22 May 1784, AGI Cuban Papers, legajo 2351, p. 3 of packet labeled "8 February 1784" in Cuban Paper transcripts, Ayer Collection, Newberry Library. The Creek-Spanish treaty of Pensacola, 1 June 1784, can be found ibid., legajo 2360, and is printed in *American State Papers, Foreign Relations*, 6 vols. (Washington, D.C.: Gales & Seaton, 1832–59)1: 278–79, and in Caughey, ed., *McGillivray*, pp. 75–76.

63. There were three of these treaties: 1 November, 1783, 12 November 1785, and 3 November 1786. For the Georgia point of view regarding the treaties, see *American State Papers, Indian Affairs*, vol. 1: 20,

23–24. The treaties are discussed by Cotterill, *Southern Indians,* p. 58, and by Chapman J. Milling, *Red Carolinians* (Chapel Hill: University of North Carolina Press, 1940), pp. 322–23.

64. Mohr, *Federal Indian Relations;* Francis P. Prucha, *American Indian Policy in the Formative Years* (Cambridge: Harvard University Press, 1962); Reginald Horsman, *Expansion and American Indian Policy, 1783–1812* (East Lansing: Michigan State University Press, 1967).

65. Knox embodied his thinking in three separate reports to President George Washington: 23 May 1789, 15 June 1789, and 6 and 7 July 1789. For these reports, see *American State Papers, Indian Affairs,* 1: 7–8, 12–14, 15–54. Some of Knox's arguments are discussed in more detail later in the text.

66. *JCC* 31: 490–93.

67. Mohr, *Federal Indian Relations,* pp. 94–97.

68. Report of the Committee on Indian Affairs, 28 May 1784, *JCC* 27: 456.

69. A convenient summary of influences on United States policy, and official statements issued, is in Reginald Horsman, "American Indian Policy in the Old Northwest, 1783–1812," *William and Mary Quarterly,* 3d ser., 18 (1961): 35–53. Washington's boundary recommendation is in a letter to James Duane, 7 September 1783, printed in *The Writings of George Washington,* ed. John C. Fitzpatrick, 39 vols. (Washington, D.C.: 1931–44) 27: 138–40. The congressional resolution of 12 August 1783 is in *JCC* 24: 503, and the proclamation of 22 September 1783 is in ibid., vol. 25: 602. On October 15, 1783, Congress made its first spe cific recommendation for an Indian-white boundary north of the Ohio River. The recommendation, based on George Washington's proposal, can be found in the report of the Committee on Indian Affairs, 15 October 1783, ibid., p. 686.

70. The four treaties that had to be renegotiated were: Six Nations–United States, 22 October 1784; Wyandot, Delaware, et al.–United States, 21 January 1785; Cherokee–United States, 12 November 1785; Shawnee–United States, 31 January 1786.

71. Brant to General Philip Schuyler, via the messengers Skenoda and Petrus, bearing messages to Schuyler on behalf of the Six Nations, 21 July 1783, Ayer MS 803, Ayer Collection, Newberry Library. For a copy of the Six Nations–United States Treaty of Fort Stanwix, 22 October 1784, see Kappler, *Treaties* 2: 5–6, and *CTS* 49: 169. Aaron Hill's speech is quoted in Kent, *Pennsylvania Purchases,* p. 88 (Garland).

72. A copy of the Wyandot, Delaware, et al.–United States Treaty of Fort McIntosh, 21 January 1785, is in Kappler, *Treaties* 2: 6–8, and *CTS* 49: 217–18. The Shawnee–United States Treaty of Fort Finney, 31 January 1786, is in Kappler, *Treaties* 2: 16–18, and *CTS* 49: 477–78. Minutes of the Fort Finney treaty proceedings are in the Frontier Wars MSS (U), 3U186–202, Draper Manuscript Collection, State Historical Society of Wisconsin.

73. *JCC* 22: 456.

74. Ibid., p. 455.

75. Ibid.

76. Franchimastabe, Choctaw, to Spanish officials at a meeting held jointly with the Chickasaws at Yazoo in late 1787, quoted in Manuel Serraño y Sanz, *España y los Indios Cherokis y Chactas* (Seville: Tip de la "Guia Oficial," 1916), p. 37. The three postwar treaties with the southern Indians, with the location of printed copies, are: Cherokee–United States, Treaty of Hopewell, 28 November 1785, Kappler, *Treaties* 2: 8–11, and *CTS* 49: 443–46; Choctaw–United States, Treaty of Hopewell, 3 January 1786, Kappler, *Treaties* 2: 11–14, and *CTS* 49: 453–56; Chickasaw–United States, Treaty of Hopewell, 10 January 1786, Kappler, *Treaties* 2: 14–16, and *CTS* 49: 459–61. State protests are in the report of Benjamin Hawkins and other United States commissioners to the southern Indians to Richard Henry Lee, president of Congress, 2 December 1785, printed in *American State Papers, Indian Affairs* 1: 38, and in the "Journal of Proceedings" of the Chickasaw–United States negotiations, January 1786, Frontier Wars Manuscripts (U), 14U102–103, Draper Manuscript Collection. The Cherokee request for the return of Kentucky is in the "Journal of Proceedings" of the Cherokee–United States negotiations, November 1785, ibid., 14U42–43. The protests of groups from all three southern Indian nations and their attempts to enlist Spanish aid can be found as follows: Cherokees, *American State Papers, Foreign Relations* 1: 280–81; Choctaws, Serraño y Sanz, *España y los Indios*, pp. 36–40; Chickasaws, ibid.

77. For instances of McGillivray's transmitting American messages to the Spanish, see McGillivray to the Spanish governor at Pensacola, Arturo O'Neill, 8 November 1785, and 8 October 1786, AGI, Cuban Papers, legajo 2360, no. 209, p. 3, and no. 54, pp. 23–26, in Cuban Papers transcripts, Ayer Collection, Newberry Library; see also ibid., no. 283, pp. 6–14.

78. Ibid., no. 209, pp. 3–5.

79. *American State Papers, Indian Affairs* 1: 20, 23.

80. Authorization was given by Don Esteban Miró, governor of Louisiana, in a letter to Conde de Galvez, captain-general of the Floridas, 28 June 1786, a document summarized in "Desavenencias entre los Indios y Americanos," AGC, Ministero de Estado, legajo 3891, no. 136 in vol. 5: 229–30, Gardoqui Dispatches, transcripts of which are in Special Collections, Regenstein Library, University of Chicago. Governor Miró sent a copy of this correspondence and a copy of the Creek-Spanish Treaty of Pensacola, 1 June 1784, to Diego de Gardoqui in New York, the Spanish representative who was engaged in negotiations with the United States at that time. Ibid., p. 230.

81. Confederated Council of the United Indian Nations to the Congress of the United States, 2 December 1786, *American State Papers, Indian Affairs* 1: 8.

Chapter Seven

1. For Dorchester's resignation and his defense of his speech to the Indians, see Dorchester to Henry Dundas, secretary of state for war,

October 1794, British Public Record Office, War Office 1, vol. 14, pt. 1: 49–56, photostat, Manuscript Division, Library of Congress. Bemis, *Pinckney's Treaty*, is the standard account of the United States–Spanish negotiations that culminated in the Treaty of 1795.

2. A. P. Whitaker, *The Spanish-American Frontier, 1783–1795* (Boston: Houghton Mifflin Co., 1927) treats these intrigues in detail.

3. British maneuvers in this period are thoroughly covered by J. Leitch Wright, Jr., in his *Britain and the American Frontier*.

4. J. Leitch Wright, Jr., *William Augustus Bowles* (Athens: University of Georgia, 1967), pp. 57–60.

5. Richard K. Murdock, "French Intrigue along the Georgia-Florida Frontier, 1793–1796," (Ph.D. dissertation, University of California, Los Angeles, 1947), pp. 114–40.

6. J. G. M. Ramsey, *The Annals of Tennessee to the End of the Eighteenth Century* (Philadelphia: J. B. Lippincott & Co., 1860), pp. 344–46.

7. For example, the British advised and provisioned the Indians from the western nations and the Six Nations who assembled for a meeting with the American peace commission in 1793, and refused an American request to provide food for the Indians on the grounds that it was "our invariable System as Possessors of the Forts to assist the Indians, from whatever Cause they may be assembled, with Provisions." Colonel John Simcoe to Captain Alexander McKee, 23 January 1793, Public Archives of Canada, Q62 from the British Public Record Office, CO42, vol. 93: 155, document no. 5062 in transcripts, Ethnohistory Collection, Special Collections, Regenstein Library, University of Chicago.

8. Downes, *Council Fires*, pp. 315–20, 324–36; "Correspondence of General Anthony Wayne and Major William Campbell, 24th Regiment, commanding the British Fort Miamis," British Public Record Office, War Office 1, vol. 14, pt. 1: 31–46, photostats, Manuscript Division, Library of Congress.

9. Serraño y Sanz, *España y los Indios*, pp. 33–34.

10. For the treaty that marked McGillivray's rapprochement with Spain, see Treaty of New Orleans, 6 July 1792, AGI Cuban Papers, legajo 2362, pp. 84–86 in Cuban Papers transcripts, Ayer Collection, Newberry Library. The treaty is printed in English translation in Caughey, ed., *McGillivray*, pp. 329–30.

11. The Indians benefited briefly from Anglo–United States hostilities during the War of 1812, then dropped back again on the scale of European concerns.

12. In any standard text of United States history, and in detail in Horsman, *Expansion and American Indian Policy*.

13. For an expression of some of these feelings about the significance of land to the future of the American nation, see the various reports of Alexander Hamilton, especially the First Report on the Public Credit, in *Papers on Public Credit, Commerce, and Finance*, ed. Samuel McKee, Jr. (1934; reprinted, New York: Liberal Arts Press, 1957), pp. 28–30.

14. The inability of Congress to get its representatives into the territory north of the Ohio in 1783 has already been mentioned (Downes,

Council Fires, pp. 287–88). The situation continued until after the defeat of the Indians at Fallen Timbers and the signing of Jay's Treaty, both in 1794. United States emissaries such as Captain Pierre Gamelin (1790), Thomas Proctor (1791), and Captain Hendrick Aupaumut (1792) were entirely dependent upon the will of the Indians and the British for entry into the area. As Downes has pointed out, of six United States emissaries sent to the Indians in 1792, two were turned back by the British and two were killed by the Indians. Two managed to meet with the Indians, but did not secure any agreement that either the Indians or the United States would honor (p. 321). This was five years after the passage of the Northwest Ordinance for the governing of the territory north of the Ohio.

15. Cappon, ed., *Atlas of Early American History,* pp. 128, 130.

16. Based on figures in Jonathan Elliot, *The Funding System of the United States and Great Britain* (1845; reprinted New York: A. M. Kelley, 1968), p. 19.

17. Proclamation of 1 September 1788: *JCC* 34: 476–79. For the Trade and Intercourse Acts: *United States Statutes at Large,* vols. 1–17 (Boston: Little Brown & Co., 1845–73) 1: 137–38 (22 July 1790); 329–33 (1 March 1793); 469–75 (19 May 1796); 743–49 (3 March 1799). For a discussion of the place of these acts in United States policy, see Prucha, *American Indian Policy,* pp. 45–50.

18. Quoted in Prucha, *American Indian Policy,* p. 37.

19. *JCC* 34: 124–26, 285–86; *American State Papers, Indian Affairs* 1: 9.

20. Report, "Relative to the Northwestern Indians," 15 June 1789, *American State Papers, Indian Affairs,* 1: 13.

21. Ibid.

22. Ibid.

23. Report, "Relating to the Southern Indians," 6–7 July 1789, ibid., p. 53.

24. Robert F. Berkhofer, Jr., *The White Man's Indian* (New York: Alfred A. Knopf, 1978), p. 143.

25. *American State Papers, Indian Affairs* 1: 52.

26. Ibid.

27. The Ohio River was the hard-line position of Indian militants, the sine qua non they maintained for eleven years in talks with the Americans. Several times, Joseph Brant and some other Indian leaders were willing to settle for a boundary along the Ohio and Muskingum rivers, which would have been a considerable concession on the part of the Indians, but this was not adopted by enough Indians to make it a possible negotiating position. The 1793 peace negotiations foundered on the Indians' insistence on the Ohio River boundary line. For the location of the Muskingum River boundary compromise, see "Proposed Boundary Line between United States and American Indians," Lord Dorchester to Henry Dundas, 23 November 1793, Public Archives of Canada, Q67, p. 30, printed in *Michigan Historical Collections* 24: 616–17.

28. "Unclaimed Lands in the Territory Ceded by North Carolina," 8 November 1791, *American State Papers, Public Lands* 1: 18.

29. For more than forty years the federal government balanced competing claims in the area, until the passage of the Indian Removal Act in 1830 tipped the weight of advantage toward the states and away from the Indians.

30. Treaty of the Holston, 2 July 1791: Kappler, *Treaties* 2: 29–33, and Parry, ed., *CTS* 51: 169–73.

31. Treaty of New York, 7 August 1790: Kappler, *Treaties* 2: 25–29, and Parry, ed., *CTS* 51: 37–41. For McGillivray's explanation of why he agreed to this treaty with the Americans, see his letter to William Panton, 8 May 1790, in Caughey, ed., *McGillivray*, pp. 259–62. For discussion, see J. Leitch Wright, Jr., "Creek-American Treaty of 1790: Alexander McGillivray and the Diplomacy of the Old Southwest," *Georgia Historical Quarterly* 51 (1967): 379–400.

32. *"...y elegido por su cabeza al rey de los Chicachas."* Franchimastabe, Choctaw, at a treaty council at Nogales, 12 May 1792 (a year prior to the grand congress at the same place), quoted in Serrano y Sanz, *España y los Indios,* p. 51. The Spanish took great pains with the grand congress at Nogales in the fall of 1793. For Carondelet's preliminary instructions, see 26 February 1793., AGI, Cuban Papers, legajo 2353, no. 4 in Cuban Papers transcripts, pp. 9–13, Ayer Collections, Newberry Library. A journal of the congress can be found ibid., no. 12, pp. 11–62. For a copy of the treaty, see ibid., legajo 42, no. 317, pp. 89–96. It is printed in Parry, ed., *CTS* 52: 177–78.

33. *JCC* 34: 285–86; *American State Papers, Indian Affairs* 1: 9. For the treaties, see Kappler, *Treaties* 2: 18–23, 23–25, and *CTS* 50. 403–10, 411–14.

34. Report of 15 June 1789, *American State Papers, Indian Affairs* 1: 13.

35. John Cleve Symmes to "Shawanoes, Delawares, Miamis, and Waweauchtenois [Weas]," 22 September 1789, Public Archives of Canada, Indian Records, vol. 16: no. 5063 in Ethnohistory Collection, Special Collections, Regenstein Library, University of Chicago.

36. Kappler, *Treaties* 2: 42. For the treaty in its entirety, see ibid., pp. 39–45, and *CTS* 52: 439–45. For a full discussion of the context and background of the treaty see Helen H. Tanner, "The Greenville Treaty, 1795," report before the Indian Claims Commission, dockets 13G, 29C et al. Printed in Tanner and Erminie Wheeler-Voegelin, *Indians of Ohio and Indiana Prior to 1795,* 2 vols. (New York: Garland Publishing Co., 1974) 1: 51–128 (Garland pagination).

37. Kappler, *Treaties* 2: 39–41.

38. For the boundary as established by the Trade and Intercourse Act of 22 May 1796, see *United States Statutes* 1: 469. For the boundary segments as established by treaty, see Kappler, *Treaties* 2: 26, 29–30, 39–40, respectively, the Treaty of New York (7 August 1790), the Treaty of Holston (2 July 1791) and the Treaty of Greenville (3 August 1795).

39. Secretary of War Henry Knox to Timothy Pickering, 9 April 1791 and 2 May 1791, Pickering Papers 60: 41–47; 61: 172–73.

40. Pickering to Knox, 16 July 1791, Pickering Papers 60. 116. Pickering's journals of his negotiations with the Six Nations have frequent references to the various strategems the Indians used to persuade Pickering to give them rum.

41. The Senecas resisted Pennsylvania's attempts to survey the Erie Triangle in the early 1790s, but resistance did not come to open fighting, and the matter was eventually settled by negotiation.

42. Speech of Farmer's Brother at Tioga Point, 21 November 1790, Pickering Papers 61: 84A.

43. Washington to Knox, 14 January 1791, in Writings 31: 194.

44. Washington to the chiefs of the Seneca nation, 19 January 1791, ibid., p. 198.

45. Washington to Thomas Jefferson, Alexander Hamilton, and Edmund Randolph, 17 February 1793, ibid., 32: 349.

46. Jefferson's record of the cabinet meeting, quoted in ibid., p. 359n.

47. Downes, Council Fires, pp. 320–21, records a large gathering of Indians from the western nations in August and September 1792. This congress rejected any compromise boundary, and insisted that all the land north of the Ohio belonged to the Indians and should remain in their possession.

48. Pickering to Joseph Brant, 20 November 1794, Pickering Papers, 62: 108; Pickering to Henry Knox, 26 December 1794, ibid., p. 192.

49. Journal of the Executive Proceedings of the Senate, vol. 1: 170. For a copy of the Treaty of Canandaigua, 11 November 1794, see Kappler, Treaties 2: 34–37, and CTS 52: 239–42.

50. For the Six Nations–Pennsylvania treaty of 23 October 1784: Minutes of the Second Session of the Ninth General Assembly [of Pennsylvania], Appendix, "Proceedings of the Treaties held at Fort Stanwix and Fort McIntosh," pp. 318–20, cited by Kent, Pennsylvania Purchases, p. 98 (Garland). For the treaty of 19 January 1785: "Proceedings," pp. 325–27; Kent, p. 125 (Garland). For the treaty of 9 January 1789: Pennsylvania Archives, 1st ser., vol. 11: 529–33, and vol. 12: 100–103, cited by Kent, p. 213 (Garland). This January 1789 agreement and deed of cession can also be found in Kappler, Laws, vol. 3: 698–701.

51. The total for New York treaties may well have to be revised upward as more research is done. Some of the records cited as sources for table 14 contain references to other treaties which are not included here because copies of them could not be located. A summary of New York's postwar policy is in Barbara Graymont, "New York State Indian Policy after the Revolution; New York History 57 (1976): 438–74.

52. New York Indian Commissioners, Proceedings of the Commissioners of Indian Affairs, compiled and edited by Franklin B. Hough, two vols. in one (Albany, N.Y.: Joel Munsell, 1861)1: 198–203.

53. Orasmus Turner, History of the Pioneer Settlement of Phelps

and Gorham's Purchase (Rochester, N.Y.: Wm. Alling, 1852) gives a detailed account of the purchase.

54. At the Treaty of Big Tree, 15 September 1797. For a copy, see *Indian Treaties and Laws and Regulations Relating to Indian Affairs* (Washington, D.C.: Way & Gideon, 1826), pp. 33–37.

55. Washington to Hamilton, 4 April 1791, in *Writings* 31: 274. Hamilton's reply is quoted in ibid., in a note.

56. Washington to Senate, 26 October 1791, *American State Papers, Indian Affairs* 1: 124; Knox to Clinton, 17 August 1791, ibid., p. 169.

57. Treaty of Canandaigua, Kappler, *Treaties* 2: 35: Pickering to Knox, 26 December 1794, Pickering Papers, vol. 62: 192.

58. "Journal of the Treaty at Newtown Point on the Tioga River, New York," Pickering Papers, vol. 60: 111–12; Pickering to James B. Mowrer, 5 August 1818, ibid., vol. 15: 163.

59. "Captain Hendrick's Narrative of his Journey from Geneseo to Grant River, commencing Feb. 18, 1792," ibid., vol. 59: 21A.

60. Onondaga and Cayuga chiefs to Timothy Pickering, 16 November 1794, ibid., vol. 62: 104.

Selected Bibliography

Treaties

There are two reasons for putting treaties into a separate category in this bibliography. Much of the analysis in the foregoing study rests on an assumption of the importance of treaties in understanding what happened in North America between 1763 and 1796. Since treaties figure so largely in the text, they need to be separated out in the sources to provide access for scholars who may wish to pursue the subject. Treaties between North American Indian groups and various groups of Europeans and Americans during this period are, however, not easy to locate, and that is the second reason for providing a separate category. In it a few signposts can be set up to point the way to sources that might not otherwise be examined.

Two major publishing projects will, when completed, make much easier the task of scholars in search of early Indian treaties. The Iroquois Project of the Newberry Library Center for the History of the American Indian, Chicago, was nearing completion as this book went to press. This project to compile, annotate, and publish a documentary political history of the Iroquois League and its tributary tribes was conducted by Francis Jennings, now director emeritus of the Center, and jointly edited by William N. Fenton, professor of anthropology, State University of New York, Albany. The guide to this important collection of treaties has been included in the following list of references, even though it was not available at the time of this writing, in order to make the bibliography as complete and useful as possible.

The goal of the second project, under the direction of Alden T. Vaughan, professor of early American history at Columbia University, is the publication, from the period before 1789, of all the documents that pertain to American Indians. This includes the laws passed by colonial, state, and national governments, as well as the diplomatic documents that are the focus of this portion of the bibliography. The first volume in the series, *Early American Indian Documents: Treaties and Laws, 1607-1789*, was published in 1979, and three additional volumes were promised before this book will appear. Plans call for the publication of twenty volumes. Volume One is included in the bibliography.

Until these projects are completed, Indian treaties from the colonial period will continue to be difficult to find.

The DePuy bibliography, listed below, summarizes the texts of fifty-four treaties signed between 1677 and 1768. Complete tests of thirteen of these treaties, which were printed by Benjamin Franklin, are included in the work edited by Julian P. Boyd. Texts of many other treaties known to have been negotiated in the colonial period must be sought in scattered locations. A few are in the standard treaty compilations included here. Most are either in manuscript collections, or in sets of printed documents drawn from the official records of various governmental bodies. A scholar interested in colonial Indian treaties should, therefore, consult not only the works listed in this section but those in the sections on manuscript collections and printed documents as well. The location of specific treaties mentioned in the text is, of course, indicated in the source notes and in appendix A.

Similar ingenuity must be exercised for Indian treaties in the early national period. For United States-Indian treaties, scholars can consult the standard compilation by Charles J. Kappler, listed below, but even it is not complete for the period when the Continental Congress was negotiating with the Indians. Furthermore, Kappler does not include treaties that the Indians made with each other, with Spain, Great Britain, individual states, and private individuals. Again, the manuscript collections and printed documents must be consulted. Only thus will scholars begin to piece together an accurate picture of the complex system of treaty agreements that helped to structure the relations between the many different groups of peoples in eastern North America.

Annual Register of World Events: A Review of the Year. London: 1758–.
Sometimes includes terms of treaties with North American Indians.
Boyd, Julian P., ed. *Indian Treaties Printed by Benjamin Franklin, 1736–1762.* Introduction by Carl Van Doren. Philadelphia: Historical Society of Pennsylvania, 1938.
Canada. *Indian Treaties and Surrenders, 1680–1890.* 2 vols. in one. Ottawa: Brown Chamberlin, 1891.
DePuy, Henry F. *A Bibliography of the English Colonial Treaties with the American Indians.* New York: for the Lenox Club, 1917.
Indian Treaties and Laws and Regulations relating to Indian Affairs. Washington, D.C.: Way & Gideon, 1826.
     Includes material on New York treaties with members of the Iroquois League.
Jennings, Francis; Fenton, William N.; Druke, Mary A. *A Reference Guide to the Treaties of the Iroquois Nations and Their League.* Syracuse, N.Y.: Syracuse University Press, forthcoming.

Kappler, Charles J., comp. and ed. *Indian Affairs, Laws, and Treaties.*
5 vols. Washington, D.C.: Government Printing Office, 1904–41.
Volume 2, *Treaties,* is the most useful, but volumes 3–5 also
contain treaty material, including lists of unratified treaties.
Kent, Donald H., ed. *Pennsylvania and Delaware Treaties, 1629–1737.*
Early American Indian Documents, edited by Alden T. Vaughan,
vol. 1. Washington, D.C.: University Publications of America, 1979.
Martens, Georg Friederich von, ed. *Recueil des principaux traités
d'alliance, de paix, de trêve . . . conclus par les puissances de l'Eur-
ope.* 7 vols. Goettingue: J. C. Dieterich, 1791–1802.
Parry, Clive, ed. *The Consolidated Treaty Series, 1648–1918.* 175 vols.
Dobbs Ferry, N.Y.: Oceana Publishing Co., 1969.
*Treaties between the United States of America and the Several Indian
Tribes, from 1778 to 1837.* Washington, D.C.: Langtree and O'Sulli-
van, 1837.

Manuscript Collections

Boston, Mass. Massachusetts Historical Society. Timothy Pickering
Papers.
Chicago, Ill. Newberry Library. Edward E. Ayer Collection.
————. Regenstein Library, The University of Chicago. Special Col-
lections: Ethnohistory Collection.
London. British Library. The Military Papers of Colonel Henry Bouquet,
1754–65. Additional MSS 21631–21660.
————. British Library. Sir Frederick Haldimand: Unpublished Papers
and Correspondence, 1758–84. Additional MSS 21661–21892.
————. British Public Record Office. Colonial Office Records: Amer-
ica and the West Indies.
Madison, Wis. State Historical Society of Wisconsin. Lyman C. Draper
Collection, especially the Brant MSS, the Brodhead Papers, the
George Rogers Clark MSS, the Frontier Wars MSS, the Kentucky
MSS, the William Preston Papers, and the Tennessee Papers.
Ottawa. Public Archives of Canada. Series M: Daniel M. Claus Papers;
Miscellaneous Collections, Reserved Papers: Indian Affairs, 1761–
1780.
Seville, Spain. Archivo General de Indias. "Papeles Procedentes de
Cuba." Transcripts in the Edward E. Ayer Collection, the Newberry
Library, Chicago.
Simancas, Spain. Archivo General de Simancas. Ministero de Estada.
Dispatches of Diego de Gardoqui. Transcripts in the Reuben T.
Durrett Collection, Special Collections, Regenstein Library, the
University of Chicago.
Washington, D.C. Library of Congress. Thomas Jefferson Papers.
————, National Archives. Record Group 360. "Papers of the Con-
tinental Congress, 1774–89." National Archives Microfilm Publica-
tion M247.

————. National Archives. Record Group 11. "Ratified Indian Treaties, 1722–1869." National Archives Microfilm Publication M668.

Printed Documents

Atkin, Edmond. *The Appalachian Indian Frontier: The Edmond Atkin Report and Plan of 1755*. Edited and with an introduction by Wilbur R. Jacobs. Columbia: University of South Carolina Press, 1954; reprint ed., Lincoln: University of Nebraska Press, Bison Books, 1967.

Connolly, John. "A Narrative of the Transactions, Imprisonment, and Sufferings of John Connolly, an American Loyalist and Lieut. Col. in His Majesty's Service." *Pennsylvania Magazine of History and Biography* 12 (1888): 310–24, 407–20; 13 (1889): 61–70, 153–83. 281–91.

Franklin, Benjamin. *The Papers of Benjamin Franklin*. Edited by Leonard W. Labaree. 19 vols. (continuing). New Haven, Conn.: Yale University Press, 1959–.

Georgia. *The Colonial Records of the State of Georgia*. Compiled by Allen D. Candler. 25 vols. Atlanta: State Printer, 1904–15.

Great Britain. Colonial Office. *Documents of the American Revolution*. Edited by K. G. Davies. 19 vols. (continuing). Shannon, Ireland: Irish University Press, 1972–.

Hamilton, Alexander. *The Papers of Alexander Hamilton*. Edited by Harold C. Syrett. 27 vols. (continuing). New York: Columbia University Press, 1961–.

————. *Papers on Public Credit, Commerce, and Finance*. Edited by Samuel McKee, Jr. New York: Columbia University Press, 1934; reprint ed., New York: Liberal Arts Press, 1957.

Illinois. *The New Regime, 1765–1767: Illinois State Historical Society Library Collections*. Vol. 11. Edited by Clarence W. Alvord and Clarence E. Carter. Springfield, Ill.: Illinois State Historical Society, 1916.

Johnson, William. *The Papers of Sir William Johnson*. Edited by James Sullivan. 13 vols. Albany: University of the State of New York, 1921–62.

Kellogg, Louise P., ed. *Frontier Advance on the Upper Ohio, 1778–1779: Wisconsin Historical Collections*. Vol. 23. Draper Series, vol. 4. Madison: State Historical Society of Wisconsin, 1916.

————, ed. *Frontier Retreat on the Upper Ohio, 1779–1791: Wisconsin Historical Collections*. Vol. 24. Draper Series, vol. 5. Madison: State Historical Society of Wisconsin, 1917.

Lockey, Joseph B. *East Florida, 1783–1785*. Berkeley: University of California Press, 1949.

McGillivray, Alexander. *McGillivray of the Creeks*. Edited and with an introduction by John W. Caughey. Norman: University of Oklahoma Press, 1938; 2d printing, 1958.

Michigan. *Michigan Pioneer and Historical Collections.* 40 vols. Lansing: Michigan Historical Commission, 1877–1929.

Mississippi. *Mississippi Provincial Archives: English Dominion, 1763–1766.* Edited by Dunbar Rowland. Nashville, Tenn.: Mississippi Department of Archives and History, 1911.

New York. *Documents Relative to the Colonial History of the State of New York.* Edited by Edmund B. O'Callaghan. 15 vols. Albany, N.Y.: Weed, Parsons & Co., 1853–87.

————. Indian Commissioners. *Proceedings of the Commissioners of Indian Affairs.* Compiled and edited by Franklin B. Hough. 2 vols. Albany, N.Y.: Joel Munsell, 1861.

————. State Legislature. *Report of the Special Committee to Investigate the Indian Problem of the State of New York.* Albany, N.Y.: Troy Press, 1889.

North Carolina. *The Colonial Records of North Carolina.* Edited by William L. Saunders. 10 vols. Raleigh, N.C.: State Printer, 1886–90.

————. *The State Records of North Carolina.* Compiled and edited by Walter Clark. 17 vols. Winston, N.C.: M. I. and J. C. Stewart, 1895–1905.

Pennsylvania. *Minutes of the Provincial Council of Pennsylvania, 1693–1776, and Colonial Records of Pennsylvania, 1683–1790.* 16 vols. Philadelphia: Theo. Fenn & Co., 1852–53.

————. *Pennsylvania Archives.* Edited by Samuel Hazard. 12 vols., 1st ser. Philadelphia: J. Severns & Co., 1852–56.

Simcoe, John Graves. *The Correspondence of Lieut. Governor John Graves Simcoe.* Edited by E. A. Cruikshank. 5 vols. Toronto: Ontario Historical Society, 1923–31.

Spain. *España y los Indios Cherokis y Chactas.* Edited by Manuel Serraño y Sanz. Sevilla: Tip de la Guia Oficial, 1916.

Thwaites, Reuben G., and Kellogg, Louise P., eds. *Documentary History of Dunmore's War, 1774.* Draper Series, vol. 1. Madison: State Historical Society of Wisconsin, 1905.

————, eds. *The Revolution on the Upper Ohio, 1775–1777.* Draper Series, vol. 2. Madison: State Historical Society of Wisconsin, 1908.

U.S. Continental Congress. *American Archives.* Compiled by Peter Force. 6 vols., 4th ser. Washington, D.C.: M. St. Clair Clarke & Peter Force, 1837–46.

————. *American Archives.* Compiled by Peter Force. 3 vols., 5th ser. Washington, D.C.: M. St. Clair Clarke & Peter Force, 1848–53.

————. *Journals of the Continental Congress, 1774–1789.* Edited by Worthington C. Ford. 34 vols. Washington, D.C.: Government Printing Office, 1904–37.

————. *The Revolutionary Diplomatic Correspondence.* Edited by Francis Wharton. 6 vols. Washington, D.C.: Government Printing Office, 1889.

————. "A Speech to the six confederate nations, Mohawks, Oneidas, Tuscaroras, Onondagas, Cayugas, Senecas, from the twelve united colonies, convened in council at Philadelphia, July 13, 1775." In

The American Museum or Repository of Ancient and Modern Fugitive Pieces 5 (1789): 88–91.

U.S. Congress. *American State Papers: Documents, Legislative and Executive of the Congress of the United States.* 38 vols. Washington, D.C.: Gales and Seaton, 1832–61. Especially: *Foreign Relations,* 6 vols.; *Indian Affairs,* 2 vols.; *Military Affairs,* 7 vols.; *Public Lands,* 8 vols.

————. Senate. *Journal of the Executive Proceedings of the Senate.* Vol. 1. Washington, D.C.: Duff Green, 1828.

Virginia. *Calendar of Virginia State Papers, 1652–1869.* 11 vols. Richmond, Va.: Superintendent of Public Printing, 1875–93.

Washington, George. *The Writings of George Washington from the Original Manuscript Sources, 1745–1799.* Edited by John C. Fitzpatrick. 39 vols. Washington, D.C.: Government Printing Office, 1931–44.

Wayne, Anthony. *Anthony Wayne, a Name in Arms: The Wayne-Knox-Pickering-McHenry Correspondence.* Edited by Richard C. Knopf. Pittsburgh: University of Pittsburgh Press, 1960.

General Sources

Abernethy, Thomas P. *Western Lands and the American Revolution.* University of Virginia Institute for Research in the Social Sciences Monograph no. 25. New York: D. Appleton-Century, for the Institute, 1937.

Alden, John R. "The Eighteenth Century Cherokee Archives." *The American Archivist* 5 (1942): 240–44.

————. *John Stuart and the Southern Colonial Frontier.* University of Michigan Publications in History and Political Science, vol. 15. Ann Arbor: University of Michigan Press, 1944.

Alvord, Clarence W. *The Mississippi Valley in British Politics.* 2 vols. Cleveland, Ohio: Arthur H. Clark Co., 1917.

American Ethnological Society. *Essays on the Problem of Tribe.* Proceedings of the 1967 annual spring meeting. Edited by June Helm. Seattle: University of Washington Press, 1968.

Andrews, Charles M. *The Colonial Period in American History.* Vol. 4: *England's Commercial and Colonial Policy.* New Haven, Conn.: Yale University Press, 1938; Yale paperbound, 1964.

Balandier, Georges. "La Situation Coloniale: Approche Théorique." In *Social Change: The Colonial Situation,* pp. 34–61. Edited by Immanuel Wallerstein. New York: John Wiley & Sons, 1966.

Barth, Fredrik. *Ethnic Groups and Boundaries.* London: George Allen & Unwin, 1969.

Beauchamp, William M. *Civil, Religious and Mourning Councils and Ceremonies of Adoption of the New York Indians.* New York State Museum Bulletin 113. Albany: New York State Museum, 1907.

Bemis, Samuel Flagg. *Jay's Treaty.* 2d ed. New Haven, Conn.: Yale University Press, 1962.

239   Bibliography

———. *Pinckney's Treaty.* 2d ed. New Haven, Conn.: Yale University Press, 1960.
———. *The Diplomacy of the American Revolution.* Rev. ed. Bloomington: Indiana University Press, 1957; Midland Books, 1965.
———. "The Rayneval Memoranda of 1782 on Western Boundaries, and Some Comments on the French Historian Doniol." *Proceedings of the American Antiquarian Society* 47 (1937): 15–41.
Berkhofer, Robert F., Jr. *The White Man's Indian.* New York: Alfred A. Knopf, 1978.
Berry, Jane M. "The Indian Policy of Spain in the Southwest, 1783–1795." *Mississippi Valley Historical Review* 3 (1917): 462–77.
Brown, James A. "The Impact of the European Presence on Indian Culture." In *Context for Empire, 1500–1775,* pp. 6–24. Edited by John B. Elliott. Indianapolis: Indiana Historical Society, 1975.
Cappon, Lester J., ed. *Atlas of Early American History.* Princeton, N.J.: Princeton University Press for the Newberry Library and the Institute of Early American History and Culture, 1976.
Carter, Charles H. "The New World as a Factor in International Relations, 1492–1739." In *First Images of America.* 2 vols. Edited by Fredi Chiapelli. Berkeley: University of California Press, 1976. Vol. 1, pp. 231–63.
Clarfield, Gerard H. *Timothy Pickering and American Diplomacy, 1795–1800.* Columbia: University of Missouri Press, 1969.
Coe, Stephen Howard. "Indian Affairs in Pennsylvania and New York, 1783–1794." Ph.D. dissertation, American University, 1968.
Cohen, Felix S. "The Spanish Origin of Indian Rights in the Law of the United States." In *The Legal Conscience,* pp. 230–52. Edited by Lucy K. Cohen. New Haven, Conn.: Yale University Press, 1960.
Corkran, David H. *The Cherokee Frontier: Conflict and Survival, 1740–1762.* Norman: University of Oklahoma Press, 1962.
———. *The Creek Frontier, 1540–1783.* Norman: University of Oklahoma Press, 1967.
Cotterill, R. S. *The Southern Indians: The Story of the Civilized Tribes before Removal.* Norman: University of Oklahoma Press, 1954.
Cosby, Alfred W., Jr. *The Columbian Exchange.* Westport, Conn.: Greenwood Publishing Co., 1972.
Cumming, William P. *The Southeast in Early Maps.* Chapel Hill: University of North Carolina Press, 1962.
Davis, Ralph. "English Foreign Trade, 1700–1774." *Economic History Review* 15 (1962): 285–303.
———. *The Rise of the Atlantic Economies.* Ithaca, N.Y.: Cornell University Press, 1973.
Deer, A. Brian. *The Papers of Sir John Johnson.* Montreal: McGill University Press, 1973.
Denevan, William M. *The Native Population of the Americas in 1492.* Madison: University of Wisconsin Press, 1976.
Deserontyon, John. "A Mohawk Form of Ritual of Condolence, 1782." Museum of the American Indian, Heye Foundation. *Indian Notes*

and Monographs 10 (1928): 83–110.
DeVorsey, Louis, Jr. *The Indian Boundary in the Southern Colonies, 1763–1775.* Chapel Hill: University of North Carolina Press, 1961.
Dobyns, Henry F. "Estimating Aboriginal American Population; Part One: An Appraisal of Techniques with a New Hemispheric Estimate." *Current Anthropology* 7 (1966): 395–416.
————. *Native American Historical Demography.* Bloomington: Indiana University Press for the Newberry Library, 1976.
————. "Brief Perspectives on a Scholarly Transformation: Widowing the 'Virgin' Land." *Ethnohistory* 23 (1976): 95–104.
Downes, Randolph C. "Cherokee-American Relations in the Upper Tennessee Valley, 1776–1791." *East Tennessee Historical Society Publications,* no. 8 (1936): 35–53.
————. *Council Fires on the Upper Ohio.* Pittsburgh: University of Pittsburgh Press, 1940.
Elliott, Jonathan. *The Funding System of the United States and Great Britain.* Reprint ed., New York: A. M. Kelley, 1968.
Fairbanks, Charles H. "Ethnographic Report on Royce Area 79: Chickasaw, Cherokee, Creek." Report to the Indian Claims Commission. Docket 275. Printed in *Cherokee and Creek Indians,* pp. 34–285. By Charles H. Fairbanks and John H. Goff. New York: Garland Publishing Co., 1974.
Farrand, Max. "The Indian Boundary Line." *American Historical Review* 10 (1905): 782–91.
Fenton, William N. "Problems Arising from the Historic Northeastern Position of the Iroquois." In *Essays in Historical Anthropology of North America,* pp. 159–251. Smithsonian Miscellaneous Collections, vol. 100. Washington, D.C.: Smithsonian Institution, 1940.
————. "Indian and White Relations in Eastern North America: A Common Ground for History and Ethnology." In *American Indian and White Relations to 1830,* pp. 3–27. Edited by William N. Fenton. Chapel Hill: University of North Carolina Press, 1957.
————, ed. *Parker on the Iroquois.* Syracuse, N.Y.: Syracuse University Press, 1968.
Fogelson, Raymond D. "Cherokee Notions of Power." In *The Anthropology of Power,* pp. 185–94. Edited by Raymond D. Fogelson and Richard N. Adams. New York: Academic Press, 1977.
Ford, Amelia C. *Colonial Precedents of Our National Land System as It Existed in 1800.* University of Wisconsin bulletin 352. Madison: University of Wisconsin Press, 1910.
Franklin, W. Neil. "Virginia and the Cherokee Indian Trade, 1753–1775." *East Tennessee Historical Society Publications,* no. 5 (1933): 22–38.
Gates, Paul W. "The Role of the Land Speculator in Western Development." *Pennsylvania Magazine of History and Biography* 66 (1942): 314–33.
Gibson, Arrell M. *The Chickasaws.* Norman: University of Oklahoma Press, 1971.

Gibson, Charles. "Conquest, Capitulation, and Indian Treaties." *American Historical Review* 83 (1978): 1-15.

Gilbert, Felix. *The Beginnings of American Foreign Policy.* First published as *To the Farewell Address.* Princeton, N.J.: Princeton University Press, 1961; reprint ed., New York, Harper Torchbook, 1965.

Gipson, Lawrence H. *The Coming of the Revolution, 1763-1775.* New York: Harper & Row, 1954; reprint ed., Harper Torchbook, 1962.

————. *The British Empire before the American Revolution.* 14 vols. New York: Alfred A. Knopf, 1958-69.

Graymont, Barbara. *The Iroquois in the American Revolution.* Syracuse, N.Y.: Syracuse University Press, 1972.

Graymont, Barbara. "New York State Indian Policy After the Revolution." *New York History* 57 (1976): 438-74.

Grisel, Etienne. "The Beginnings of International Law and General Public Law Doctrine: Francisco de Vitoria's *De Indiis prior.*" In *First Images of America.* 2 vols. Edited by Fredi Chiapelli. Berkeley: University of California Press, 1976, Vol. 1, pp. 305-25.

Grotius, Hugo. *De Jure Belli ac Pacis.* The Classics of International Law series. 2 vols. Oxford: Clarendon Press, 1925.

Gunther, Gerald. "Governmental Power and New York Indian Lands— A Reassessment of a Persistent Problem of Federal-State Relations." *Buffalo Law Review* 8 (1958): 1-26.

Guzzardo, John C. "The Superintendent and the Ministers: The Battle for Oneida Allegiances, 1761-75." *New York History* 57 (1976): 255-83.

Haan, Richard L. "The Covenant Chain: Iroquois Diplomacy on the Niagara Frontier, 1697-1730." Ph.D. dissertation, University of California, Santa Barbara, 1976.

Hale, Horatio, ed. *The Iroquois Book of Rites.* Introduction by William N. Fenton. Toronto: University of Toronto Press, 1963.

Hamilton, Milton W. "Sir William Johnson: Interpreter of the Iroquois." *Ethnohistory* 10 (1963): 270-86.

————. *Sir William Johnson, Colonial American, 1715-1763.* Port Washington, N.Y.: Kennikat Press, 1976.

Hanke, Lewis. *The Spanish Struggle for Justice in the Conquest of America.* Philadelphia: University of Pennsylvania Press, 1949.

Harlow, Vincent T. *The Founding of the Second British Empire, 1763-1793.* 2 vols. London: Longmans, Green, 1952-64.

Hayden, Ralston. *The Senate and Treaties, 1789-1817.* New York: Macmillan, 1920.

Heckewelder, John. *A Narrative of the Mission of the United Brethren among the Delaware and Mohegan Indians.* Philadelphia: M'Carty & Davis, 1820.

Henderson, Archibald. *The Conquest of the Old Southwest.* New York: Century Co., 1920.

Henry, Alexander. *Travels and Adventures in Canada and the Indian Territories between the Years 1760 and 1776.* New York: I. Riley, 1809.

Hibbard, Benjamin Horace. *A History of the Public Land Policies*. Introduction by Paul W. Gates. Madison: University of Wisconsin Press, 1965.

Hodge, Frederick W., ed. *Handbook of American Indians North of Mexico*. 2 vols. Bureau of American Ethnology bulletin 30. Washington, D.C.: Government Printing Office, 1907-10.

Horsman, Reginald. "American Indian Policy in the Old Northwest, 1783-1812." *William and Mary Quarterly* 18 (1961).

————. *Matthew Elliott, British Indian Agent*. Detroit: Wayne State University Press, 1964.

————. *Expansion and American Indian Policy, 1783-1812*. East Lansing: Michigan State University Press, 1967.

————. *The Frontier in the Formative Years, 1783-1815*. New York: Holt, Rinehart and Winston, 1970.

Hudson, Charles. *The Southeastern Indians*. Knoxville: University of Tennessee Press, 1976.

Hunt, George T. *The Wars of the Iroquois: A Study in Intertribal Trade Relations*. Madison: University of Wisconsin Press, 1940.

Goff, John H. "Land Cessions of the Cherokee Nation in Tennessee, Mississippi, North Carolina, Georgia, Alabama." Report before the Indian Claims Commission. Docket 282. Printed in *Cherokee and Creek Indians*, pp. 287-581. Charles H. Fairbanks and John H. Goff. New York: Garland Publishing Co., 1974.

Jacobs, Wilbur R. *Diplomacy and Indian Gifts: Anglo-French Rivalry Along the Ohio and Northwest Frontiers, 1748-1763*. Stanford University Publication, vol. 6. Stanford, Calif.: Stanford University Press, 1950.

Jennings, Francis. "A Vanishing Indian: Francis Parkman versus His Sources." *The Pennsylvania Magazine of History and Biography* 87 (1963): 306-23.

————. "Miquon's Passing: Indian-European Relations in Colonial Pennsylvania, 1674-1755." Ph.D. dissertation, University of Pennsylvania, 1965.

————. "The Delaware Interregnum." *The Pennsylvania Magazine of History and Biography* 89 (1965): 174-98.

————. "The Constitutional Evolution of the Covenant Chain." *Proceedings of the American Philosophical Society* 115 (1971): 88-96.

————. *The Invasion of America*. Chapel Hill: University of North Carolina Press for the Institute of Early American History and Culture, 1975.

————. "The Indians' Revolution." In *The American Revolution: Explorations in the History of American Radicalism*, pp. 319-48. Edited by Alfred F. Young. DeKalb: Northern Illinois University Press, 1976.

————. *Ambiguous Empire: The Iroquois League and Its Covenant Chain*. New York: W. W. Norton, forthcoming.

Johnson, Richard R. "The Search for a Usable Indian: An Aspect of the Defense of New England." *Journal of American History* 64 (1977): 623-51.

Kaplan, Lawrence S. *Colonies into Nation: American Diplomacy, 1763–1801.* New York: Macmillan, 1972.

Kent, Donald H. "Historical Report on Pennsylvania's Purchases from the Indians in 1784, 1785, and 1789, and on Indian Occupancy of the Areas Purchased." Report before the Indian Claims Commission. Docket 344. Printed as *Iroquois Indians I: History of Pennsylvania Purchases from the Indians.* New York: Garland Publishing Co., 1974.

Kinnaird, Lawrence. "Spanish Treaties with Indian Tribes." *Western Historical Quarterly* 10 (1979): 39–48.

Lewis, George E. *The Indiana Company, 1763–1798.* Old Northwest Historical Series no. 4. Glendale, Calif.: Arthur H. Clark Co., 1941.

Livermore, Shaw. *Early American Land Companies: Their Influence on Corporate Development.* New York: The Commonwealth Fund, 1939.

Marshall, Peter. "Lord Hillsborough, Samuel Wharton, and the Ohio Grant, 1769–1775." *The English Historical Review* 80 (1965): 717–39.

———. "Sir William Johnson and the Treaty of Fort Stanwix, 1768." *Journal of American Studies* 1 (1967): 149–79.

———. "Colonial Protest and Imperial Retrenchment: Indian Policy, 1764–1768." *Journal of American Studies* 5 (1971): 1–17.

Martens, Georg Friedrich von. *Précis du droit des gens.* 1788. Reprint edition, 2 vols. (Paris: Guillaumin et Cie, 1864). Translated into English by William Cobbett and published as *Summary of the Law of Nations.* Philadelphia: Thomas Bradford, 1795.

Mathur, Mary E. Fleming. "The Iroquois in Ethnography." *The Indian Historian* 2 (1969): 12–18.

McDermott, John Francis, ed. *The Spanish in the Mississippi Valley, 1762–1804.* Urbana: University of Illinois Press, 1974.

Michelson, Gunther. "The Covenant Chain in Colonial History." *Man in the Northeast* 21 (Spring 1981): 115–26.

Milling, Chapman J. *Red Carolinians.* Chapel Hill: University of North Carolina Press, 1940.

Mohawk Nation. *The Great Law of Peace of the Longhouse People.* Akwesasne via Rooseveltown, N.Y.: Mohawk Nation at Akwesasne, 1971.

Mohr, Walter H. *Federal Indian Relations, 1774–1788.* Philadelphia: University of Pennsylvania Press, 1933.

Morgan, Lewis H. *League of the Ho-dé-no-sau-nee or Iroquois.* Rochester, N.Y.: Sage & Bros., 1851.

Mowat, Charles L. *East Florida as a British Province, 1763–1784.* Berkeley: University of California Press, 1943.

Murdoch, Richard K. "French Intrigue Along the Georgia-Florida Frontier, 1793–1796." Ph.D. dissertation, University of California, Los Angeles, 1947.

Nash, Gary B. "The Image of the Indian in the Southern Colonial Mind." *William and Mary Quarterly,* 3 ser., 29 (1972): 197–230.

Newbold, Robert C. *The Albany Congress and Plan of Union of 1754.*

Bibliography

New York: Vantage Press, 1955.
O'Donnell, James H., III. *Southern Indians in the American Revolution.* Knoxville: University of Tennessee Press, 1973.
Pares, Richard. *King George III and the Politicians.* Oxford: Oxford University Press, 1953.
Parker, Arthur C. *The Code of Handsome Lake, the Seneca Prophet.* New York State Museum bulletin 163. Albany: New York State Museum, 1912.
Parkman, Francis. *The Conspiracy of Pontiac.* 2 vols. Frontenac edition. New York: Charles Scribner's Sons, 1915.
Pastore, Ralph Thomas. "The Board of Commissioners for Indian Affairs in the Northern Department and the Iroquois Indians, 1775-1778." Ph.D. dissertation, University of Notre Dame, 1972.
Pearce, Roy Harvey. *Savagism and Civilization.* Originally published as *The Savages of America.* Baltimore: Johns Hopkins Press, 1953; rev. ed., Johns Hopkins Paperbacks, 1967.
Peckham, Howard H. *Pontiac and the Indian Uprising.* Princeton, N.J.: Princeton University Press, 1947.
Phillips, Edward Hake. "Timothy Pickering at His Best: Indian Commissioner, 1790-1794." *Essex Institute Historical Collections* 102 (1966): 163-202.
Pickering, Octavius, and Upham, C. W. *The Life of Timothy Pickering.* 4 vols. Boston: Little, Green & Co., 1867-73.
Prucha, Francis Paul. *American Indian Policy in the Formative Years.* Cambridge, Mass.: Harvard University Press, 1962.
Ramsey, J. G. M. *The Annals of Tennessee to the End of the Eighteenth Century.* Philadelphia: J. B. Lippincott & Co., 1860.
Robinson, W. Stitt. "Virginia and the Cherokees." In *The Old Dominion,* pp. 21-40. Edited by Darrett B. Rutman. Charlottesville: University Press of Virginia, 1964.
Royce, Charles C. "The Cherokee Nation of Indians." In *Annual Report of the Bureau of Ethnology, 1883-1884,* pp. 121-378. Washington, D.C.: Government Printing Office, 1887.
————, comp. *Indian Land Cessions in the United States; Eighteenth Annual Report of the Bureau of American Ethnology, 1896-1897.* Part 2. Washington, D.C.: Government Printing Office, 1899.
Savelle, Max. "The American Balance of Power and European Diplomacy, 1713-78." In *The Era of the American Revolution,* pp. 140-69. Edited by Richard B. Morris. New York: Columbia University Press, 1939; reprint ed., Harper Torchbooks, 1965.
Schlesier, Earl H. "Epidemics and Indian Middlemen: Rethinking the Wars of the Iroquois, 1609-1653." *Ethnohistory* 23 (1976): 129-45.
Scott, James Brown. *The Spanish Conception of International Law and Sanctions.* Washington, D.C.: Carnegie Endowment for International Peace, 1934.
————. *The Spanish Origin of International Law, Part One: Francisco de Vitoria and His Law of Nations.* Oxford: Clarendon Press, 1934.
Snyderman, George S. "Behind the Tree of Peace: A Sociological Analy-

sis of Iroquois Warfare." *Pennsylvania Archaeologist* 18 (1948): 2-93.

————. "Concepts of Land Ownership among the Iroquois and Their Neighbors." In *Bureau of American Ethnology Bulletin 149*, pp. 13-34. Washington, D.C.: Government Printing Office, 1951.

Sosin, Jack M. *Whitehall and the Wilderness.* Lincoln: University of Nebraska Press, 1961.

————. "Britain and the Ohio Valley, 1760-1775: The Search for Alternatives in a Revolutionary Era." In *Contest for Empire*, pp. 60-76. Edited by John B. Elliott. Indianapolis: Indiana Historical Society, 1975.

Stourzh, Gerald. *Benjamin Franklin and American Foreign Policy.* Chicago: The University of Chicago Press, 1954.

Sturtevant, William C., ed. *Handbook of North American Indians.* 20 vols. (projected). Washington, D.C.: Smithsonian Institution, 1978-. Vol. 15: *Northeast,* Bruce Trigger, ed.

Swanton, John R. *Early History of the Creek Indians and Their Neighbors.* Bureau of American Ethnology Bulletin 73. Washington, D.C.: Government Printing Office, 1922.

————. *The Indians of the Southeastern United States.* Bureau of American Ethnology Bulletin 137. Washington, D.C.: Government Printing Office, 1946.

————. *The Indian Tribes of North America.* Bureau of American Ethnology Bulletin 145. Washington, D.C.: Government Printing Office, 1947.

Tanner, Helen H. "Vicente Manuel de Zéspedes and the Restoration of Spanish Rule in East Florida, 1784-1790." Ph.D. dissertation, University of Michigan, 1961.

————. "The Greenville Treaty, 1795." Report before the Indian Claims Commission. Dockets 13G, 29C, et al. Printed in *Indians of Ohio and Indiana Prior to 1795.* 2 vols. By Helen H. Tanner and Erminie Wheeler-Voegelin. New York: Garland Publishing Co., 1974. Vol. 1, pp. 51-128.

————, et al. *Atlas of Great Lakes Indians.* Norman, Okla.: University of Oklahoma Press, forthcoming.

TePaske, John J. "Spanish Indian Policy and the Struggle for Empire in the Southeast, 1513-1776." In *Contest for Empire*, pp. 25-40. Edited by John B. Elliott. Indianapolis: Indiana Historical Society, 1975.

Tooker, Elizabeth. "The League of the Iroquois: Its History, Politics, and Ritual." In *Handbook of North American Indians.* Vol. 15: *Northeast,* pp. 418-41. Edited by Bruce G. Trigger. Washington, D.C.: Smithsonian Institution, 1978.

Vattell, Emmerich de. *Le droit des gens.* Classics of International Law series. 3 vols. Washington, D.C.: Carnegie Institution, 1916.

Wainwright, Nicholas B. *George Croghan, Wilderness Diplomat.* Chapel Hill: University of North Carolina Press, 1959.

Wallace, Anthony F. C. "Political Organization and Land Tenure among the Northeastern Indians." *Southwest Journal of Anthropology* 13 (1957): 301–21.

————. "The Dekanawideh Myth Analyzed as the Record of a Revitalization Movement." *Ethnohistory* 5 (1958): 118–30.

————. *The Death and Rebirth of the Seneca.* New York: Alfred A. Knopf, 1970.

Wallace, Paul A. W. *The White Roots of Peace.* Philadelphia: University of Pennsylvania Press, 1946.

Washburn, Wilcomb E. *Red Man's Land/White Man's Law.* New York: Charles Scribner's Sons, 1971.

Weslager, C. A. *The Delaware Indians.* New Brunswick, N.J.: Rutgers University Press, 1972.

Wheeler-Voegelin, Erminie. "An Ethnohistorical Report on the Indian Use and Occupancy of Royce Area 11 in Ohio and Indiana. Report before the Indian Claims Commission. Docket 13G. Printed in *Indians of Ohio and Indiana Prior to 1795.* 2 vols. New York: Garland Publishing Co., 1974. Vol. 1: 129–463; vol. 2: 7–468.

————. "An Ethnohistorical Report on the Wyandot, Potawatomi, Ottawa, and Chippewa of Northwest Ohio." Report before the Indian Claims Commission. Docket 139. Printed as *Indians of Northwest Ohio.* New York: Garland Publishing Co., 1974.

Whitaker, Arthur Preston. *The Spanish-American Frontier: 1783–1795.* Boston: Houghton Mifflin, 1927; reprint ed., Gloucester, Mass.: Peter Smith, 1962.

Williams, Samuel Cole. *History of the Lost State of Franklin.* Johnson City, Tenn.: The Watauga Press, 1924.

Wright, J. Leitch, Jr. *William Augustus Bowles.* Athens: University of Georgia Press, 1967.

————. "Creek-American Treaty of 1790: Alexander McGillivray and the Diplomacy of the Old Southwest." *Georgia Historical Quarterly* 51 (1967): 379–400.

————. *Britain and the American Frontier, 1783–1815.* Athens: University of Georgia Press, 1975.

————. *The Only Land They Knew.* New York: The Free Press, 1981.

Index